The Commonwealth Block, Melbourne

Studies in Australasian Historical Archaeology

Martin Gibbs and Angela Middleton, Series Editors

The Studies in Australasian Historical Archaeology series aims to publish excavation reports and regional syntheses that deal with research into the historical archaeology of Australia, New Zealand and the Asia-Pacific region. The series aims to encourage greater public access to the results of major research and consultancy investigations, and it is co-published with the Australasian Society for Historical Archaeology.

An Archaeology of Institutional Confinement: The Hyde Park Barracks, 1848–1886
Peter Davies, Penny Crook and Tim Murray

Archaeology of the Chinese Fishing Industry in Colonial Victoria
Alister M Bowen

The Commonwealth Block, Melbourne: A Historical Archaeology
Tim Murray, Kristal Buckley, Sarah Hayes, Geoff Hewitt, Justin McCarthy, Richard Mackay, Barbara Minchinton, Charlotte Smith, Jeremy Smith and Bronwyn Woff

Flashy, Fun and Functional: How Things Helped to Invent Melbourne's Gold Rush Mayor
Sarah Hayes

Good Taste, Fashion, Luxury: A Genteel Melbourne Family and Their Rubbish
Sarah Hayes

Port Essington: The Historical Archaeology of a North Australian 19th-Century Military Outpost
Jim Allen

The Shore Whalers of Western Australia: Historical Archaeology of a Maritime Frontier
Martin Gibbs

The Commonwealth Block, Melbourne
A Historical Archaeology

Tim Murray, Kristal Buckley, Sarah Hayes,
Geoff Hewitt, Justin McCarthy, Richard Mackay,
Barbara Minchinton, Charlotte Smith,
Jeremy Smith and Bronwyn Woff

Studies in Australasian Historical Archaeology
Volume 7

SYDNEY UNIVERSITY PRESS

Published 2019 by Sydney University Press
In association with the Australasian Society for Historical Archaeology
asha.org.au

© Tim Murray, Kristal Buckley, Sarah Hayes, Geoff Hewitt, Justin McCarthy, Richard Mackay, Barbara
   Minchinton, Charlotte Smith, Jeremy Smith and Bronwyn Woff 2019
© Sydney University Press 2019

Reproduction and communication for other purposes
Except as permitted under the Copyright Act, no part of this edition may be reproduced, stored in a retrieval system, or communicated in any form or by any means without prior written permission. All requests for reproduction or communication should be made to Sydney University Press at the address below:

Sydney University Press
Fisher Library F03
University of Sydney NSW 2006
AUSTRALIA
sup.info@sydney.edu.au
sydney.edu.au/sup

A catalogue record for this book is available
from the National Library of Australia.

ISBN 9781743323694 paperback
ISBN 9781743322246 epub

Cover images: Mahlstedt fire insurance plan of the city block, Map 8a (1923); Casselden Place Site, aerial perspective, looking northeast from Lonsdale Street during phase 1, 2002 (Photo: Tony Jenner).

Cover design by Miguel Yamin and Ming Wei
Layout by Ming Wei

Contents

List of Figures		vii
List of Plates		ix
About the Authors		xi

1. **Introduction and Context** — Tim Murray — 1
2. **Agencies of Change: Government Perspectives on Little Lon** — Kristal Buckley and Jeremy Smith — 7
3. **The First Campaign: Little Lon** — Justin McCarthy — 19
4. **Assemblage Analysis and Outcomes: Phase 1** — Tim Murray — 43
5. **Smaller Investigations between Phase 1 and Phase 2** — Tim Murray — 53
6. **The Second Campaign: Casselden Place** — Richard Mackay — 55
7. **Assemblage Analysis and Outcomes: Phase 2** — Tim Murray — 69
8. **Little Lon and Museum Victoria: A Tale of Benign Neglect, Restoration and a Bright Future** — Charlotte Smith — 87
9. **Diversity and Change in Little Lon: Ongoing Historical and Archaeological Research** — Sarah Hayes and Barbara Minchinton — 99
10. **An Update on the Commonwealth Block Project: A Second Phase of Targeted Feature Cataloguing** — Bronwyn Woff — 113
11. **The 2017 Excavations: 271 Spring Street, Melbourne** — Geoff Hewitt — 119
12. **Little Lon and the Archaeology of the Modern World** — Tim Murray — 139

Plates	143
Index	147

List of Figures

Figure 2.1: Commonwealth Block site plan. 9
Figure 3.1: Location plan. 20
Figure 3.2: Commonwealth Block Site Plan. 21
Figure 3.3: Former Commonwealth Centre Building (so-called Green Latrine) on Site D, corner Spring Street and Victoria Parade, Melbourne 1968. 21
Figure 3.4: Melbourne and Metropolitan Board of Works Plan 27 East Melbourne (1895). 23
Figure 3.5: Mahlstedt fire insurance plan of the city block. Map 8a (1923). 23
Figure 3.6: Twin gabled building at right is the former Lugton and Sons, Engineers old boiler factory, 27–29 Little Lonsdale Street looking southwest in the early 1980s. 24
Figure 3.7: Trench Location Plan showing the basic 10-metre grid established across the site. 28
Figure 3.8: Early stages of the excavation showing cottage footings in Trench 01; view is to east northeast. 29
Figure 3.9: Volunteers in Trench 04; view is to northwest. 29
Figure 3.10: Backhoe at work in Trench 16; view is to east with Spring Street in the background. 29
Figure 3.11: General view of Trenches 16–19 and Pits G–J in Trench 19. View is to north with Spring Street in background. 29
Figure 3.12: Close up view of artefacts in Pit J in Trench 19 / Location 57B during excavation; view is to north. 29
Figure 3.13: General view to east of Pits I & J after excavation in Trench 19 / Locations 57A & B. 29
Figure 3.14: General view of CCS Site towards south east (corner of Lonsdale and Spring Streets) after first phase of excavation has been completed and demolition has commenced. 30
Figure 3.15: The large red gum stump *in situ* under footings in Trench 06 / Location 73A & B; view is to south. 30
Figure 3.16: Volunteers and archaeologists pose on the stump after removal from Trench 06; view is to west. 30
Figure 3.17: General view to east of Pits M, N, O and P during excavation in Trench 27 / Locations 30 and 31A & B. 30
Figure 3.18: Close up view of Pit N in Trench 27 / Location 31A during excavation showing some of the numerous bottles and corks recovered. 30
Figure 3.19: From left Justin McCarthy and the three Davids (David Ellson, David Knox and David Bannear) with a convoy of barrows full of artefacts retrieved from Pit N in Trench 27 / Location 31A. 30
Figure 3.20: 'Space Locator' showing subdivisions of the block with the Black Eagle Hotel (Location 42) and Oddfellows Hotel (Location 80A & B) highlighted. 32
Figure 3.21: 'Space Locator' subdivision plan overlaid with excavated bluestone footings, rubbish pits and cesspits drawn in blue. 33
Figure 3.22: Black Eagle Hotel Excavation Plan. 37
Figure 3.23: Oddfellows Hotel Excavation Plan. Note Area 76 is the cellar and lies below Area 75. 37
Figure 4.1: The Commonwealth Block showing Sites A, B and C. 46
Figure 4.2: Structure of spatial comparison of Australian material culture, form urban settings, in a global context. 50
Figure 6.1: The Casselden Place Site, with excavated features shown and allotments superimposed. 58
Figure 6.2: Archaeological excavation in progress: trench supervisor and community participants. 59
Figure 6.3: Excavation of allotments 33 and 34. 59
Figure 6.4: Excavated 'barrel' cesspit. 60
Figure 6.5: Onsite processing of artefacts by specialists and community participants. 61
Figure 6.6: Faunal remains included mutton beef, pork and lamb. 63
Figure 6.7: Casselden Place Archaeological Excavation Project media launch May 2002. 65
Figure 6.8: Cessation of Transportation Medal: obverse and reverse. 67
Figure 8.1: The Historical Archaeology collections at Museum Victoria before commencement of the ARC-funded Commonwealth Block rehabilitation project. 89
Figure 8.2: The Commonwealth Block assemblage at Museum Victoria after four years of labour-intensive rehabilitation. 90

Figure 8.3: The second of three EMu Historical Archaeology tabs. 91
Figure 8.4: Museum staff member registering CUB finds onsite, direct into EMu. 92
Figure 9.1: The contents of the Moloneys' cesspit on display at Museum Victoria as part of the *Commonwealth Block* project. 105
Figure 9.2: Absinthe bottle from Mrs Bond's rubbish pit. 106
Figure 9.3: Henry Cornwell's houses in Westgarth Street Northcote, 'Aliceville', 'Edithville' and 'Belleville'. 108
Figure 10.1: Status of all significant features. 114
Figure 11.1: Location of the 271 Spring Street site. 119
Figure 11.2: Subdivision of CA7 and CA9 of Section 25. 120
Figure 11.3: Overlay of lot boundaries onto a detail of Thomas Bibbs' ca. 1856 map of Melbourne. 120
Figure 11.4: Overlay of allotment boundaries onto a detail from the 1895 MMBW block plan 1019. 121
Figure 11.5: Detail from Charles Nettleton's ca. 1861 photograph of Spring Street from Parliament House, view towards the north-west. 121
Figure 11.6: View west down Little Lonsdale Street from Spring Street in ca. 1870. 121
Figure 11.7: Detail from Paterson Brothers' *'Bird's-eye view of Melbourne, taken from the top of Scots' Church spire, Collins Street'* (1875). 121
Figure 11.8: Detail from Charles Nettleton's 1883 photograph *View of Melbourne (south west) from the terrace of the Exhibition Building, Carlton Gardens*. 121
Figure 11.9: A view of the northern part of the phase one area looking towards Little Lonsdale Street. 122
Figure 11.10: Lot 67AB partially excavated (for legend see text). 123
Figure 11.11: Schematic plan of lot 67C and the north end of lot 68AB. 124
Figure 11.12: Part of the rear yard of 21 Little Lonsdale Street looking north. 126
Figure 11.13: Detail from De Gruchy and Leigh's 1866 *Isometrical plan of Melbourne and suburbs*. Alexander Morison's house on lot 68 is arrowed. 127
Figure 11.14: Brick-lined cesspit 5 on lot 63. 127
Figure 11.15: Detail from Mahlstedt Plan section 2 sheet 8A 1910–1915 showing internal details of Porta's bellows factory. 128
Figure 11.16: The positions of the phase two trenches are shown, together with the outlines of remaining buildings, the historic buildings and lot boundaries. 128
Figure 11.17: View of trench 2 looking towards Little Lonsdale Street, within the standing walls of the Elms Hotel (Photo: GML Heritage). 129
Figure 11.18: Subsequent view of trench 2 looking towards Little Lonsdale Street, clearly showing the later wall of rectangular basalt blocks. 129
Figure 11.19: View towards the east of trench 1 showing the disturbed western wall of the Little Lonsdale Street wing and the double cask cesspit 6. 130
Figure 11.20: The Spring Street end of trench 11 on lot 61, showing the *in situ* brickwork of the dividing wall between rooms and the passage wall joining to the rear wall of the boarding house and an asphalt surface. 130
Figure 11.21: Excavation in progress revealed the the clay capping within stone-lined cesspit 7 associated with the boarding house on lot 61. 131
Figure 11.22: Stone-lined cesspit 7 associated with the boarding house on lot 61. 131
Figure 11.23: Part of the hearth and footing at the south wall of the pre-1850 brick house at 161 Spring Street revealed in trench 12. 133
Figure 11.24: Fragment of the stone-lining of the southern wall of a cesspit in the rear yards of lot 60 adjacent to the boundary with lot 59. 133

List of Plates

Plate 2.1: The Casselden Place site interpretation scheme, installed 2004.   143
Plate 6.1: The Casselden Place Site, 50 Lonsdale Street, Melbourne.   144
Plate 6.2: Casselden Place Site, aerial perspective, looking northeast from Lonsdale Street during Phase 1, 2002.   145
Plate 6.3: Artefacts such as this gold pendant and 19th-century 'moralising china' provide alternative perspectives about the socio-ecomonic status and morals of the 'Little Lon' community.   145
Plate 8.1: Stories from a City: Little Lon, Australia Gallery, Melbourne Museum, 2000–2007.   146
Plate 8.2: Artefacts displayed in cabinets outside Little Lon's recreated cottages, The Melbourne Story, Melbourne Museum, 2007.   146

About the Authors

Kristal Buckley AM is a lecturer in cultural heritage at Deakin University in Melbourne, Australia. Her teaching and research interests focus on global cultural heritage practices and world heritage. She holds professional qualifications in the fields of archaeology, anthropology and public policy, and has worked in government, private practice and in the community sector. She is a former international Vice-President of ICOMOS and a former President of Australia ICOMOS. She currently works as a world heritage adviser for ICOMOS and is a board member of the Port Arthur Historic Site Management Authority (Tasmania).

Sarah Hayes is an *Australian Research Council* 'Discovery Early Career Researcher Award' recipient in archaeology and history at La Trobe University. Her current research is on how the gold rush shaped quality of life in Victoria and the factors that determine individual participation in employment and society. Sarah's previous research focused on class construction and social mobility in early Melbourne. In addition, Sarah has worked as a tutor at La Trobe University, as an artefact specialist in consulting archaeology and in the management of moveable heritage in the museum and cultural heritage contexts. She is an editor of the *Australasian Historical Archaeology* journal.

Geoff Hewitt first graduated in metallurgy and pursued an engineering career in the shipbuilding and repair industry. An active diver, his first taste of archaeology was shipwreck excavation as a volunteer. This led to undergraduate and post-graduate studies in archaeology at La Trobe University and a new career as a contract and consulting archaeologist. Geoff's broad interests include historical archaeologies of landscape, confinement, defence, urbanism, pastoralism and utopianism, together with histories of maritime and industrial technology.

Justin McCarthy is an archaeologist and the managing director of heritage consulting firm Austral Archaeology Pty Ltd. After graduating from Sydney University in 1982, Justin was appointed as archaeological consultant to the South Australian State Heritage Branch from 1983 to 1987. He then founded Austral Archaeology in Adelaide with offices opening in Sydney and Hobart in the early to mid-1990s. The creation of heritage legislation from the late 1970s into the early 1980s provided opportunities to work around Australia in many aspects of cultural heritage management. In terms of urban archaeology, Justin directed some of the earliest and largest excavations in South Australia, Queensland, Victoria and Tasmania. One of these projects was the Little Lon excavation in Melbourne in 1988 and then the follow-up season in 2003 in collaboration with Godden Mackay Logan heritage consultants and La Trobe University. Justin has also directed regional and thematic heritage surveys, undertaken environmental impact assessments, conservation plans, heritage assessments, research projects, industrial archaeological surveys, interpretative design for historic sites, assessment of cultural landscapes and project management. He has been a member of Australia ICOMOS since 1981 and served as an Executive Member of that organisation for two terms and is currently an Adjunct Research Fellow at Flinders University. Justin has held many positions including deputy member of the former South Australian Heritage Authority, a member of the Heritage Advisory Council of the National Trust of South Australia, an expert advisor on industrial heritage to the Queensland Heritage Council, and an independent assessor for the former Australian Heritage Commission. Austral Archaeology is currently an industry partner with Flinders University.

Richard Mackay AM is the founder and 'Director of Possibilities' at Mackay Strategic and an adjunct professor in the archaeology program at La Trobe University. Richard has worked in cultural heritage management for more than 30 years. He was a founding Partner of GML Heritage, and was an ICOMOS cultural advisor at recent Sessions of the World Heritage Committee. He is currently a Member of the National Executive Committee of Australia ICOMOS and a Casual Member of the NSW Planning Assessment Commission. He has pioneered public archaeology and community participation programs, and was the Project Director of the 'Big Dig' at the Cumberland / Gloucester Streets Site in Sydney's Rocks district in 1994 and the 'Casselden Place' archaeological investigation project in the Little Lon area of Melbourne in 2002. He was the co-editor of the Getty 'Readings in Conservation' volume *Archaeological Sites: Conservation and Management*. In 2013 Richard was the inaugural winner of the Australian Heritage Council 'Sharon Sullivan Award' for his contribution to Australia's national heritage. In 2003 he was made a Member in the General Division of the Order of Australia for services to archaeology and cultural heritage.

Barbara Minchinton is an independent researcher and volunteer at the Public Record Office Victoria. Since completing her doctorate on settlement in the Otways under Victoria's 19th century land acts she has worked on projects including the urban archaeology of Little Lon, soldier settlement in Victoria after the First World War, and women as landowners in Victoria.

Tim Murray is Charles La Trobe Professor of Archaeology at La Trobe University. As a practising archaeologist with an interest in history and epistemology, his research and publication have focused on the history and philosophy of archaeology, the archaeology of the modern world and heritage archaeology. His most recent books include *World Antiquarianism Comparative Perspectives* (co-edited with Alain Schnapp, Lothar von Falkenhausen and Peter Miller, Getty Research Institute, 2013), *An Archaeology of Institutional Confinement: The Hyde Park Barracks, 1848–1886* (co-authored with Peter Davies and Penny Crook, Sydney University Press, 2013), and *From Antiquarian to Archaeologist: The History and Philosophy of Archaeology* (Pen and Sword Press, 2014). His current projects are based around the general theme of transnational archaeologies in the long 19th century, with particular focus on 'contact' archaeology, urban archaeology and technology transfer, and demonstrating the importance of the history of archaeology for building more robust archaeological theory.

Charlotte Smith is Curator Emeritus, Museums Victoria. Before her retirement in 2016, Charlotte was Senior Curator, Politics & Society; a significant aspect of this role was the curation and management of the museum's extensive historical archaeology collection. Charlotte has over 20 years' experience working in museums and universities in England and Australia. She has a PhD from the University of Canberra and an MA from City University, London. She was a Chief Investigator on the ARC Linkage Project *An Historical Archaeology of the Commonwealth Block* and is currently a Partner Investigator on the ARC Linkage Project *How Meston's 'Wild Australia Show' Shaped Australian Aboriginal History*.

Jeremy Smith is Heritage Victoria's Principal Archaeologist, and has been a member of the Archaeology Advisory Committee of the Victorian Heritage Council since 2002. He has worked on sites throughout Australia and the Middle East, and has contributed to a number of publications on significant excavation projects in Victoria, with a focus on the archaeology of early Melbourne. He was also a key contributor to the award-winning book *Ned Kelly: Under the Microscope* (CSIRO Publishing, 2014).

Bronwyn Woff graduated from La Trobe University with a Bachelor of Archaeology, and completed Honours in 2014. Her Honours thesis explored the reuse of glass bottles in early Melbourne. Bronwyn has several years of experience working as a freelance material culture specialist and archaeologist throughout the eastern states of Australia, mostly in Victoria and Tasmania. She specialises as an artefact cataloguer and analyst, and worked as the research assistant for the La Trobe University Commonwealth Block project between 2015 and 2017.

1
Introduction and Context

Tim Murray

This book is best described as an interim report on nearly three decades of excavation and analysis conducted on the Commonwealth Block in Melbourne, Australia. Each of its constituent chapters is written by those who had the most direct responsibilities for the management and execution of the excavation and analysis that had occurred on the Block since the late 1980s, and which continue to this day.

In essence *The Commonwealth Block, Melbourne* describes the cumulative history of the work of many historical archaeologists and historians who have slowly revealed the historical riches of a city precinct that has often been described in the popular and professional literature as a slum.

The authors outline their theoretical concerns and the links they made to a developing archaeology of the city in Australia. Importantly both elements of theory and method (and indeed inspiration and aspiration) changed over time as excavators and analysts responded to previous work, and to the changing disciplinary context of urban archaeology in Australia and elsewhere (see e.g. Bairstow 1990; Birmingham 1988, 1990; Fitts 1999; Green and Leech 2006; Karskens 1997, 1999, 2001; Kelly 1979; Mayne and Murray 2001; Pearson 1979; Praetzellis and Praetzellis 1992, 2005; Rimmer et al. 2011; Wall 1992; Yamin 2000, 2001a, 2001b). There is every possibility that further work will see additional developments in approach and perspective as the shortcomings of previous approaches are revealed and responded to.

Given the scale of the site and the historical and archaeological components of its database, this book does not present a comprehensive reporting of all that has been found there. One important outcome of such a long-running project has been the continuous publication of fundamental data (a process that will continue as the project moves forward) and the development of a regime of open access to its core data, which are now held at Museum Victoria, with a limited amount also available at tDAR: https://core.tdar.org/project/407136/casselden-place-archaeological-excavations. We plan to deposit more of our core data on tDAR in the future as funds allow. It is our earnest hope that making our data openly available will assist the development of a comparative archaeology of the modern city on a global scale, as well as expanding the pool of analysed data for more local aspirations. This has been a major goal since the conclusion of the first phase of detailed analysis (Murray 2003; Murray and Mayne 2001, 2003; Williamson 1999) and comparative work undertaken by Murray and Crook in The Rocks, Sydney (see e.g. Crook and Murray 2004; Godden Mackay 1999; Murray and Crook 2005, *in press*), and more recently by Riccardi (2015) between Melbourne and Buenos Aires, has begun to demonstrate the potential of this multiscalar approach to the archaeology of the modern city in Australia.

Archaeological research at the Commonwealth Block began as an exercise in heritage archaeology, specifically to mitigate the impact of major redevelopment of the site. All subsequent excavations on the Block have also been funded by the development process. It is significant that while some analysis of the important excavated assemblages was funded by developers, the vast bulk of the detailed work of assemblage analysis has been funded through a series of major grants from the Australian Research Council and by La Trobe University. I see this as being particularly significant as Australian taxpayers, rather than the financial beneficiaries of urban development, have played a vital role in enhancing the cultural capital of the city of Melbourne, and through this have made possible the gift of significant analysed urban assemblages to world archaeology. Although the experience of the Cumberland Gloucester Street site in The Rocks, Sydney, saw more developer-funded analysis, once again it was the Australian Research Council (through the Exploring the Archaeology of the Modern City project) that supported the detailed assemblage analysis of much of the original excavations there (see e.g. Crook et al. 2005; Murray 2013). As a result of this extended period of post-excavation analysis the histories of both Sydney and Melbourne have been enhanced, as it has now become possible for the specifically Australian context of migration, nation-building, and the growth of the modern city in Sydney and Melbourne, to join much better known examples from the United States (see e.g. Praetzellis and Praetzellis 2005; Yamin 2000). In the closing chapter of this book I will reflect a little further on the funding of post-excavation analysis but, put simply, without these major funds there would have been no detailed analysis and the assemblages would have most likely remained in their boxes with their secrets intact.

The archaeology of the Commonwealth Block has made an important contribution to the archaeology of the modern city in Australia, joining the justly famous excavations in The Rocks, Sydney as one of the very few instances where archaeologists, historians and members of the general public have been given relatively easy access to the documentary records (and associated material culture) linked with urban archaeological sites in Sydney and Melbourne. It is a bit disappointing to note that over 20 years later with some notable exceptions such as First Government House (Proudfoot et al. 1991), Sarah Hayes' work on the reanalysis of 300 Queen Street in Melbourne, and the work of Mary Casey in Sydney (see e.g. Casey 2005; Casey and Lowe 2000), that important elements of the archaeology of both cities to all intents and purposes, remain unpublished. I am not so naïve to expect that the publication of our book (or indeed the comparative analysis created by Murray and Crook in press) will lead to a major change of heart among practitioners of heritage archaeology or their developer funders that would result in a more widespread published engagement with the many historical and archaeological issues raised by the archaeology of the modern city. Indeed the economics (and contemporary practice) of heritage archaeology militate against such an outcome. Nonetheless I am hopeful that urban archaeology in Australia (especially) will be enhanced by practitioners responding to the work our contributors have done, and in this way contribute directly to the development of the archaeology of the modern city on a global scale.

Each of the constituent chapters effectively create a history of research on the Block. Chapters 2 and 8 explore the genesis of the project as a major instance of heritage archaeology, and the response of Museum Victoria to the challenges of curating what has proved to be an extensive artefact assemblage. An important element of the management of excavated assemblages was the creation of databases that could capture the specifics of the site and its assemblages. Bronwyn Woff's discussion of our project cataloguing processes in Chapter 10 provides additional background to Dr Charlotte Smith's tale of loss and redemption in Chapter 8. These are critical learnings that derive directly from two additional related projects funded by the Australia Research Council where it became possible to make significant process on artefact analysis linking the outcomes of the two major phases of excavation and analysis.

In Chapter 3 Justin McCarthy provides a detailed account of phase 1 of excavation on the Commonwealth Block which took place on the Little Lon site. Justin creates a very clear picture of a large-scale excavation carried out under considerable time pressure in a city that was fundamentally unused to meeting the challenges proposed by major urban excavations. It is particularly noteworthy that the site reports for phase 1 and for subsequent work on limited sections of the remainder of the Block (McCarthy 1989, 1990) were so comprehensive and so quickly available for wide circulation.

Chapter 4 reports analyses that were undertaken nearly a decade after McCarthy finalised phase 1. This research was funded via a grant to Alan Mayne and myself through the Australian Research Council. The difference between our historical and archaeological goals and those of the historians who had supported McCarthy's original research was stark. In large part driven by Mayne's revisionist history of the slum, our goal was to try to establish whether there were stories locked up in all of those fundamentally unanalysed assemblages that could add more than an archaeological exclamation point to received historical wisdom about the social history of the Block. 'Telling a different story' became an important goal for Mayne and Murray which developed into the Vanished Communities project, which employed new modes of historical presentation using multimedia visualisation technologies delivered via a CD Rom (Murray and Mayne 2002).

Chapter 5 reports smaller excavations undertaken at 17 Casselden Place and elsewhere on the Block by other consultants that further established the archaeological potential of the unexcavated parts of the Block. These laid the foundations for the major phase 2 excavations at Casselden Place undertaken by a consortium comprising Godden, Mackay Logan Pty Ltd, Austral Archaeology, led by Justin McCarthy, and La Trobe University, reported in Chapter 6. The analysis (especially its theoretical underpinnings) of the work done at Casselden Place is briefly summarised in Chapter 7, and builds on major publications flowing directly from the excavation and analysis funded by the developer (see GML et al. 2004; and contributors to the issue of the *International Journal of Historical Archaeology*, Murray ed. 2006).

Chapters 9 and 10 report new analyses funded via two further grants from the Australian Research Council and represent the outcomes of significant collaborations between Murray and Museum Victoria, especially Dr Charlotte Smith (Murray 2011; Smith and Hayes 2010; Smith and Murray 2011). This research was undertaken by Dr Sarah Hayes as a post-doctoral fellow and by historian Dr Barbara Minchinton, and has borne additional fruit in publications related to the history of waste disposal in the city, and the ownership of property by women in mid-to-late 19th-century Melbourne (Hayes 2011; Hayes and Minchinton 2016; Minchinton 2017).

Chapter 11 reports the outcomes of the latest excavations on the Commonwealth Block undertaken by Geoff Hewitt for GML which made significant new discoveries in a small unexcavated area of the Block. Chapter 12 concludes the volume.

CHANGES AND TRANSFORMATIONS

Little Lonsdale Street, in central Melbourne, was notorious for much of the 19th and 20th centuries as a foul slum and brothel district. Little Lon, as the neighbourhood was locally known, became entrenched in national Australian popular culture from the time of the First World War when it was featured by the well-known poet and journalist, C.J. Dennis (1915). In 1948 two entire city blocks at the eastern end of Little Lonsdale Street were resumed by the Commonwealth Government. This precinct, a mosaic of houses, shops, warehouses and factories, was almost totally razed and rebuilt.

Notwithstanding half-a-century of 'renewal', traces of this vanished community and of its forgotten history remained for McCarthy and others to uncover. Research by historians and archaeologists came to reveal a working-class and immigrant community that was much more than just a slum occupied by the itinerant and the criminal. It was a place with a long and complex history of social, cultural and economic transformation.

Today, apart from an incomplete shell of late 19th-century buildings along the southern side of Little Lonsdale Street, and around the perimeter formed by Spring, Lonsdale and Exhibition Streets, the surface physical markers of this former community had been obliterated. The internal laneways, and the entire block north from Little Lonsdale Street to Latrobe Street, have gone. The homeplaces, workspaces, and with them the inhabitants of Little Lon were swept away by the public policies designed to clear central Melbourne of its 'slums'.

In 1948 the Commonwealth Government compulsorily acquired the blocks on either side of Little Lonsdale Street, from Latrobe Street in the north to Lonsdale Street in the south, and from Spring Street in the east to Exhibition Street in the west. Most of the northern block to Latrobe Street – including Cumberland Place – was bulldozed in the late 1950s and 1960s to make way for an enormous government office tower. Because of its green ceramic cladding, the Commonwealth Centre became known to Melburnians as the 'green latrine'. It was demolished in the late 1980s and is now the site of yet another high rise apartment block. Much of the rest of the Commonwealth Block has since been cleared and developed by the organisations that have funded all of the excavations (and some of the analyses) we report here.

However the stereotype of slumdom, so effectively described by Mayne (1993, 2017) came to define the essence of Little Lon in the minds of Melburnians, and one of the most remarkable outcomes of our research has been the longevity of such perceptions – even in the face of detailed archaeological and historical data demonstrating the contrary (see e.g. Murray 2005). This was the realm of Madame Brussels, Chinese opium dens and sly grog outlets now being seen as a strong marketing ploy for contemporary gin distillers and local bars. Nonetheless it is also the case that the historical narrative of the precinct has changed to include a more nuanced account of life on the Block. This is perhaps the most significant transformation of the historical context of archaeological analysis of inner-city Melbourne that has happened over the last 30 years. Gone has been the total reliance on the old narrative of slumdom which has now been joined with engaging alternative stories competing for public and professional attention (see e.g. Annear 1996; Arnold 1997; Brown-May 1998; Canon 1975; Davison 1978; Davison et al. 1985; McConville 1980, 2000; Mayne 2006; Mayne and Murray 1999; Mayne et al. 2000). In its place we have constructed a truer representation of the lives of so many people who lived at the margins of Melbourne society from 1850 to 1950 and restored something of a vanished community lying at the heart of this great city.

Nonetheless it is also the case that our attention as historical archaeologists has moved away from just demonstrating the shortcomings of what Mayne has called the 'slum myth'. Our attention is also drawn to seeking a deeper understanding of social and cultural transformations in 19th century urban migrant communities in Australia (and elsewhere), as well as sharpening a focus on political economy of places at the margins of new societies being born at the uttermost ends of the earth. We have barely begun.

ACKNOWLEDGEMENTS

Each of the authors has made their own acknowledgements. I here acknowledge the great skill and commitment of Mr Wei Ming, Archaeology, La Trobe who was responsible for the production of this book, and many of its images. I am very happy to acknowledge my extensive debt to long-time collaborators historian Professor Alan Mayne and archaeologist Dr Penny Crook. They have done their level best to inject some creative history-making and empirical rigour into my work on the modern city. I also acknowledge the great contributions of Dr Sarah Hayes and Dr Barbara Minchinton to the work at Little Lon. I thank the readers of the draft chapters for their speedy and careful work. Last I thank the Getty Research Institute, Los Angeles, California, for the award of a Fellowship during the last quarter of 2017. During this time I was able to make real progress towards completing the long term research project of which the archaeology of the Commonwealth Block forms an important part.

REFERENCES

Annear, R. 1996. *Bearbrass: Imagining Early Melbourne*. Melbourne: Reed Books.

Arnold, J. 1997. The Laneways of Melbourne. In Finch, L. and C. McConville (eds.) *Images of the Urban*, pp. 78–84, Sunshine Coast University College.

Bairstow, D. 1990. Urban Archaeology: American Theory, Australian Practice. *Australian Archaeology* 33: 52–58.

Birmingham, J. 1988. The Refuse of Empire: International Perspectives on Urban Colonial Rubbish. In Birmingham, J. et al. (eds.) *Archaeology and Colonisation: Australia in the World Context*, pp. 149–171, Sydney: Australian Society for Historical Archaeology Incorporated.

Birmingham, J. 1990. A Decade of Digging: Deconstructing Urban Archaeology. *Australian Historical Archaeology* 8: 13–22.

Brown-May, A. 1998. *Melbourne Street Life: The Itinerary of Our Days*. Melbourne: Australian Scholarly Publishing.

Canon, M. 1975. *Life in the Cities: Australia in the Victorian Age*. Melbourne: Nelson.

Casey, M. 2005. Material Culture and the Construction of Hierarchy at the Conservatorium Site, Sydney. *Australasian Historical Archaeology* 23: 97–113.

Casey & Lowe Associates, 2000. Archaeological Investigation: CSR Site, Pyrmont (Jacksons Landing). Unpublished report prepared for Lend Lease Development, 3 vols, December 2000.

Crook, P. and T. Murray, 2004. The Analysis of Cesspit Deposits from The Rocks, Sydney. *Australasian Journal of Historical Archaeology* 22: 44–56.

Crook, P., L. Ellmoos and T. Murray, 2005. *Keeping up with the McNamaras: A Historical Archaeological Study of the Cumberland and Gloucester Streets Site, The Rocks, Sydney*. Sydney: Historic Houses Trust of NSW.

Davison, G. 1978. *The Rise and Fall of Marvellous Melbourne*. Melbourne: Melbourne University Press.

Davison, G., D. Dunstan and C. McConville, 1985. *The Outcasts of Melbourne: Essays in Social History*. Sydney: Allen & Unwin.

Fitts, R. 1999. The Archaeology of Middle-Class Domesticity and Gentility in Victorian Brooklyn. *Historical Archaeology* 33(1): 39–62.

Godden Mackay Heritage Consultants, 1999. *The Cumberland/Gloucester Streets Site, The Rocks: Archaeological Investigation Report*, Volumes 1, 3–5, prepared for the Sydney Cove Authority. Sydney: Godden Mackay Logan Pty Ltd.

Godden Mackay Logan, La Trobe University and Austral Archaeology, 2004. Casselden Place, 50 Lonsdale Street, Melbourne: Archaeological Excavations – Research Archive. HV report collection no. 3916.

Green, A. and R. Leech (eds.), 2006. *Cities in the World, 1500–2000: Papers Given at the Conference for Post-Medieval Archaeology, April 2002*. Leeds: Maney Publishing.

Hayes, S. 2011. Amalgamation of Archaeological Assemblages: Experiences from the Commonwealth Block Project Melbourne. *Australian Archaeology* 73: 13–24.

Hayes, S. and B. Minchinton, 2016. Melbourne's Waste Management History and Cesspit Formation Processes: Evidence from Little Lon. *Australian Archaeology* 82(1): 12–24.

Karskens, G. 1997. *The Rocks. Life in Early Sydney*. Melbourne: Melbourne University Press.

Karskens, G. 1999. *Inside The Rocks: The Archaeology of a Neighbourhood*. Alexandria, NSW: Hale and Iremonger.

Kelly, M. 1979. Roads to Yesterday. In Stanbury, P. (ed.) *10,000 Years of Sydney Life: A Guide to Archaeological Discovery*, pp. 2–9, Sydney: Macleay Museum.

McCarthy, J. 1989. Archaeological Investigation – The Commonwealth Block Melbourne, Victoria. HV report collection no. 198.

McCarthy, J. 1990. Archaeological Investigation – The Black Eagle & Oddfellows Hotels (Site B), The Commonwealth Block Melbourne, Victoria.

McConville, C. 1980. The Location of Melbourne's Prostitutes, 1870–1920. *Historical Studies* 19(74): 86–97.

McConville, C. 2000. Big Notes from a Little Street: Re/newing Social History in Melbourne? *Australian Historical Studies* 32: 325–327.

Mayne, A. 1993. *The Imagined Slum: Newspaper Representation in Three Cities, 1870–1914*. Leicester: Leicester University Press.

Mayne, A. 2017. *Slums: The History of a Global Injustice*. London: Reaktion Press.

Mayne, A. and T. Murray, 1999. 'In Little Lon … Wiv Ginger Mick': Telling the Forgotten History of a Vanished Community. *Journal of Popular Culture* 33(1): 49–60.

Mayne, A. and T. Murray (eds.), 2001. *The Archaeology of Urban Landscapes: Explorations in Slumland*. Cambridge: Cambridge University Press.

Mayne, A., T. Murray and S. Lawrence, 2000. Historic Sites: Melbourne's Little Lon. *Australian Historical Studies* 31(114): 131–151.

Minchinton, B. 2017a. 'Prostitutes' and 'Lodgers' in Little Lon: Constructing a List of Occupiers in Nineteenth-Century Melbourne. *Australasian Historical Archaeology* 35: 64–70.

Minchinton, B. 2017b. Women as Landowners in Victoria: Questions from Little Lon. *History Australia* 14(1): 67–81.

Murray, T. 2005, Images of Little Lon: Making History, Changing Perceptions. In Murray, T. (ed.) *Object Lessons: Archaeology and Heritage in Australia*, pp. 167–185, Melbourne: Australian Scholarly Publishing.

Murray, T. 2006. Integrating Archaeology and History at the Commonwealth Block: Little Lon and Casselden Place. *International Journal of Historical Archaeology* 10(4): 395–413.

Murray, T. 2011. Research Using Museum Collections Need Not Be a 'Vale of Tears', Though It Often Is. In Smith, C.H.F. and T. Murray (eds.) *Caring for Our Collections: Papers from the Symposium 'Developing Sustainable, Strategic Collection Management Approaches for Archaeological Assemblages'*, pp. 79–88, Melbourne: Museum Victoria.

Murray, T. 2013. Expanding Horizons in the Archaeology of the Modern City: A Tale in Six Projects. *Journal of Urban History*, 6 March 2013, doi:10.1177/0096144213479308.

Murray, T. (ed.) 2003. *Exploring the Modern City: Recent Approaches to Urban History and Archaeology*. Sydney: Historic Houses Trust of NSW.

Murray, T. (ed.) 2006. *International Journal of Historical Archaeology* 10(4).

Murray, T. and P. Crook, 2005. Exploring the Archaeology of the Modern City: Issues of Scale, Integration and Complexity. *International Journal of Historical Archaeology* 9(2): 89–109.

Murray, T. and P. Crook, in press. *The Archaeology of the Modern City in 19th Century Australia: In Search of the McNamaras*. New York: Springer.

Murray, T. and A. Mayne, 2001. Imaginary Landscapes: Reading Melbourne's Little Lon. In Mayne, A. and T. Murray (eds.) *The Archaeology of Urban Landscapes: Explorations in Slumland*, pp. 89–105, Cambridge: Cambridge University Press.

Murray, T. and A. Mayne, 2002. *Vanished Communities: Investigating History at Little Lon, An ARC Funded CDROM*. Melbourne: La Trobe University and Swish Group.

Murray, T. and A. Mayne 2003. (Re)Constructing a Lost Community: Little Lon, Melbourne, Australia. *Historical Archaeology* 37(1): 87–101.

Pearson, M. 1979. Historic Sites: Themes and Variations. In Stanbury, P. (ed.) *10,000 years of Sydney Life: A Guide to Archaeological Discovery*, pp. 96–105, Sydney: Macleay Museum.

Praetzellis, A. and M. Praetzellis, 1992. Faces and Facades: Victorian Ideology in Early Sacramento. In Yentsch, A.E. and M.C. Beaudry (eds.) *The Art and Mystery of Historical Archaeology: Essays in Honor of James Deetz*, pp. 75–99, Florida: CRC Press.

Praetzellis, M. and A. Praetzellis (eds.), 2005. *Putting the 'There' There: Historical Archaeologies of West Oakland, 1-880 Cypress Freeway Replacement Project*. California: Anthropological Studies Center, Sonoma State University.

Proudfoot, H., A. Bickford, B. Egloff and R. Stocks, 1991. *Australia's First Government House*. Sydney: Allen & Unwin and the Department of Planning.

Riccardi, P. 2015. A Tale of Two Cities: Nineteenth Century Consumer Behaviour in Melbourne and Buenos Aires. Unpublished PhD dissertation, La Trobe University.

Rimmer, J., P. Connelly, S. Rees Jones and J. Walker (eds.) 2011. Special Collection: Poverty in Depth: New International Perspectives. *International Journal of Historical Archaeology* 15: 533–636.

Smith, C.H.F. and S. Hayes, 2010. Managing the Commonwealth Block Assemblage: An Australian Case Study. *Collections: A Journal for Museum and Archive Professionals* 6(3): 171–188.

Smith C.H.F. and T. Murray (eds.), 2011. *Caring for Our Collections: Papers from the Symposium 'Developing Sustainable, Strategic Collection Management Approaches for Archaeological Assemblages'*. Melbourne: Museum Victoria.

Wall, D.D. 1992. Sacred Dinners and Secular Teas: Constructing Domesticity in Mid-19th-Century New York. *Historical Archaeology* 25: 69–81.

Williamson, C. 1998. Slums and Sluts: Lonsdale Street Project Report. Unpublished report for the La Trobe University, Melbourne.

Yamin, R. 2001a. Becoming New York: The Five Points Neighbourhood. *Historical Archaeology* 35(3): 1–5.

Yamin, R. 2001b. Alternative Narratives: Respectability at New York's Five Points. In Mayne, A. and T. Murray (eds.) *The Archaeology of Urban Landscapes: Explorations in*

Slumland, pp. 154–170, Cambridge: Cambridge University Press.

Yamin, R. (ed.) 2000. Tales of Five Points: Working-Class Life in Nineteenth-Century New York. Reports prepared for Edwards and Kelcey Engineers, Inc. and General Services Administration (Region 2), 6 vols. John Milner Associates, West Chester, Pennsylvania.

2
Agencies of Change: Government Perspectives on Little Lon

Kristal Buckley and Jeremy Smith

The project better known as Little Lon began with a handwritten note from Rosemary Buchan, Manager – Archaeology at the Victoria Archaeological Survey (VAS), dated 9 September 1987. It reads:

> Kristal – Ivar Nelsen, C'wealth Dept. of Housing & Construction rang. They are developing property they own in the city ... for office complex. They have a sizeable historical dossier on the area including plans of previous buildings. Area was once focus of Chinese occupancy and red light district (?). Are concerned to ensure no impt. archaeological material is disturbed. They have funding for consultant but need advice on (a) what work they should do; (b) who should do it. Would require c. 1/2 day of your or Iain's time to eyeball it for them & advise. Could you ring him [number] and discuss after your return from 4-wheel driving course?[1]

Humble beginnings for a project that would extend over a period of two decades, and provide some direction-setting challenges for historical archaeology in Victoria. But in fact, such notes and contacts are commonplace in the work of the government historical archaeologists, and not all of them result in such significant outcomes.

VAS Historical Archaeologists Iain Stuart and Kristal Buckley visited the site on 21 September 1987, initiating a range of complex negotiations between several Victorian and Commonwealth departments, and a steep learning curve for all concerned. By December 1987, an excavation team led by Justin McCarthy of Austral Archaeology began salvage excavations which continued through the summer months into early 1988, ahead of impossibly tight development timelines for parts of the Commonwealth Block, bounded by Spring, Lonsdale, Exhibition and Latrobe Streets in Melbourne's central city grid.

This paper is about the two major phases of the Little Lon archaeological excavations – one that took place in the late 1980s and the other that occurred in the early years of the 2000s. The contexts of these very different timeframes are considered, and the legacies of the two digs within the changing and developing landscape of archaeology in Victoria.

The project has been the subject of many media reports (especially in the second stage, as will be discussed later), but also in the writing of both academic and professional archaeologists that were involved (*cf.* chapters in this volume; Mackay et al. 2006; Mayne and Lawrence 1998; Mayne and Murray 1999; Mayne, Murray and Lawrence 2000; McConville 2000; McKenzie 2003; Murray 2003, 2006; Murray and Mayne 2001; Smith 2002; Smith and Tout-Smith 2010). In this paper, we do not seek to repeat or revisit those other accounts, but to focus on a rarely considered part of these processes: our own roles over time as the archaeologists employed by the Victorian state heritage apparatus; and the interplay between government requirements, client/owner non-negotiables and concerns, consultants (providing a wide variety of professional services), and interested observers (including the public, the media, but also our peers in academia).

HISTORICAL ARCHAEOLOGY IN 1980S VICTORIA

Recalling the state of play for historical archaeology in the 1980s is an important part of this account. At that time, legislation for the protection and regulation of all 'land' archaeology was provided by the *Archaeological and Aboriginal Relics Preservation Act* 1972 ('Relics Act'), administered by the then Victoria Archaeological Survey (VAS), which had been variously located within government structures, and was in 1987 part of the Victorian Ministry of Planning and Environment.

From the 1970s, historic buildings, shipwrecks and Aboriginal and 'historical' archaeological sites and artefacts were protected by different state legislative frameworks, and there were separate government branches for each of them. Although the 'Relics Act' did not easily read as applying to the archaeological resources associated with the post-contact history of Victoria, a High Court ruling in 1981 determined that this was the case, leaving historical archaeological material well protected in

---

[1] Victoria Archaeological Survey file note from Rosemary Buchan to Kristal Buckley (9/9/87).

some ways (via the 'blanket protection' determined by the state), but without any workable mechanisms that might be employed when development processes aimed to proceed without detrimental impact on archaeological sites and materials.

The late 1980s was a time of significant changes to shift decision making for Aboriginal heritage to Aboriginal community organisations (rather than the state minister or his/her delegated officials). Political barriers in the Victorian Parliament at the time frustrated the Minister, the Hon. Jim Kennan, and he sought assistance from the Commonwealth Parliament, resulting in the 1987 Part IIa amendments to the *Aboriginal and Torres Strait Islander Protection Act* 1984 (Commonwealth), leaving the 'Relics Act' with limited operational effect overall.

Suffice to say that the legal requirements for historical archaeology were not clear or well understood by their users – inside or outside of government – at the time that Ivar Nelsen contacted the VAS to initiate a discussion about the archaeological potential of the Commonwealth Block.

An added dimension of complexity is that the Commonwealth Block was owned by the Commonwealth Government, and therefore not subject to state heritage laws. The Commonwealth legislation for 'historic' heritage was the *Australian Heritage Commission Act* 1975, which had been introduced by the Whitlam government following the landmark Hope Inquiry into the National Estate (see Veale and Firestone 2012). Many archaeological sites were included in the Register of the National Estate, but there were no specific legal or policy provisions for archaeological interventions. While the Australian Heritage Commission was an influential national champion of progressive heritage practices, the act itself was not strong in its ability to protect heritage places, nor did it outline the responsibilities of government developers when planning work that could impact on heritage values.

It is quite conceivable that the development of the Commonwealth Block could have proceeded without any archaeology being undertaken at all. In our view, a number of factors fortuitously aligned, enabling the project to be established.

While the VAS had conducted some excavation and survey projects for historical archaeology for more than a decade under the leadership of its first Director, Dr Peter Coutts, the establishment of a new unit and two positions for historical archaeology occurred in mid-1987, only a few months before Ivar Nelsen's phone call. It was therefore a time when there were dedicated staff able to respond to the request.

There was no legislative basis for the VAS to be involved at the Commonwealth Block. Involvement in an 'advisory' capacity was agreed by the director with both excitement and trepidation given the degree to which it ultimately diverted significant resources. The potential public interest of the project, and the capacity to establish a baseline for the newly created historical archaeology unit were deciding factors. While the Commonwealth ownership of the site created extra complexities, it also brought into play the Australian Heritage Commission and the Commonwealth Department's heritage architect (Ivar Nelsen), both familiar with issues of archaeological potential, the precautionary principles of the Australia ICOMOS Burra Charter (2013),[2] and the need to engage in pre-development testing and salvage in historically important areas.

The 1980s also marked a period when social histories and recognition and interest in Australian history and identity were on the rise. In 1985, the 150th anniversary of the establishment of the colony that became Victoria was marked by the commissioning of new histories; and many heritage conservation and interpretation projects were supported in the lead-up to the 1988 bicentennial of the non-Indigenous 'settlement' of the Australian continent through the processes of European colonisation and invasion of Indigenous lands. New staff and academic programs in historical archaeology began at La Trobe University in Melbourne around this time, joining the established academic programs there and at the University of Melbourne that focused on the long history of Indigenous peoples and interests in art history and classical archaeology. In other words, the time was right for a strong mix of professional, academic and public interest in the early history of Melbourne, including early neighbourhoods like Little Lon. The assessment of the archaeological potential was cursory by today's standards, but was considered to be substantial due to the lack of post-Second World War re-development on the site and the opportunity to research the lives of Melbourne's 19th-century urban poor. The possibility of excavating a large assemblage of artefacts with research significance was also recognised, despite the lack of precedents in Melbourne.

From the 'Commonwealth Block' to 'Little Lon' (1987–1988)

The Commonwealth Government had acquired the Commonwealth Block bounded by Spring, Lonsdale, Exhibition and Latrobe Streets in 1948. Over time, many of the small 19th and early 20th century buildings on the block (including those that faced

---

[2] While the current version of the Burra Charter is dated 2013, its first version was adopted in 1979 and there were some amended versions released during the 1980s.

2. Agencies of Change

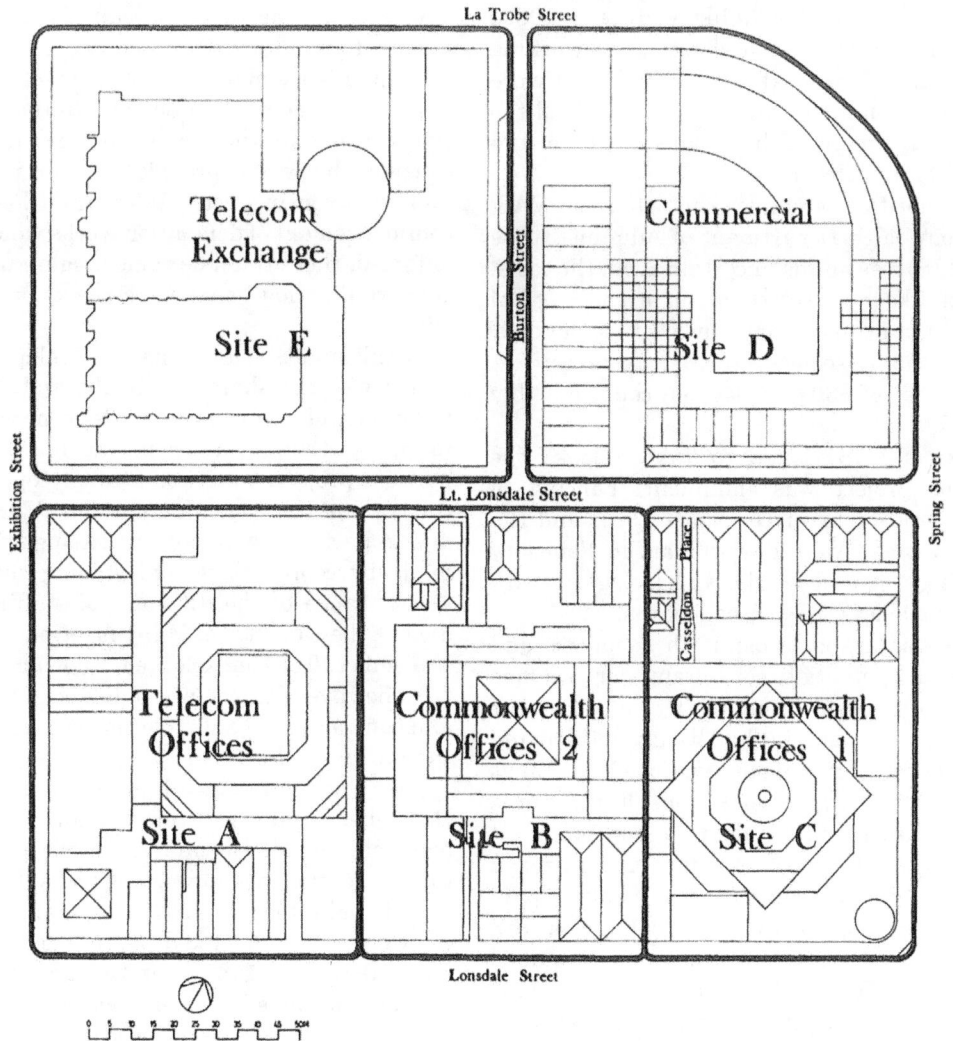

Figure 2.1: Commonwealth Block site plan (source: Parliamentary Standing Committee on Public Works 1988: Fig. 2).

the main streets, but also a number of cross-cutting laneways) had been demolished – and most of the remaining small single and double-storey structures that fringed the 'block' were in fair/poor condition and unused (other than for storage). A large area in the central part of the 'block' was surfaced and used for car parking. The Commonwealth Government's policy at this time was to improve the standard of government-owned office accommodation and to reduce its reliance on expensive leased office space elsewhere in the city. In the 1980s plans were developed to build several new office towers on the Commonwealth Block.

Possibly the most imposing building on the Commonwealth Block at this time was a large office building tagged the 'green latrine'[3] (on Site D).[4] The Commonwealth had determined that this building could not be refurbished in a cost-effective manner because of asbestos removal costs. It was sold in March 1988 (and later demolished), and was to be superseded by a new 42-storey building to house the offices of Commonwealth Government departments (on Site C). A new building was to be constructed on Site A for Telecom, alongside a recently established Telecom exchange building on Site E. Site B – in the centre of the block facing Lonsdale Street – was scheduled for later redevelopment, as will be discussed in this paper.

There was little experience or information for the Commonwealth owners and/or VAS staff to guide the consideration, costing or timing of an urban archaeological project on this scale in Victoria. The most urgently looming questions concerned how much the project might cost, how long it would take and who could lead it. The VAS had directed excavations throughout Victoria, but the scale

---

[3] The distinctive colour was provided by thousands of 'Wunderlich' tiles, manufactured in Victoria. A tile from the building is held by the Sunshine District Historical Society (Victorian Collections online).

[4] Sites A–E were designated by the Commonwealth as part of the project proposal, and are shown in Figure 2.1.

of this project made this unlikely. In the 1980s there were few consultant archaeologists working in Victoria, and those that were established were sole traders or small enterprises unable to lead the project (although many of them joined the team and contributed to its outcomes).

When its heritage architect contacted the VAS, the Commonwealth Department of Administrative Services (DAS) was just as uncertain about the costs, timing and likely outcomes of an archaeological investigation, but had some awareness of 'digs' in Sydney, and it seemed worth looking into. A notional budget of $30,000–$40,000 could possibly be allocated.

By the time VAS visited to 'take a look', the development project was imminent. Fencing of the block would occur in December 1987, and the construction works were due to start in February 1988, leaving a period for the archaeological work on site of a little less than three months.

The VAS was asked to establish a budget, and to identify a potential consultant for salvage excavations of Sites A, B, and C. By early October 1987, a principal consultant had been identified and three budget scenarios were developed. Costings included a director/principal consultant, three trench supervisors and an artefacts supervisor. It was assumed that the vast amount of labour needed would be provided by volunteers (who would be paid a small daily allowance to cover their expenses). In order for the budgets to work, it was assumed that the 'client' (DAS and Telecom) would provide needed materials, equipment, services, onsite offices and historical research.

The budgets at this point ranged from $114,000–$154,000 depending on various timing and other contingencies, but this was in excess of the DAS's expectations. A revised scenario was presented, which eliminated Site B, since the development would not proceed there for several years at least; and ensuring that the work could be completed on Site C by the end of January 1988. The Commonwealth preferred to contract a principal consultant, who would then engage all other personnel and purchase the needed equipment.

DAS sought a second opinion from Dr Michael Pearson, an archaeologist and senior official at the Commonwealth Government's Australian Heritage Commission, who visited Melbourne for that purpose in late October. He advised that the estimated costs seemed reasonable, and reinforced the need for funding of the post-excavation analysis and reporting.

In case it is not already clear, the ticking time clock added a particular edge to these negotiations. Dr Pearson raised concerns about the difficulty of meeting the time expectations of the DAS given that the project itself was not yet agreed or funded. A revised total budget of $165,000 was finalised by the VAS at this time – considered to be a sufficient but modest figure.

By mid-November, DAS confirmed that it could not allocate more than $50,000 to the project until the hearing of the Parliamentary Inquiry could consider the need to provide funds for report writing and other contingencies. While the 1 February 1988 commencement of demolition works would be rigidly enforced, there could be some staging within Site C that would allow some extra weeks on parts of the site.

At this point, Telecom had a development agenda which was not shared as freely, and did not wish to be part of a joint project. Telecom was planning to engage their own consultant and commission a parallel project. This was strongly opposed by the Australian Heritage Commission, VAS and DAS, due in part to the loss of cost savings that could be made by coordinating and staging the work, but also because of the difficulty of staffing two such digs at the same time. Many meetings later, in late November, Telecom relented, allowing Sites A and C to be investigated in a single sequential project and contract. DAS and Telecom contributed $50,000 each towards the costs.

The principal consultant started work on 8 December, and the project team (including the principal consultants and VAS staff) quickly worked to set up the site office, engage sub-consultants, recruit volunteers, purchase equipment and plan the work. After only ten days, the excavations began on 18 December 1987, even though less than 2/3 of the needed funds had been secured.

Throughout this period there were many small scuffles over the provision of a variety of in-kind resources and services. For example, at this time, Telecom Australia (the precursor of Telstra) was a government-owned monopoly for telephone services, and as they were one of the project 'owners', VAS naively assumed that Telecom could provide the site office with a telephone, but this proved to be the source of long-running arguments. However, many other important contributions were made by the Commonwealth Government such as the site office space, a backhoe (and operator), fencing and site security, typing, printing and drafting. Private sponsors supplied computers and a photocopier to the project, and of course, the Victorian community contributed overwhelmingly to the call for volunteers that performed every kind of needed job.

Significant amounts of time of a number of VAS staff were provided to the project (including archaeologists, a conservator, an education officer and stores/laboratory staff), and VAS also provided a telephone message service to organise the volunteers, office furnishings and appliances, froth flotation of soil samples and some excavation equipment. VAS coordinated much of the publicity for the project, led by the dducation officer, Derek Fowell; although the Commonwealth Department and the director and key staff of the dig quickly became very involved in media and publicity activities. In November 1987, a seminar with academic colleagues in the fields of history and archaeology sought to fast-track the research plan for the excavations. At this time, the project team began to refer to the area as Little Lon, drawn from the literary references that were included in recent books (Davison 1979; Davison, Dunstan and McConville 1985).

A timeline was adopted that allowed the archaeologists to work ahead of the demolition program. While parts of Site C had to be completed by the end of January 1988 (as always planned), other parts of Site C were able to be worked on until the end of February. Site A was planned for March and April 1988, and the report writing and artefact analysis was scheduled to occur by the end of 1988.

From the beginning of the discussions about this project, VAS recognised that it could generate significant public interest and provide an unusual opportunity for the community to experience archaeological excavations. Public viewing of the excavations was arranged wherever safety and practical site management issues allowed, and there were often people standing at the fence, watching the work and chatting to the workers. Interpretive signs were installed, and there was a lot of media contact.

As noted already, the public response to the project was very positive. In terms of volunteer contribution, the team reported that 600 person-days of volunteer labour had been contributed in January 1988 alone.

In terms of publicity, the project was viewed as a success by VAS and the Victorian Ministry. There were numerous newspaper articles, radio news, and many interviews with people working on the site. The project was covered by TV News and current affairs, including the local Chinese language press. The Victorian Film Corporation produced a documentary about the project.

Parliamentary Inquiry (1988)

In February 1988, after the project was already well underway, a Commonwealth Parliamentary Standing Committee on Public Works held an inquiry into the construction of the new Commonwealth offices building, which now stands at the Spring Street end of the Commonwealth Block (Site C). The VAS, Australian Heritage Commission (AHC) and National Trust provided written submissions about heritage issues, and the VAS and the Australian Heritage Commission appeared at the Hearing in Melbourne on 11 February 1988 to assist the committee.

Many issues were discussed, including the need for the Commonwealth to allow for more time for archaeological investigations to occur prior to developing its own sites in future. The most pressing issue raised with the committee was the need for the project to be fully funded so that all areas of archaeological potential could be investigated prior to the development, and the necessary artefact processing, analysis and report writing could be completed. The submissions argued for the importance of the post-excavation processes and the resources they would require, and highlighted the need for the long-term conservation and storage of the excavated material. The AHC submission, in particular, stressed the importance of linking the excavation and post-excavation funding, rather than allowing a hiatus to occur between them (reflecting an awareness of problems that had arisen on other Australian projects).

Underlying all of these interactions were questions about why an archaeological excavation on the site justified the expenditure of precious public funds. Although the members seemed to appreciate the importance of the 19th-century urban heritage, the representatives of the heritage organisations did not meet with an especially sympathetic committee and the tone of the interaction was challenging. There was not an automatic acceptance that proponents of developments should pay for pre-development archaeological investigations. The committee raised the valid point that the value of the site should have been identified at an earlier moment, giving Victorian and Commonwealth officials more opportunity to explore them without impeding the process of redevelopment. One member suggested that a map be developed that plotted all the important archaeological sites in the city, and VAS described its plans to develop an archaeological zoning plan for that purpose.

Despite some apparent scepticism, in the end the committee found that the 'block' had 'considerable cultural significance due to its archaeological remains' (Parliamentary Standing Committee on Public Works 1988: 11) and that the archaeological potential was remarkable due to the lack of new developments affecting the ground surface since the acquisition of the block by the Commonwealth in 1948. While both DAS and Telecom had provided $50,000 each for the project, the committee seemed to accept the validity of the project budget prepared by the VAS ($165,000 plus significant in-kind contributions by VAS and the two Commonwealth agencies); and acknowledged the significant shortfall. The committee proposed that the DAS should continue to consult with the VAS and the AHC concerning the costs for the analysis of the artefacts, reporting and storage of the artefacts, although the specific means of doing so were left unidentified. Following the completion of the committee's report in May, the additional funds were finally provided in June 1988, by which time the fieldwork was complete and demolitions on Site C well advanced.

After the Excavations

By October 1988, meetings were still occurring to sort out the long-term storage and conservation of the records from the excavation (artefacts, documents, photographs).

Justin McCarthy reported that despite a limited retention strategy during the excavation, there were 482 large boxes and 168 small boxes of artefacts stored at the site office, and that the collection of coins had been moved to the VAS lab for conservation treatment.

The two Commonwealth Government agencies were keen to transfer the material to Museum Victoria, and there were many discussions about the packing and cataloguing needs of the collection. The museum was generally agreeable, but was itself in a period of transition, in the midst of proposals to establish a new Melbourne Museum at Southbank (this did not proceed). It was therefore not in a good position to accept and store the large quantity of materials involved. By July 1990, all the records were deposited with Museum Victoria, with the photographic record to follow after copying by the Commonwealth.

Modest Gains?

The outcomes of this project have been the subject of reflection by many of its observers and participants (*cf.* chapters in this volume; Mayne and Lawrence 1998; Mayne and Murray 1999; Mayne, Murray and Lawrence 2000; McConville 2000; Murray and Mayne 2001).

From the point of view of the government-based archaeologists, there is no doubt that the excavation did 'new things' for historical archaeology in Victoria. It opened a new dialogue between government-based historical archaeologists and our academic colleagues in the universities, and between archaeologists and historians, exposing at the same time some enduring points of inter-disciplinary friction (*cf.* McConville 2000). It heightened awareness for the VAS of the research and public interest potential of such places – especially in the processes of excavation and the power of the materiality of small objects left behind. It started discussions with the museum and other institutions about the value of such collections and what to do about their long-term curation. It opened a new avenue of passionate public interest in the city's history, especially in the lives of the people outside the 'elites' of society.

For the staff of the VAS, the project elicited equal measures of excitement and terror as we launched into quite unfamiliar terrain. The sharp learning curve revealed that huge numbers of artefacts might be recovered from urban digs, and the large scale of the costs required to embark on such projects (in human, financial, time and political terms). While these ideas were not entirely new, the project increased the pressures on the VAS to find ways to be predictive and proactive in its work. And, it helped in a small way to begin the development of consulting in historical archaeology in Victoria, but perhaps not as dramatically as expected at the time.

Most of all, it opened – ever so slightly – the idea that 'our' history and heritage could be worth this kind of serious engagement, research and care. As a supportive article in Victoria's 'Trust News' proclaimed in June 1988: 'Archaeologists don't just look for tombs or dinosaur bones. Objects of everyday life can be just as important ...'.

In the Wake of Little Lon (1989–1995)

Given the success and high profile of the Little Lon dig, it may have been expected that the project would lead to more frequent archaeological work in the city in the following months and years, and to the establishment of a dynamic urban archaeology profession. But, in the decade that followed the Little Lon dig, from 1989 to 1999, there was only one other excavation conducted in the city, at the Queen Victoria Market site (former Old Melbourne Cemetery) in 1991. Another major dig did follow soon after Little Lon, at the Saltwater Crossing site in Footscray, but the excavation landscape remained almost empty in the city itself. It was not until a decade later that archaeology became a relatively common sight in the Melbourne landscape; from 2000 to 2010, there were 87 historical archaeological projects conducted in the city, and there have now been more than 200.

Little Lon did not lead directly to an outbreak of archaeological activity in the city but significant changes to heritage management practices took place in the years after the dig, and perhaps the legacy of the project lies in the legislative and policy reforms that followed.

The Little Lon dig was significant because it revealed to an unsuspecting public that the Melbourne city contained an archaeological record; for the first time the layers of the city's history were exposed, and Melbourne's status as a major metropolis was, in some way, affirmed. As noted already, in the 1980s very little historical archaeology had taken place in Victoria, with only a handful of research projects being undertaken by the state heritage agency and by university teams, and some work by a small number of archaeology consultancies. There was more activity in the field of Aboriginal archaeology, but in the public mind archaeology was largely something that happened overseas. The Little Lon project engaged the public and placed archaeology on the agenda for policy developers and law-makers, but it was not directly a catalyst for increased archaeological work in the city.

To some degree, the most significant advances in archaeology in the late 1980s and early 1990s were taking place in the area of strategic policy development, rather than on excavation sites. David Bannear's landmark project researching and documenting the state's gold mining sites started in 1990. At the same time Gary Vines conducted an assessment of industrial heritage in Melbourne's west, and Karen Townrow completed a study of Victorian sealing and whaling sites. Behind the scenes government archaeologists at the Victoria Archaeological Survey were analysing laws and practice beyond Victoria and developing an understanding of what might constitute strong archaeological legislation. It was a changeable time in Victorian politics with ministers, departments and state agencies being shuffled and reshaped regularly, and it was difficult to establish and progress a clear agenda for legislative reform. The existence of clearly defined legislation for maritime heritage, the *Historic Shipwrecks Act* 1981, was cited to policy-makers as a successful precursor for laws that would specifically relate to historical archaeology.

The election of the Kennett (Liberal) government in 1992 led to the formation of Heritage Victoria, which included the maritime and historical archaeological management divisions from the former VAS. The archaeologists joined new colleagues from the Heritage Branch and Historic Buildings Council pushing for improved legislation, which was well received by the planning minister, Robert MacLellan, and the detailed framing of the new *Heritage Act* began.

It is too simplistic to say that the success and profile of the Little Lon dig directly precipitated the development of strong archaeology legislation in the new act. Ideas about the protection and management of archaeological sites were coalescing and developing among the key state agencies in the years leading up to the dig, and the profession was maturing in other ways at the same time. Lobbying and advocacy was taking place with ministers and within government departments with varying degrees of success. Projects such as the state-wide survey of Victoria's gold mining heritage led to an understanding of historical archaeology and support from key stakeholders such as the Minerals Council of Australia, which proved invaluable when feedback was sought on the new *Heritage Act* provisions. But Little Lon played its part as a very real demonstration of a significant and substantial archaeological site in the heart of the city, at a time when large excavations were almost unknown in Australia, and archaeology was poorly understood. The strength of the public response at Little Lon, and at the Saltwater Crossing site in Footscray, demonstrated that these places were engaging and important, and should be appropriately protected and managed.

THE NEW *HERITAGE ACT* (1995–2001)

Six years after the completion of the Little Lon dig, the *Heritage Act* 1995 was enacted. Part 6 of the *Heritage Act*, titled the *Protection of Archaeological Places* addressed the shortcomings of the previous legislation and guaranteed blanket protection for all historical archaeological sites in the state. The new act also established a process for mandatory recording and reporting of sites, and included permitting (or *Consent*) requirements that enabled the executive director of Heritage Victoria to set conditions for archaeological investigations, post-excavation analysis and report production as part of any excavation or site disturbance work. These *Heritage Act* approvals, that enabled the setting of conditions on permits for archaeological work, would underpin the developments of a strong historical archaeology profession in Victoria.

While Little Lon did not result in a large number of urban excavations taking place in the city in the years directly after its completion, in the opinion of Mike McIntyre[5] the Little Lon experience was an 'eye-opener' that identified a need for legislative controls that included specific historical archaeology protection mechanisms beyond the broader heritage-place management provisions of acts such as the *Historic Buildings Act* 1981 and the *Planning and Environment Act* 1987. For example, the objectives of the *Planning and Environment Act* included a direction to 'conserve and enhance those buildings, areas or other places which are of scientific, aesthetic, architectural or historical interest, or otherwise of special cultural value' – archaeology might find a place somewhere in this description, but it was not a central consideration in the minds of the administrators and politicians who framed the act.

Although the new *Heritage Act* came in to being in the mid-1990s, it took a few years for the requirements of the legislation to be understood by developers, planners and other key stakeholders. In 1998, Heritage Victoria developed a mapping layer that showed the location of potential archaeological sites in the city. The plan was based on an earlier study (Fels, Lavelle and Mider 1993), which was partly a response to recommendations from the Little Lon Parliamentary Inquiry in 1988. At the same time, the Archaeology Advisory Committee of the Victorian Heritage Council worked with Heritage Victoria to promote an awareness of the city's archaeology and the requirements of the *Heritage Act*, particularly to statutory planners at the key local government agency, the City of Melbourne. Statistics show that the framework for the effective management of Melbourne's historical archaeology started to take shape three to four years after the establishment of the *Heritage Act* 1995. In the ten years following the completion of

---

[5] Pers. comm. McIntyre was director of the VAS to 1993 and a senior officer of Heritage Victoria in 1994–2001.

the Little Lon dig in 1989 there had been only one other dig in the Melbourne CBD; in the three years from 1998 to 2000 there were 13. As archaeology began to find its place in Melbourne's planning and heritage management landscape, the stage was set for the next big project. The Casselden Place dig in 2002 took place at exactly the right time to consolidate the growth in the awareness and profile of archaeology in Melbourne.

MANAGING CASSELDEN PLACE (2001–2005)

The new *Heritage Act* processes meant that the owners of the Casselden Place site that adjoined the land where the Little Lon dig had taken place, were aware that the project area was a listed archaeological site early in the planning process. The owners were also aware of the significance of the Little Lon dig, and of the way that the earlier project had captivated public opinion. Following initial contact after the Industry Superannuation Property Trust (ISPT) acquired the site from the Commonwealth Government, Heritage Victoria's archaeologists met representatives from the developer early in 2001 and outlined the scope of the archaeological investigations that would be required, particularly in relation to timeframes. Planning for the project was underway more than a year before the commencement of the excavation, and the legacy of Little Lon was a constant reference point as the scope of the project was established.

In general terms, the most useful learnings from Little Lon related to an understanding of the site's archaeological potential. In 2001 there was confidence or knowledge that the site would contain extensive, significant, and intact deposits and artefacts. Accordingly, the level of required resourcing (in terms of time and money) was understood to be considerable, in order to avoid the constraints that had added so much uncertainty to the Little Lon fieldwork. Finally, Little Lon had demonstrated that the public and the media would have a sizeable appetite for the new project – the engagement and involvement of the public in various forms, and a strategy for media management and project communications were important considerations for the Casselden Place project, based on the Little Lon experiences.

In June 2001 Heritage Victoria convened a meeting of the Archaeology Advisory Committee of the Heritage Council and a number of archaeologists who had worked on the Little Lon project or had undertaken low-level testing on the Casselden Place site. The Archaeology Advisory Committee was an advisory committee formed by the Victorian Heritage Council in the late 1990s to advise council on the protection, management and promotion of the state's historical archaeology. The expertise of the committee members proved invaluable during all phases of the Casselden Place dig, and is a clear example of a form of support that existed in 2002, that was not available when the Little Lon project was taking shape in 1987 and 1988. A wide range of project approaches, aims and key deliverables were discussed when the archaeologists met with the advisory committee. Initially, discussions focused on the likely archaeological condition and character of the Casselden Place site; the experience of the Little Lon excavation from the neighbouring site meant that the potential high-level significance of Casselden Place was clearly understood, and justified the development of a complex investigation strategy. Other issues that were discussed included excavation methodologies, research frameworks, the importance of integrating historical research with archaeological evidence, artefact cataloguing, artefact analysis and conservation, and project reporting and publications.

Heritage Victoria was also very keen to place one other item on the agenda for discussion. The Casselden Place project was seen as a unique opportunity to engage the public and promote historical archaeology to the community. One of the defining characteristics of the Little Lon dig had been the way in which the community was involved in many aspects including excavation, artefact processing and even research. Heritage Victoria wanted the Casselden Place project to continue the tradition of public archaeology that had been so successful on the Little Lon dig nearly 15 years earlier.

Following the June meeting, Heritage Victoria assisted the site developer with the preparation of the invitation to tender for the archaeology consultants, which outlined the key project deliverables. In April 2002, *Heritage Act* Consent C0173 was issued to the ISPT to authorise the Casselden Place dig. In 2002, the complexity of establishing indicative budgets, contracts, insurance provisions, engaging qualified archaeology consultants, obtaining statutory approvals, and addressing other project requirements was fundamentally different to the situation that has confronted the Little Lon team 14 years earlier. The broader development of the heritage industry and the maturing of the historical archaeology profession allowed the logistics of the project planning to progress comparatively easily and with greater rigour.

Early in 2002, as the project team prepared for the fieldwork program, Heritage Victoria was working on aspects of the public engagement strategy. In recognition of the importance of the project, it was decided that Heritage Victoria, perhaps unusually for a state agency, would play an active role in the promotion of the project. Heritage Victoria archaeologist Jeremy Smith was assigned to the Casselden Place project full time, and his substantive role was back-filled. In the weeks leading up to the start of the dig a number of community engagement programs were discussed by the site owner, the archaeology team, and Heritage Victoria. The initiatives included the development of a media strategy, including a project launch, an education partnership with Melbourne Museum, a program of site tours for school groups and the general public, and the construction of an onsite viewing platform.

Heritage Victoria's communications officer Jane Thomas worked with the archaeology team to develop a media strategy, which required all enquiries to be initially directed to her before being forwarded to the most suitable project member. As a result, requests for television, radio and newspaper articles were shared between the senior project archaeologists (Richard Mackay, Justin McCarthy and Tim Murray), Heritage Victoria and occasionally the site owner. A series of key media events were programmed consisting of the project launch, a mid-season update and the project close. This strategy of carefully managed media responses marked a significant improvement from the earlier Little Lon project, when reporters had unrestricted access to onsite workers, and where messaging was sometimes confused, contradictory or inflammatory.

Heritage Victoria also worked with education officers at Melbourne Museum to develop an archaeology education program, which consisted of school groups visiting the museum for an archaeology-themed discussion and viewing of parts of the archaeology collection, followed by a tour of the Casselden Place excavation and dig house. Heritage Victoria and Museum Victoria ran a similar program for the general public that consisted of a museum visit followed by a guided site tour. All tour bookings were organised by the museum, which enabled Heritage Victoria and the project archaeologists to avoid having to commit time and resources to the scheduling process. In all, Heritage Victoria conducted 78 site tours during the excavation, with an average number of 40–50 participants per tour. In addition to the tours, the excavation was made accessible to the public by the construction of a viewing ramp and platform, running off Lonsdale Street into the heart of the site. Particularly at lunchtime, the platform would frequently be filled with city office-workers watching the site being uncovered, and engaging with the archaeologists at close hand.

As the excavation proceeded through July and August 2002, the strong level of public interest continued to build. The places that were allocated for public participation in the dig were snapped up as soon as they mere made available, and Heritage Victoria scheduled additional site tours for school groups and the general public. Media interest culminated in a final site open day, with key artefacts on display, against the backdrop of Melbourne's newly uncovered 19th-century archaeological landscape. As had been the case at the launch, the project received saturation media coverage on its final day.

For Heritage Victoria, the professionalism and expertise of the archaeology project team, led onsite by Graeme Wilson, meant that there were no concerns with the way the fieldwork was conducted. The archaeologists managed the complex logistics of a major urban dig, ensured that potentially significant deposits were given appropriate time and resourcing for their investigation and recording, and stayed on track with the agreed project timeframes. The site owner, the ISPT, was reassured by the efficient management of the project, and embraced the level of public and media interest that was generated. A few weeks after the dig commenced, the owner produced site signage stating that the Casselden Place dig was 'proudly sponsored by ISPT'. Rather than play the compliance and mediation role that is often the lot of the state heritage agency, at Casselden Place Heritage Victoria's archaeologists were able to focus on education and promotion outcomes through the coordination of the media, site tours, and other initiatives.

Conservation, Collection and Site Interpretation Outcomes

In Victoria, more than in any other state, artefact conservation and management has always been a fundamental requirement of any historical excavation. Condition 3 of the project consent required the ISPT to provide funding for the conservation, management and storage of significant artefacts recovered during the excavation. Heritage Victoria staff, led by conservator Karina Acton, worked on site during the excavation, and for 18 months following the completion of the fieldwork, to identify and provide conservation treatments for the tens of thousands of artefacts unearthed at Casselden Place. Heritage Victoria is the only state agency that administers heritage legislation and operates an archaeology conservation laboratory, where artefacts recovered from historical and maritime archaeological sites are conserved and stored. Once Heritage Victoria's conservators had completed the artefact conservation process, the Casselden Place collection was lodged with Museum Victoria to sit alongside the earlier collection from Little Lon as the state's most significant historical archaeological assemblage. For more than 10 years, the collection has enjoyed high profile as an integral element of the permanent Melbourne Story exhibit at the museum.

Heritage Victoria's last major involvement in the Casselden Place project took place in the year after the completion of the excavation, with the development of the site interpretation scheme. The project's *Heritage Act* approval required the development of an onsite display that presented the history of the Little Lon neighbourhood and the findings from the archaeological investigations, and included some key artefacts from the dig. The initial challenge for the team designing the interpretation scheme was how to integrate the findings from 19th-century Melbourne into the foyer of a new, 21st-century commercial building. Understandably, the building designers, John Wardle Architects, did not want dusty artefacts in glass cases or information panels crowding the central spaces of the modern foyer. Initially, the site owner wanted to address the interpretation requirement with a predominantly artistic display, that only obliquely referenced the history and archaeology of the place. Heritage Victoria required a scheme that clearly detailed the historical and archaeological significance of the place, and presented stories about the place that were engaging and accessible. In the end, a balance was found that relied on the use of high-quality materials and finishes, with artefacts displayed artistically but not in ways that compromised their historical integrity or capacity to demonstrate key aspects of the site investigation (Plate 2.1). Artist Rosslynd Piggott worked closely with historian Michele Summerton to find a balance between the artistic interpretation of Casselden Place and Little Lon, and a more down-to-earth presentation of the neighbourhood's history and recently uncovered archaeology.

Perhaps the clearest sign that the right balance had been struck came with the announcement that the new 'Urban Workshop' building constructed on the Casselden Place site was the winner of the Royal Australian Institute of Architects Commercial Architecture Award 2005, with the citation acknowledging the successful integration of the place's unique heritage character within its innovative new design.

Conclusion

Even though Little Lon did not lead to a direct increase in the number of urban archaeological investigations in Melbourne in the early 1990s, the success and profile of the project assisted policy makers who were developing a framework for the effective management of the state's historical archaeology. This structure was largely in place by the time of the Casselden Place dig in 2002 which meant that Heritage Victoria and the project team did not have to focus on whether an archaeology program could be justified and required, but on what the optimum outputs might be. The Little Lon and Casselden Place sites demonstrate how the role of the state agency, whether as the Victoria Archaeological Survey or Heritage Victoria, has changed over the last 25 years. In many ways, the various stages of the excavations reflect the changes that have taken place to the management of Victoria's historical archaeology.

In the late 1980s, the agency managed to justify and support an archaeology program at Little Lon, in the absence of a clear policy and legislative framework, and without any significant precedents for large scale urban archaeology in Victoria. In the early 1990s ideas about effective archaeology legislation began to coalesce among agency staff; the success and profile of Little Lon enabled this reform agenda to be pursued successfully with politicians and legislators, and found clear expression in the *Heritage Act* 1995. From 1998 onwards, Heritage Victoria actively promoted the archaeology requirements of the act to developers, planners and other key stakeholders, and excavation projects began to take place on an increasingly regular basis across the city. In 2001 Heritage Victoria's archaeologists faced a much easier task than their VAS predecessors, when they met with the ISPT to discuss the proposed Casselden Place project. The focus of the meetings with ISPT, and with the members of the Heritage Council's Archaeology Advisory Committee who convened to discuss the project, was not on whether it might be possible to require and resource a dig at Little Lon, but on what the best project outcomes might be. Heritage Victoria ensured that the involvement and engagement of the community, which was so successful at Little Lon, was continued at Casselden Place, and the findings from the investigation were presented to the public in a number of dynamic and innovative ways.

There is one final, perhaps cautionary, point to be made that relates to the heritage environment and the role of the state agency in major archaeology projects. If the Little Lon dig took place in an uncertain legislative framework, by the time of Casselden Place strong historical archaeology legislation was in place. One of the strengths of the *Heritage Act* is that it protects sites based on their potential, not just demonstrated capacity, to contain archaeological remains, and the subject site does not have to address a state-level threshold of significance. The act provides protection for a range of sites, of varying levels of significance and condition. The legislation gives a clear head of power for requirements that relate to field and post-excavation outcomes, including artefact conservation, to ensure the delivery of optimal and wide-ranging project results. In the current development environment it is hard to envisage a large, complex urban archaeology project obtaining significant outcomes in the absence of strong, underlying heritage legislation. Laws that provides strong protection for historical archaeological sites, and promotes detailed and meaningful outcomes from investigations, do not exist across all Australian jurisdictions.

At the time of the Little Lon and Casselden Place digs, both the VAS and Heritage Victoria were agencies whose core operation focused on the protection, management and promotion of heritage places, including archaeological sites.

Neither agency was, for example, a planning unit with secondary responsibilities for historic cultural heritage management. Within the agencies the key staff members who worked on the projects were qualified archaeologists, with specifically designated archaeology titles and roles. Increasingly, there has been a push for state agencies to employ generic 'heritage officers' to fill a wide range of roles, which may include the administration of archaeology legislation. At Little Lon and Casselden Place, the archaeology expertise of the VAS and Heritage Victoria staff was an important part of many aspects of the project successes. As archaeologists, the staff could explain site significance and project requirements to the site owners and developers, prepare the legislative approvals, liaise with the project archaeologists about excavation methodologies and other requirements, generate interest and support for the project at senior government and ministerial level, and communicate with media and the general public in an informed and enthusiastic way about the value of the site's unique archaeology.

The archaeology landscape in Victoria has changed considerably since Rosemary Buchan's note of September 1987 alerted the archaeology team to a site of possible interest in town. The Little Lon site has played a major role in the recognition and protection of Victoria's archaeological heritage during this time. The existence of a state agency with relevant expertise and clear responsibilities for the management and promotion of the state's archaeology has contributed significantly to the success of the Little Lon and Casselden Place projects.

References

Allom Lovell & Associates, 1984. 300 Queen Street Archaeological Report. HV report collection no. 40.

Austral Archaeology, 1991. Archaeological Investigation of the Proposed J Shed Site, Queen Victoria Market, Melbourne. HV report collection no. 69.

Austral Archaeology, 1999. Archaeological Report on the Franklin Street Stores, Queen Victoria Market, Melbourne. HV report collection no. 858.

Australia ICOMOS, 2013. *The Australia ICOMOS Charter for Places of Cultural Significance: The Burra Charter*. Burwood.

Australian Construction Services (Archaeology Consultant Justin McCarthy), 1989. Archaeological Investigation – The Commonwealth Block Melbourne, Victoria. HV report collection no. 198.

Davison, G. 1979. *The Rise and Fall of Marvellous Melbourne*. Carlton: Melbourne University Press.

Davison, G., D. Dunstan and C. McConville 1985. *The Outcasts of Melbourne: Essays in Social History*. Sydney: Allen & Unwin.

Fels, M., S. Lavelle and D. Mider, 1993. Melbourne Central Activities District Archaeological Management Plan. Maritime and Historical Archaeology Unit, Victorian Archaeological Survey.

Godden Mackay Logan, La Trobe University and Austral Archaeology, 2004. Casselden Place, 50 Lonsdale Street, Melbourne: Archaeological Excavations – Research Archive. HV report collection no. 3916.

Heritage Victoria, 2004. Archaeological Artefacts Management Guidelines. Heritage Victoria. Melbourne.

Heritage Victoria, 2014. Guidelines for Investigating Historical Archaeological Artefacts and Sites. Heritage Victoria. Melbourne. Version 2.

Mackay, R., J. McCarthy, A. Sneddon and G. Wilson, 2006. Down Little Lon: An Introduction to the Casselden Place Archaeological Excavations, Melbourne. *International Journal of Historical Archaeology* 10(4): 299–310.

Mayne, A. and S. Lawrence, 1998. An Ethnography of Place: Imagining Little Lon. *Journal of Australian Studies* 22(57): 93–107.

Mayne, A. and T. Murray, 1999. 'In Little Lon ... Wiv Ginger Mick': Telling the Forgotten History of a Vanished Community. *Journal of Popular Culture* 33(1): 49–60.

Mayne, A., T. Murray and S. Lawrence, 2000. Historic Sites: Melbourne's Little Lon. *Australian Historical Studies* 31(114): 131–151.

McConville, C. 2000. Big Notes from a Little Street: Re/newing Social History in Melbourne? *Australian Historical Studies* 32 (October 2000): 325–327.

McKenzie, L. 2003. *The Casselden Place Project – Victoria's Management of a Large Excavation Project*. Australian Association of Consulting Archaeologists Inc. Newsletter No. 92, April 2003: 6–11.

Murray, T. 2006. Integrating Archaeology and History at the "Commonwealth Block": "Little Lon" and Casselden Place. *International Journal of Historical Archaeology* 10(4): 385–413.

Murray, T. (ed.), 2003. *Exploring the Modern City: Recent Approaches to Urban History and Archaeology*. Sydney: Historic Houses Trust of New South Wales.

Murray, T. and A. Mayne, 2001. Imaginary Landscapes: Reading Melbourne's Little

Lon. In Mayne, A. and T. Murray (eds.), *The Archaeology of Urban Landscapes: Explorations in Slumland*. Cambridge: Cambridge University Press.

National Trust of Australia (Victoria). Victorian Heritage Database Place Details: 'The Commonwealth Centre, 275 Spring Street, Melbourne'. http://vhd.heritagecouncil.vic.gov.au/places/183758.

Parliamentary Standing Committee on Public Works, 1988. Report Relating to the Construction of New Commonwealth Offices, Melbourne. Fourth Report of 1988. Parliament of the Commonwealth of Australia, Canberra.

Smith, C.H.F. and D. Tout-Smith, 2010. Recreating Place: Little Lon. *Museum Management and Curatorship* 25(1): 37–51.

Smith, J. 2002. *Funds for Finds: Heritage Victoria's Artefact Conservation Bond Scheme*. AACA newsletter, issue no 91, December 2002.

Smith, J. 2002. Uncovering the Secrets of Little Lon. *The Artefact* 25.

Trust News, 1988. 'Digging for Our History'. *National Trust of Australia (Victoria)*, p. 17.

Veale, S. and R. Freestone, 2012. The Things We Wanted to Keep: The Commonwealth and the National Estate 1969–1974. *Historic Environment* 24(3): 12–18.

Victorian Collections [online]. 'Wunderlich Tile' Sunshine and District Historical Society. https://victoriancollections.net.au/items/561b6a092162f126108732fe.

3
The First Campaign: Little Lon

Justin McCarthy

In late September 1987 I received a phone call from Kristal Buckley of the Victorian Archaeological Survey (VAS) asking about my availability to undertake a large historical archaeological project at short notice in Melbourne. Was I interested? If so when could I get a team together and start? She explained that she and others from VAS were scouting around Australia to see who was available and that it would be a fixed price contract. It was a bolt from the blue. At the time I was winding up a five-year stint as an historical archaeology consultant in the Heritage Branch in the then South Australian Department of Environment and Planning in Adelaide. I was uncertain as to my future and together with my wife and two very young children, was considering returning to NSW to establish my own consultancy.

My intent in this chapter is to give a synopsis of the Little Lon project (as it became known), from my perspective as principal archaeology consultant. Given it occurred nearly 30 years ago, I will touch upon the background to the project including the lead up to it, my appointment and getting a team together, the client's project parameters and imperatives including deadlines for completion, the uncertainty of the funding arrangements, the challenges in getting the project up and running from scratch with very limited resources, the research design workshop, the approach and methodology used, the choice of the recording system, the daily management and day to day operations, the use of volunteers and the outcomes.

THE BACKSTORY

Chapter 2 has explained the background to the project and how it came about from the statutory side. The complexity of it being a Commonwealth-owned site and not subject to state laws cannot be understated and nor can the impossible timeframes which were to apply to the work. The construction schedule had already been set and all the archaeology had to be completed before construction could begin. Initially the Commonwealth Department of Administrative Services (DAS) wanted the work on Site C to commence at the beginning of November 1987 and be completed by the end of January 1988. Even with prioritising parts of the work so that partial site clearance would be achieved to allow commencement of demolition works and construction, the deadlines were impossible and hence the need for expediency in appointing a consultant.

As it happened I knew most of the main players who were behind the push to mount the investigation. Ivar Nelsen had been a heritage architect in the South Australian Heritage Branch for the first two years I was there (1983–1984). Upon arriving in South Australia to take up the archaeology position in the branch, I was thrust almost immediately into the fray and had to mount a three-week salvage excavation of extensive below ground structures that had been found during construction work at the rear of the SA Museum, off Kintore Avenue. It transpired that this structure was the furnace room beneath a laundry drying room that had been part of the Destitute Asylum for homeless mothers in the mid to late 1800s. Ivar was mightily interested in the whole project and how it was accomplished with a team of inexperienced archaeology students from Adelaide University while the bulldozers lay in wait! I also knew Rosemary Buchan well as she had been the team leader of the Aboriginal Heritage Unit at the Heritage Branch until 1986 when she left to take up the position at VAS in Victoria. I knew Kristal Buckley through Australia ICOMOS (International Council of Monuments and Sites) and connections with Port Arthur, Tasmania.

It seems strange now but there were no large size archaeology consultancy firms in existence in Australia at the time as there had been no real need for them. The development of heritage legislation in Victoria has been explained by Buckley and Smith in Chapter 2. In NSW, the *Heritage Act* was passed in 1977. This included provision for the protection of archaeological heritage and created a need for historical archaeologists to be involved in the process of gaining development approvals. This task was mainly serviced by sole traders (graduate archaeologists) who were subcontracted by larger architectural or engineering firms or developers, although Sydney University Archaeology Department did take on small archaeological surveys or excavation contracts under the guidance of the matriarch of historical archaeology in Australia, Dr Judy Birmingham. I had done some of this work for Judy in and around Sydney, in the Hunter Valley and on Norfolk Island (along with other graduate archaeologists) as well as some private consulting to the mining sector in NSW before I went to South Australia in early 1983. The historic heritage legislation gazetted in SA in 1978 did not explicitly make provision for historical archaeological heritage but archaeologists became involved in the government-sponsored regional heritage survey program and specific thematic surveys after I was appointed to the Heritage Branch in 1983.

The SA Heritage Branch was a very dynamic organisation in the early 1980s and I was privileged to work there. Apart from learning the ropes as a government archaeologist, I got to work with a highly skilled group of heritage specialists who made up our very diverse team. These people included a planner, five historians, four conservation architects, an interpretive planner, two maritime archaeologists as well as administrative support staff. It was a very cohesive team with a collaborative mindset and there was a somewhat frontier feel to the place in that we all felt we were at the leading edge of heritage conservation in Australia. The branch had a very ambitious goal to undertake regional surveys of the entire state with detailed infill surveys of specific large towns and cities. This goal has been largely achieved although it took a lot longer than envisaged back in the early 1980s when funding for heritage at both state and national levels was more generous.

One of the archaeologists I met in SA later turned out to be a key player in the Little Lon project, as it later became known. David Bannear was an Australian who had gone backpacking around the world in the 1970s and ended up as a volunteer excavator on Roman sites in the United Kingdom. In 1978 he turned it into his profession by undertaking a B.A. Hons (and later an M.A. Hons) in archaeology at Cambridge University and then began working as a qualified archaeologist. David had gained valuable experience in this role and met many of the characters of archaeology in the UK. On his return to SA in the early 1980s he despaired of not finding archaeological work and took a job as a gravedigger at the cemetery in his home town in Auburn in the mid-north of SA! Like me, David was interested in industrial archaeology and we had struck up a friendship as we both worked on different aspects of Cornish mining in SA. I approached David to be the lead archaeologist on the project and he readily accepted. So I responded to Kristal in early October that we would take the project on and try and get a team together as soon as possible.

The Planning Phase

As has been explained in Chapter 2, the Commonwealth Block was bounded by the main streets of Spring, Lonsdale, Exhibition and Latrobe Streets (see Figure 3.1). A minor street, Little Lonsdale, subdivided Sites A, B and C from Sites D and E to the north (see Figure 3.2). Sites A, B and C comprised roughly three equal land parcels with

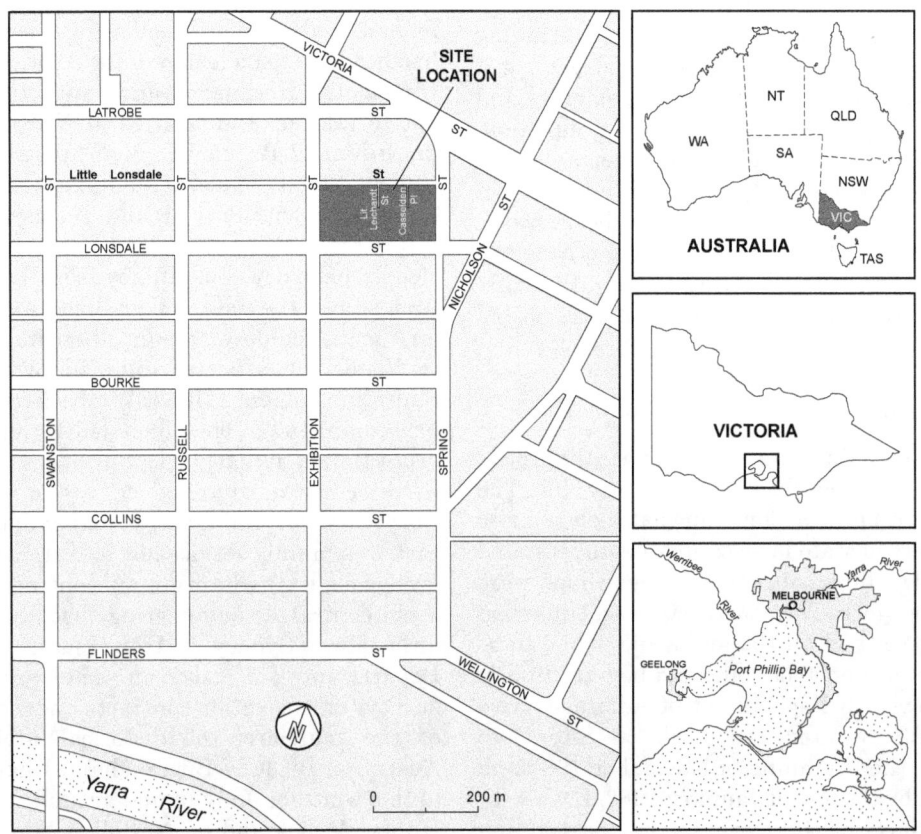

Figure 3.1: Location plan.

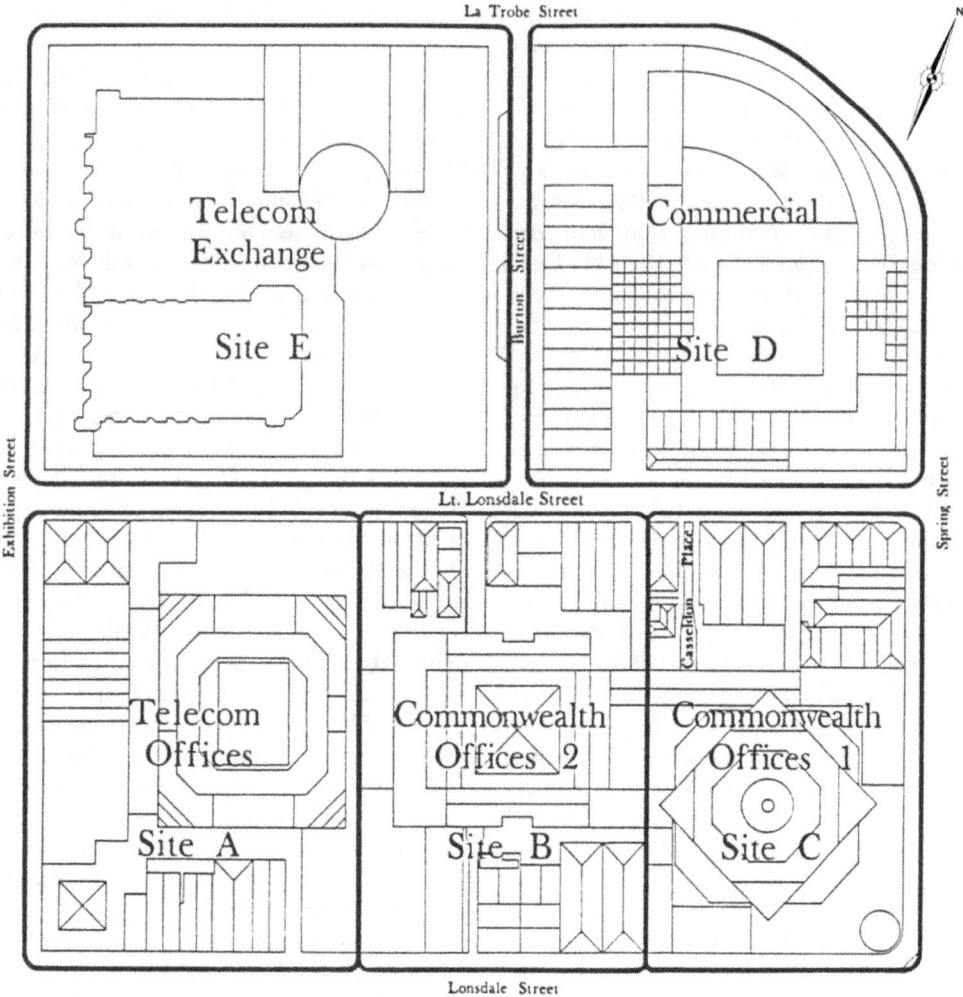

Figure 3.2: Commonwealth Block Site Plan.

Site A fronting Exhibition Street and Site C fronting Spring Street with Site B in the middle. At that time developments were only planned for Sites A and C (and these were the areas to be archaeologically investigated in the proposed scope of works) with the existing 1958 building on Site D to be demolished (the so-called Green Latrine – see Figure 3.3). The Department of Administrative Services (DAS) was planning to build on Site C while Site A was earmarked for Telecom (the forerunner to Telstra) which already had an existing exchange building on Site E that would be retained.

Throughout October, negotiations ensued with VAS and DAS to get a contract sorted out. The matter was further complicated by the fact that Telecom would not enter into discussions with DAS and were intent on appointing their own consultant. VAS had framed the budget and staffing levels which allowed for a team of three archaeologists and an artefact supervisor to act as team leaders with all the labour to be supplied by volunteers who would be paid a small daily stipend and provided with lunch! It sounds like a recipe for disaster nowadays as well as a health, safety and environment nightmare, but at the time such an ambitious large scale urban excavation had never been attempted in Australia. The very approach itself however, reflects the origins of archaeology as an academic pursuit where large scale research projects were taken on over 'seasons' by small core teams of trained archaeologists who

Figure 3.3: Former Commonwealth Centre Building (so-called Green Latrine) on Site D, corner Spring Street and Victoria Parade, Melbourne 1968. Source: Wolfgang Sievers. © National Library of Australia, nla.obj-160560931

used volunteer or paid labour to do the digging under supervision. As Buckley and Smith have pointed out in Chapter 2, Dr Peter Coutts at VAS had undertaken a number of research-orientated projects in the previous 10 years in Victoria, and the largest historical archaeology project undertaken in Australia until that time was the Port Arthur Conservation Project in Tasmania that had run over five years. But obviously with the benefit of hindsight, it is clear that this model was not the perfect fit for the task at hand.

Bannear and I had serious concerns from the outset as to how we would accomplish the work using this approach. Nevertheless, with the exuberance of youth, we accepted the challenge and started the planning process to make it all happen.

The enormity of what we were taking on as a team cannot be overstated. The scale and scope of the work was massive. The two blocks A and C comprised almost 6,000 m². As a result of a planning day in November 1987 to establish a research orientation for the project (discussed below) as well as a client requirement that there be no delays in the construction critical path, the whole site was to be totally excavated – not sampled. We had a tiny team of professionals who really only had limited experience themselves. The time allowed for the works was minimal and the clock was already ticking. Only a third of the funds had been committed by the client at that time. The project occurred almost right at the commencement of the personal computer technology wave. There was very little off-the-shelf software available, no Windows only MSDOS (Microsoft Disk Operating System), Apple Macs were new and as a point of reference, the first hand-held mobile phone call had only been made in Australia in February 1987! There was no time to do site specific historical research prior to the excavation. At the time the only comprehensive integrated site recording and artefact cataloguing system was the paper-based Port Arthur system which had been developed over the life of the Port Arthur Conservation Project (PACP) 1979–1984.

Given the tight schedule, there were a thousand small matters to get in hand even though the contract was not signed nor all the funding secured. While the team could plan some of the logistics, the lack of any available funds hampered things considerably. Remember that none of this preliminary setup work had any allocated funding under the excavation contract so the consultant staff all worked in the lead up phase for no pay. We really had no idea when the funds would start to flow. At this time, David and I became almost *de facto* members of VAS, spending large amounts of time at their offices in Albert Park in planning logistics and a phased excavation methodology as well as sourcing the availability of tools, equipment, stationery and consumable supplies. VAS kindly provided office space and phones for our use as well as key contacts and access to their library of archaeological texts and reports.

It was apparent to us that one of the single largest issues we faced was that there was no time to research and prepare a detailed site development history prior to commencing the excavation. As neither David nor I were native Melbournians, we did not have even a general background in the history of that state's colonial development. We set about sourcing as much material as possible and of necessity relied upon the available secondary sources authored by historians such as Graeme Davison (Davison 1978). A key document that we did have access to was a report that had been prepared for the then (Commonwealth) Department of Housing and Construction (Commonwealth Department of Housing and Construction 1979) entitled 'Historical and Architectural Development of the Commonwealth Centre Site bounded by Spring, Lonsdale, Exhibition and Latrobe Streets Melbourne, 1837–1978'. While the report was primarily architectural in nature and intended to determine the cultural significance of the buildings on the block and to make recommendations as to possible retention of the most significant, it also provided some specific information on the historical development of the study area within a chronological/thematic framework.

My approach to the work was influenced by my university course where we had been exposed to texts such as Robert L. Schuyler's 1978 work, *Historical Archaeology: A Guide to Substantive and Theoretical Contributions*. Schuyler promoted the development of historical archaeology and adopted an approach that embraced scrutinisation and inclusion of all available sources to the archaeologist such as archival documents including diaries, drawings, photographs, government and newspaper records, maps and plans as well as oral history.

We were all very keen to hold a seminar or workshop as a matter of urgency that would bring all knowledgeable people to the table. Kristal Buckley of VAS organised this for 12 November 1987. It was held at the VAS offices and included said social historians, VAS managers and staff, academic and consultant archaeologists, conservation architects, architectural historians, planners and others with information about the history and development of the area or the 1850 to early 1900s historical period. Attendees included Kristal Buckley (archaeologist VAS), Iain Stewart (archaeologist VAS), Rosemary Buchan (assistant director VAS), Mike McIntyre (director VAS), Derek Fowell (information officer VAS), Graeme Davison (historian), Chris McConville (historian), Ivar Nelsen (regional heritage architect DAS), Jim Allen (La Trobe University), Tim Murray (La Trobe University), and David Dunstan (Ministry of Planning and Environment).

Although the primary driver for the seminar was to provide us with immediate access to historical information about the site (or at least where to find it), it went on to become much more than that. The discussions on the day ranged far and wide from the logistical to the very theoretical. Basically it provided a research orientation that amongst other things, set up a methodological framework for the excavation. It was hoped that this approach would facilitate the excavation work to be completed in the allocated period, provide an outcome that would enable the results and recovered artefacts to be analysed in the following years, bring the public's attention to the relevancy and value of archaeology within the city, and provide interesting and thought provoking artefacts for display in a major museum. As I wrote in the final report, 'In one sense [the site] presented an opportunity to investigate the antithesis of "Marvellous Melbourne", to see how the ordinary and poorer classes were faring in Melbourne ...'.

A result of the seminar was the realisation that the level of historical research related specifically to this city block was a very small body of work indeed. Consequently, a historian, Andy May who was then undertaking his PhD, was commissioned at the commencement of the excavation phase to undertake three weeks research and to obtain copies of all the available historical maps and plans (see Figures 3.4 and 3.5). This was only partially successful given the time constraints and it was decided that further intensive historical research would have to be undertaken after the excavation phase was over.

Negotiations dragged on with DAS and Telecom through November. I continued to liaise with VAS

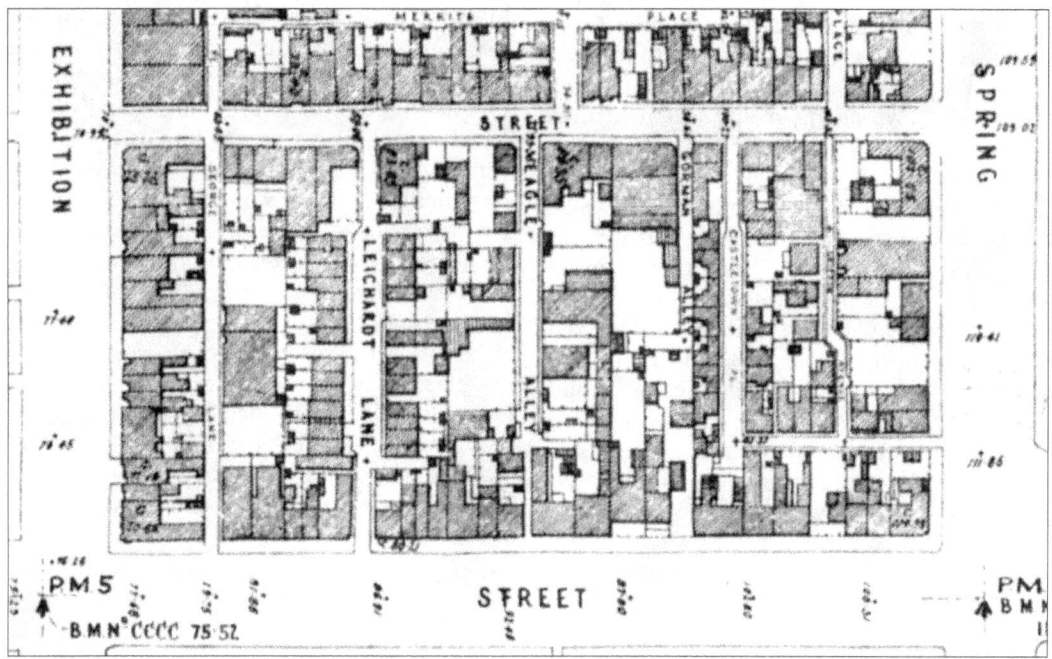

Figure 3.4: Melbourne and Metropolitan Board of Works Plan 27 East Melbourne (1895).

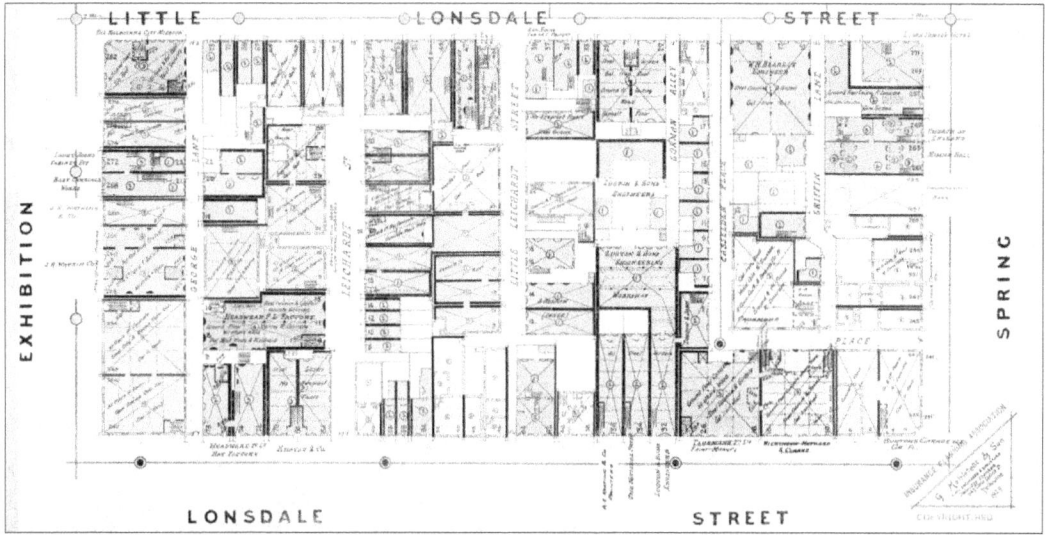

Figure 3.5: Mahlstedt fire insurance plan of the city block. Map 8a (1923).

on a number of matters related to site and logistics planning as well as detailed discussions regarding the public relations strategy, media releases, press management, target strategy for volunteers, site signage and even the production of a film by Film Victoria. Eventually I signed a contract with DAS on 1 December 1987 with work scheduled to commence on 7 December. David and I and the VAS team then embarked on a frenzied two-week period of site setup and mobilisation.

Setup

There were literally dozens of tasks that had to be organised prior to the commencement of the excavation.

Site Office

As Buckley and Smith have stated in Chapter 2, the Commonwealth Government had agreed to provide 'site office space, a backhoe (and operator), fencing and site security, typing, printing and drafting'. 'Provide' is not exactly the correct term. What they had agreed begrudgingly to do was to pay for those things, and like everything else, we had to organise them. The exception was the site office; this was an existing building on the block – the former Lugton and Sons, Engineers old boiler factory (Figure 3.6). It was a commodious, two storey, double gabled red brick building fronting Little Lonsdale Street. It was ideal as an archaeological site office as it had a couple of small offices at the back and vast open floor space at the front suitable for desks and trestle tables for sorting artefacts and plenty of space for storage shelving.

This building was to become not only the 'home' of the excavation for the next 12 months or so but

Figure 3.6: Twin gabled building at right is the former Lugton and Sons, Engineers old boiler factory, 27–29 Little Lonsdale Street looking southwest in the early 1980s. This was used as the archaeological site office for the Little Lon excavation 1988–89. Source: Melbourne Heritage Action.

an actual home for David Bannear and I after the first month. We had initially hired a caravan to live in and had placed it behind the boiler factory. But it was cramped and relatively expensive so we sent it back and moved into the boiler factory and slept on camp beds. There was one problem (apart from the rats running over us in the night) in that there were no usable showers or toilets there ... but we quickly overcame this once we got to know the security guards who were protecting the Green Latrine from vandals and squatters across the road. They let us use the facilities on the ground floor that were very well maintained even though the building had no occupants at all! Prior to the excavation commencing, we got the toilets working in the site office too.

Furnishing our site office was not accounted for in the budget either, and so demanded an alternative approach. Both the Commonwealth and Telecom sites had numerous existing buildings on them that had been used for a variety of purposes including offices, storage facilities and factories. It was a rabbit warren of late 19th- to early 20th-century two- and three-storey buildings – some with basements – and seemingly miles of corridors within old warehouses or factories that had been split up for subsequent smaller businesses or offices. All the staff and lessees had moved out before we arrived but the buildings were a virtual Aladdin's cave of necessities for resource-poor archaeologists! Items such as discarded office desks, tables, office chairs, white boards, lights, heaters, lamps, pedestal fans and even an urn, cutlery and crockery, littered the buildings and only required lugging back to the boiler factory. The most useful items however to us as archaeologists were the metres of old Dexion and Brownbuilt steel shelving suitable for storage of artefact boxes. Once we had a few volunteers we raided these buildings and moved the furniture and shelving to the boiler factory. By the end of the first week or two of excavation we had a quite well appointed site office!

Other tasks that were occurring at this time included getting all the site recording forms and stationery printed, sourcing providers of plastic artefact bags, archive boxes, suitable hand tools and sieves etc and arranging enough equipment for an army of volunteers. After many phone calls, we had recruited two other archaeologists to be team members, Hilary du Cros and David Rhodes, both of whom lived in Melbourne. Both were appointed as trench supervisors but Hilary was eventually to take on the artefact manager role and David worked both as a trench supervisor and on the artefacts.

Volunteers

VAS assisted us by publicising the upcoming excavation and providing a hotline number and message service for volunteers to register for the project. Once the project started, we quickly

3. The First Campaign

assembled a core team from this group of early volunteers, many of whom went on to play key roles in the project and some of whom went on later to forge their own careers in archaeology and history. These people, who came from diverse backgrounds and all walks of life, brought special skills or knowledge to the project and assisted in the preliminary set-up tasks and getting the project up and running.

The volunteers were destined to play a huge role in the excavation. Looking back through the archive boxes of material I have, I found some of the original telephone messages that VAS had taken from people interested in volunteering for the excavation. The first inquiry that we received is dated 26 October 1987. VAS received a steady stream of inquiries from the public and archaeology students throughout November and December 1987 and into January 1988. At some point and after protracted negotiations with Telecom, we eventually got a telephone connected to the site office (probably some time in late January or early February 1988), and our volunteer staff assisted with taking the calls and messages. We had to constantly ring volunteers each afternoon or evening to ensure we had enough labour for the following day.

One of the most enriching things about the volunteer program was the amazing range of people we met from all walks of life, and a few 'gems' who appeared and more or less worked with us throughout the whole excavation period and even afterwards. While most were keen to dig and do 'archaeological' work, they worked in a variety of other capacities as needed; these included administration, catering (especially Robyn Rawson), purchasing, preparing work rosters for the volunteers, answering the phone, data entry, moving and assembling shelving, setting up the site office, etc. At least one of these people was a qualified archaeologist with experience on prehistoric sites in the USA (Diana Coultas) while many others had tertiary qualifications in disciplines other than archaeology. We also met people who had serious medical conditions or were in remission. Many volunteers were students enrolled in archaeology or allied university courses (at La Trobe, Melbourne and Deakin) as well as some students from RMIT. All these people had either a curiosity about, or an interest in, archaeology and revelled in the opportunity to be involved in the excavation. Strong friendships formed in a very short time and a solid almost family-like bond developed amongst the core group of volunteers and archaeological staff. A massive thanks is due to all the volunteers who contributed over the project but special mention must be made of Robyn Annear, David Ellson, Diana Coultas, Robyn Rawson, Tony Jenner, Dick Moline, David Knox, Janet Cohen, and Rebecca Vandersluiys.

While there was a dedicated group of volunteers who worked at the site regularly and became quite skilled excavators in many cases, there were many who only came once or twice. There was therefore an enormous workload to induct them daily and then give them some basic safety and excavation training, depending on what was being done that day. Many of these people had never done any physical work and did not know how to use tools such as shovels, mattocks and picks. The work was hard and for much of the time in January and February – very hot. In these two months there were 10 days that were at, or over, 35 degrees Celsius. One area of the site (which was largely a car park) hosted a very large carport-style roof. We intended to reserve this covered area in case of rain but quickly found that because of the extreme temperatures in early January we needed it as a shady area to dig! Even so we had several cases of heatstroke and we were constantly reminding volunteers to wear hats, take breaks in the shade, keep up their fluid intake and ask to be re-assigned to alternative indoor tasks (such as artefact washing or helping with cataloguing) if they could not deal with the heat.

Although the present day requirements for formalised inductions and safety training sessions using Safe Work Method Statements and/or Job Safety and Environmental Assessments did not apply, we inducted all volunteers who came to work at the site. This took about an hour and included a brief background history of the site, the goals of the excavation, the work schedule, the nature of the work being undertaken at that time, the site health and safety rules including working around machines, and our expectations of them as volunteers. Once they were inducted they were taken out to the excavation area and allocated to an excavation team or supervisor who instructed them on the use of tools and excavation techniques. Generally they were started off on simple tasks e.g. removing the blue-metal car park surface which covered much of the site.

We were constantly surprised by the actions and attitudes of the volunteers – most often favourably by things such as their enthusiasm to work under hard conditions etc but sometimes the opposite. One of the latter occasions that springs to mind was the volunteer who came into the smoko (morning tea) break with a tray of artefacts he had excavated from an underfloor area. I thought he had brought the tray into the artefact room for cataloguing but I saw him decanting some of the items (including a coin) into a plastic bag. I asked what he was doing and he said that they were the artefacts he wanted to keep and he was going to put them in his bag! I explained that the artefacts were not his to take and he said he thought he could keep anything he dug up! Needless to say the induction was modified to reinforce the message that the artefacts were to stay at the site.

Another aspect to the volunteer program was the daily feeding frenzy! We had offered to supply lunch to volunteers to try and attract sufficient numbers. We had a budget of five dollars per day per person and this was sufficient if we bought food at the Victoria Markets but it necessitated someone shopping almost every day. We mainly prepared sandwiches but the shopping and preparation times were very time consuming. I don't have the figures or the log book of volunteers who worked on the site but for one item we reported to VAS that 600 volunteer person days were achieved in January 1988. So that is at least 600 lunches! We gave up on the lunches at the end of January because it was just too much work and costly and we were getting sufficient numbers of volunteers who weren't just coming because of the lunches. We replaced it with a weekly lunch or after-work barbeque to which all volunteers for the week were invited.

LIFE AT LITTLE LON - THE DOCUMENTARY FILM

Amongst other things, VAS saw the proposed excavation as an opportunity to both advertise and promote itself and to publicise the value of archaeology and heritage in the middle of a large modern city – right in people's backyards, if you will. As Buckley and Smith have stated in Chapter 2, VAS contributed in many ways but the legacy of Little Lon is that it was the genesis of a wider appreciation and understanding of the importance of historical archaeology in Melbourne and Australia. VAS had approached Film Victoria (FV) to discuss the possibility of doing a documentary on the project and after much negotiation between VAS, DAS, the film makers and ourselves (archaeology consultants), a strategy was formulated and a draft script prepared by Film Victoria. The film would include a potted background history using a mixture of text, historic pictures and paintings, voice overs and interviews with historians, intercut with progressive footage of the excavation as it occurred, interviews with the archaeologists about what was being found and footage of the artefacts and artefact processing area as they were being catalogued.

The film crew came to site regularly throughout the excavation and we became good friends with them. Unlike the news media film crews who always wanted to present a stereotyped view of archaeology and artefacts as 'treasure', the documentary crew were interested in the real story of how archaeologists use all the evidence about a place to piece together the lives of those who lived or worked there and how the place developed or changed through time. The project was a success and *Life at Little Lon* was shown on TV on a number of occasions and subsequently used by schools and even a few university archaeology courses I believe, as a teaching aid.

THE METHODOLOGY AND APPROACH

As this was a salvage excavation to be undertaken very rapidly both prior to, and then after initial archaeological clearance of specified areas, in conjunction with, demolition works occurring on the site, it was always going to rely heavily on mechanical methods to remove overburden. The plan was for all significant *in situ* deposits such as underfloors and cesspits to be excavated by hand. The Commonwealth had agreed to provide a machine (a back hoe was selected, as at that time small hydraulic excavators were not readily available). The site had already been gridded for the archaeologists on a five-metre grid pattern by staff of the Australian Survey Office so ten metre by ten metre trenches were laid out with stakes and strings. As it turned out, we had so many volunteers in January that we actually removed most of the car park gravel by hand and stockpiled it on a concrete pad behind the boiler factory. We later sold this material to a landscape company and used the proceeds for barbeques and beers for the volunteers!

It had been decided at the seminar that the Port Arthur (PA) recording system would be used for the project. The PA system was itself an adaptation of the Harris Matrix System developed by Edward Harris in Britain in the 1970s. Using 'units' (any discrete thing) as the basic recording device, they are recorded spatially – both horizontally and vertically – with their relationship to each other being recorded on a series of stratigraphic recording sheets. These are complemented by detailed plans (in our case drawn at 1:50) and keyed to a 1:200 site plan. Artefacts were recorded in one of three classes; as Accession Items, Inventory Items or Special Finds. Accession Items were generally those recovered from disturbed or demolition deposits, Inventory Items were those recovered from stratified deposits or undisturbed contexts, while Special Finds were from undisturbed contexts and deemed to be of special interest or value in terms of the research design. These recording forms were complemented by detailed photographic records. A numbering system was developed for the artefacts and their tags/labels which comprised the trench and unit number from where the artefact was excavated and an artefact number. The type of artefact (accession, inventory or special find) was identifiable at a glance (by the position of its identifier in one of three available slots on the tag).

We considered from the outset that the PA system would lend itself to computerisation. I had been using Apple computers since 1986 and thought that Apple's Hypercard database system could be developed to cross link the main streams of information being recorded on paper forms i.e. – stratigraphic, artefactual, locational as well as site plans, photographs and later, historical data. This system had a well-developed user interface that was text-based and/or utilised pull down menus and thus did not require programming skills or knowledge. This meant that any one of our volunteers could use it to transpose site and artefact data from the paper-based forms. Through various contacts I met Patrick Miller, an historian and amateur programmer. Patrick developed the beta version of the archaeological program in Hypercard (named HyperDig) and it did work. We could input all types of information associated with any particular excavation trench/unit via a series of 'hot buttons' that created cross-linked 'cards'; for example the stratigraphic information card was cross-linked to the plans and sections cards as well as the artefacts cards that showed details (and even photos) of items retrieved from that deposit. Historical information could also be entered if it related to the location of an excavation trench/unit or a known cadastral point on the site. The beauty of the system was that once all the data was entered, it could be accessed from any number of points of entry e.g. from an artefact number or description, or a stratigraphic unit number. After the dig was completed and more research done on the ratebooks to establish the former owners and occupiers of the lots, the system could also be accessed by an address, or the name of a former owner or occupier.

As it worked out, this system was only eventually used to catalogue the artefacts and the site histories of the owners and occupiers of the lots on the site. In the end this system was beaten by three factors – two of which were related to the then relatively primitive state of the available technology. These factors were the large amount of data being generated so rapidly from the excavation was very time-consuming to enter; the fact that there was no available technology such as scanners and geographic information systems to make the input of mapping and drawing data quick and simple; and the limited memory size of the available computers.

An Apple Macintosh computer and printer were purchased for the project to enable data recording and storage. Apple Australia also sponsored the team in the form of a loan of a second Mac for the duration of the project to facilitate data entry. Minolta also became sponsors and loaned a high speed office photocopier so that we could print the thousands of stratigraphic recording forms and artefact cataloguing sheets that were required. These sponsorships saved the project a considerable amount of money and were much appreciated.

THE EXCAVATION

When the archaeologists gained control of the site in late 1987, the perimeter of the block along the principal streets presented continuous facades of a range of building types from small single storey buildings to large three storey former factories. The internal areas off the laneways were comprised of standing buildings, areas of blue metal gravel car parks (where buildings had been demolished in an ongoing process since the 1960s), cobbled laneways (some of which had been covered with blue metal), a mixture of building types ranging from the small cottages in Casselden Place, through to large two and three storey former factory buildings. When excavation commenced there were 39 standing buildings on the block with many of them to be demolished during and after the excavation. The laneways included George Lane, Leichardt and Little Leichardt Streets, Gorman Alley, Casselden Place, Griffin Lane and Surrey Place. As stated above, the excavation area comprised Site A (fronting Exhibition Street) and Site C (fronting Spring Street) (Figure 3.7). The middle area between the two, Area B, was to be excavated subsequently by the Austral Archaeology, Godden Mackay Logan and La Trobe University joint venture in 2003. The whole site sloped gently from east to west with Spring Street in the east being considerably higher than Exhibition Street in the west.

To allow demolition to get underway at the southeastern side of Site C, we were required to complete excavations in that area by 31 January 1988. Work finally commenced on site in Casselden Place on Friday 18 December 1987 with a limited crew and then in earnest the next day. We decided to commence at that point as it was the site of a demolished cottage of similar design to that still standing and the thinking was we would get an idea of how the demolition process had been undertaken, whether underfloor deposits had survived, the nature of the fills that had been used and determine the level and extent of any structural remains (which in that instance could be compared to the existing standing structure).

Work was then concentrated on Trenches 03, 04, 05, 06, 07, 08, 11, 12 and 13, as these were closest to the buildings to be demolished fronting Lonsdale Street and Spring Street and the demolition crew needed this as a works area for machinery and trucks. This work was nearly all completed by 31 January 1988 as required and the demolition team then moved in to work in tandem with us. Some of these trenches required a little further work but as they were pretty close to the demolition zone we could only work there safely by agreement with the demolition team and not of course when walls were being felled.

The presence of the demolition team added a new dimension to the logistics and dynamics at the site. The crew were mainly Maoris and we got on very well with them from the outset. They were intrigued by what we were doing and we were impressed by their skills with large machines and precision of their demolition activities. They also assisted us where we needed a large machine to remove a massive red gum tree stump from Trench 06 in Casselden Place. We ended up socialising with them at smoko and lunch times and also shared a number of after work barbeques with them and the volunteers. At one

The Commonwealth Block, Melbourne

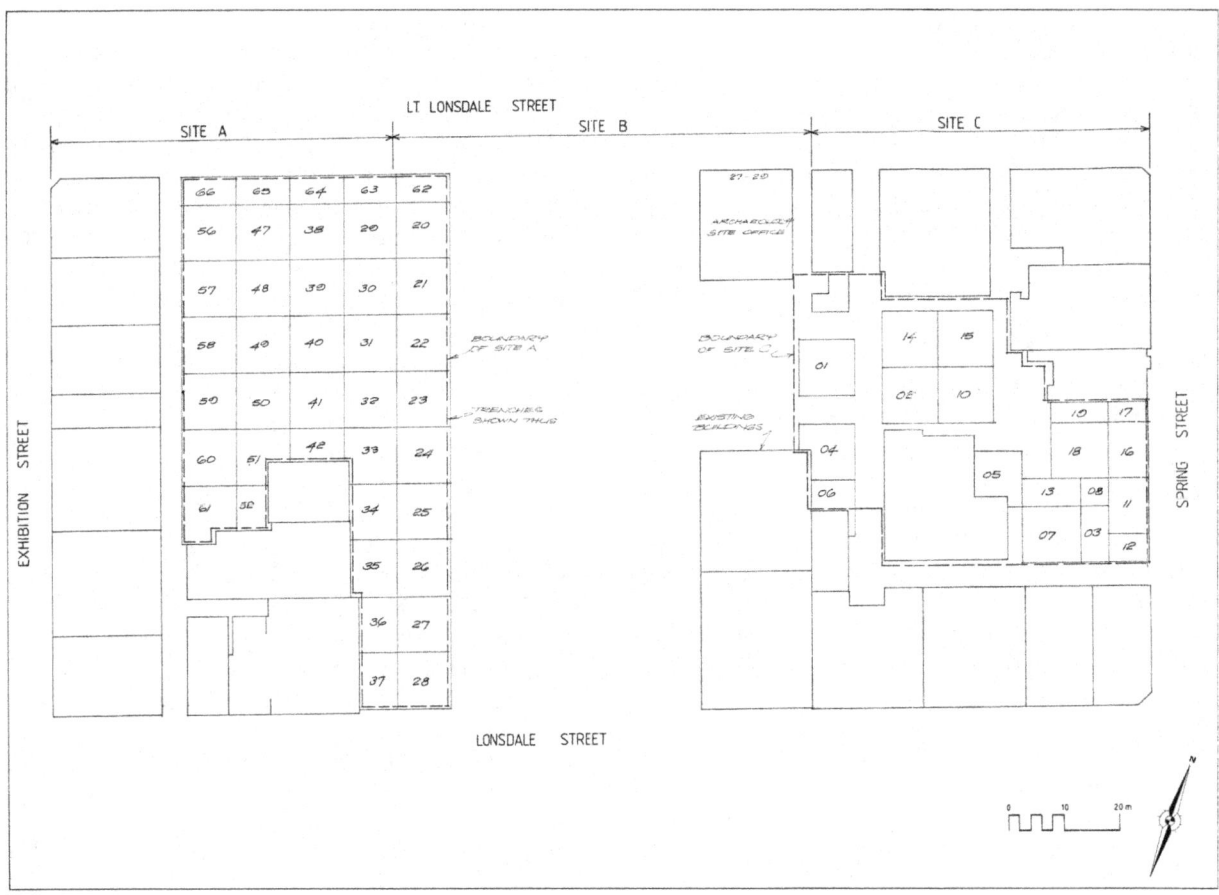

Figure 3.7: Trench Location Plan showing the basic 10-metre grid established across the site.

memorable barbeque, Hilary du Cros and Cheryl, one of our most committed volunteers, both drove a 20-tonne excavator (under guidance). Hilary dug into a massive pile of loose bricks with the bucket and managed to retrieve only one!

Excavation then centred on Trenches 02, 10 and 14–19. The work in these areas was required to be completed by 29 February to meet the DAS schedule. This was achieved.

The team then moved to Site A – the Telecom site that fronted Exhibition Street. We retained the same site office at 27–29 Little Lonsdale Street and accessed Site A through Site B which was still mainly a carpark. Excavation commenced at Little Lonsdale Street and advanced in a wide swathe along the east side of Leichardt Street to Lonsdale Street. The remaining area to the west of Leichardt Street to George Street was the last part to be excavated. By this time we had a much better grasp of the stratigraphy across the site and as the numbers of volunteers declined with the recommencement of the school and university academic years, much more work was done with the backhoe. A core group of volunteers remained and this was augmented by a smaller but continuing flow of others who worked for shorter periods or came regularly on a part-time basis. Work was completed on the Telecom site by the end of May 1988.

The stratigraphy across most of the site was fairly simple because as we discovered later after much detailed historical research into the ratebooks and land title records, most allotments had only undergone two or possibly three phases of development between subdivision of the block in 1848 and about 1900. Peak development of the site had occurred by about 1920 when much (but by no means all) of it had been turned to industrial use for factories and printeries etc. There was then a period of ongoing usage for these purposes until about the 1940s when the slow but inexorable process of attrition and removal began. Most of the sites of demolished buildings were then used for car parking. This process accelerated once the Green Latrine was built and more area was required for government employees' cars.

While it was thought likely that there had been some 'unofficial' development on the block prior to its formal subdivision and sale in 1848, no archaeological evidence of this was found. The ratebooks also indicate that there were many small timber cottages initially erected after the formal subdivision and sale; many of these were replaced fairly quickly with masonry dwellings but in some cases they survived into the 1880s or even early 1890s. While no material evidence of these actual timber structures was found, many of the cesspits and rubbish pits recorded did relate to this earliest phase of occupation. The only remnants of the original landscape were two large redgum stumps; these had been burned and then incorporated into the foundations of the later masonry cottages. One of the stumps was retained and is now located at the rear of the former Oddfellows Hotel.

The excavations mainly revealed the brick and/or stone foundations of small two- to four-room cottages and their allotment walls, yard spaces and detached outbuildings such as sheds and toilets.

Figure 3.8: Early stages of the excavation showing cottage footings in Trench 01; view is to east northeast. 12 January 1988 Photo R02_24.

Figure 3.9: Volunteers in Trench 04; view is to northwest. 23 January 1988 Photo R04_17 (Justin McCarthy).

Figure 3.10: Backhoe at work in Trench 16; view is to east with Spring Street in the background. 19 February 1988 Photo R08_26 (Justin McCarthy).

Figure 3.11: General view of Trenches 16–19 and Pits G–J in Trench 19. View is to north with Spring Street in background. 21 February 1988 Photo R09_07 (Justin McCarthy).

Figure 3.12: Close up view of artefacts in Pit J in Trench 19 / Location 57B during excavation; view is to north. 25 February 1988 Photo R09_32 (Justin McCarthy).

Figure 3.13: General view to east of Pits I & J after excavation in Trench 19 / Locations 57A & B. 27 February 1988 Photo R10_07 (Tony Jenner).

Figure 3.14: General view of CCS Site towards south east (corner of Lonsdale and Spring Streets) after first phase of excavation has been completed and demolition has commenced. The Commonwealth building now resides on this corner. 3 March 1988 Photo R11_19 (David Bannear).

Figure 3.17: General view to east of Pits M, N, O and P during excavation in Trench 27 / Locations 30 and 31A & B. Pit N is the one that yielded the famous absinthe bottles from Mrs Bond's brothel. 15 April 1988 Photo R19_22 (David Bannear).

Figure 3.15: The large red gum stump *in situ* under footings in Trench 06 / Location 73A & B; view is to south. 3 February 1988 Photo R05_26.

Figure 3.18: Close up view of Pit N in Trench 27 / Location 31A during excavation showing some of the numerous bottles and corks recovered. 12 April 1988 Photo R19_06 (David Bannear).

Figure 3.16: Volunteers and archaeologists pose on the stump after removal from Trench 06; view is to west. 5 February 1988 Photo R07_13 (Justin McCarthy).

Figure 3.19: From left Justin McCarthy and the three Davids (David Ellson, David Knox and David Bannear) with a convoy of barrows full of artefacts retrieved from Pit N in Trench 27 / Location 31A. View is to south southwest to the Leichardt Lane and Lonsdale Street corner. 30 March 1988 Photo R18_06.

Deeper below ground features associated with the cottages that were found included rubbish pits, cellars and cesspits. Other below ground features were mainly services and service trenches. The excavations also revealed evidence of the later factory buildings which had begun to replace the cottages from about 1890 but these generally had unreinforced concrete strip footings which during construction had only intersected the earlier house foundations in part and not totally obliterated them. Laneways pitched (surfaced) with bluestone blocks were also revealed where they had been covered by the car park gravel.

The stratigraphy in the areas used as car park generally comprised a 20–30cm layer of crushed bluestone screenings (gravel) that formed the car park surface. This usually overlay a demolition deposit of variable thickness (about 20–40cm) that comprised a mixture of soil fill and demolition material from the structures that had been demolished whether they were a late 19th century factory or a mid-century house or both. In the majority of trenches where bluestone footings were found (i.e. in the earlier cottage sites), lying below the demolition deposit there was an organic, grey/black silt deposit of about 10cm thickness. This was often artefact rich and appeared to be an accumulation of a typical underfloor deposit that had been infiltrated by, and covered with, a water-borne silt – hypothesised to be the result of the much publicised overflowing Melbourne cesspits of the mid to late 19th century. No discernible evidence of a 'construction deposit' from the original structures was found but this is likely a result of a combination of factors: the fact that it may have been very ephemeral and hence easily missed; the presence of the subsequent water-borne silt deposit having disturbed or modified it; the speed at which it was being excavated; or the lack of skills of the volunteer excavators (although generally an experienced archaeologist was always involved in the proceedings and doing the recording). Generally the natural soil was encountered below the underfloor/silt deposits and this comprised an orange to yellow clay (weathered silverian mudstone). The A soil horizon had been removed and this was interpreted as part of the B horizon. Rubbish pits, cesspits and all services had been cut into the B and C horizons.

Given the focus of the artefact analysis was mainly going to be on the ceramics and glass recovered from the cesspits and rubbish pits, we were keen to also gain information on any organic materials from these pits if possible. Dr Don Ranson of VAS had been experimenting with a froth floatation machine which could extract organic material from a wet-sieved deposit. A number of the cesspit and rubbish pit deposits were sieved in this manner and useful results were gained. Dr Beth Gott of Monash University analysed the material recovered and identified a wide variety of berries, fruits and grains which were obviously part of the diet of the inhabitants.

Post Excavation Tasks

Historical Research – Developing the 'Space Locator'

As stated above, only limited historical research was done before the excavation commenced due to time constraints imposed by the client's construction schedule. After the excavation was completed, we embarked on an extensive research phase in order to be able to link the houses excavated and artefacts recovered to specific people or families if possible. This work was supervised by David Bannear and undertaken by some of our most reliable long-term volunteers (Robyn Annear, David Ellson and Diana Coultas) who worked for literally months in the government and city council archives looking at thousands of primary source documents. We examined the records for the period from 1848 to 1930 (checking every fifth year) as the block appeared to have been totally developed by that latter date. All this work was done on a voluntary basis and has since proven invaluable as a starting point for subsequent researchers.

The Melbourne City Council (MCC) records which relate to the development of Melbourne are vast and virtually go back to day one of the development of the study area in 1848. These include valuation books, ratebooks, building applications, Inspector of Nuisances reports, Health Committee reports and the Town Clerk's files. Sketch plans included in many of the original valuation and ratebook assessors notebooks also proved invaluable. Other available records include land titles records, directories (such as Sands) and plans including the Metropolitan Board of Works plans (incredibly accurate sewerage and drainage plans dated 1895 and 1899), the Mahlstedt fire insurance plans (1923) and plans from the Lands Department (various dates). At that time (1988) digitisation was hardly dreamt of and all the research was done manually and it literally took hundreds of hours of work. As well as these records there are the newspaper accounts of the day. While these are comparatively easy to access now through the National Library of Australia's Trove website, back in 1988 it was an incredibly time consuming and hit or miss process to research newspapers using microfilm or microfiche readers. As Hayes and Minchinton point out in Chapter 9, before digitisation of the MCC ratebook records 'making these comparisons for the twenty-two sites of this study through 50 years of rate records was previously unthinkable'. Well that is what we attempted and the results probably played a big part in the subsequent recognition of the potential of this resource not to mention the value of the block subdivision plan that was created at the time and which was used in the investigation of Site B (Casselden Place) in 2002 and is still in use by researchers today.

The task of trying to trace the development of each individual land parcel and record what happened to it in terms of subdivision or amalgamation, if and when houses were built and demolished on it, and who the owners and occupiers were at any given time was extremely difficult and could not be achieved by looking at any single source or set of records. Even identifying each land parcel or allotment from the rate and valuation records was fraught because there were no house or lot numbers in the early period and when they did come into use the numbering system changed dramatically from time to time. This was compounded by the fact that individual rate assessors walked around the blocks in different directions from year to year and it required a lot of patient research to correlate the results from one year to the next.

The initial formal subdivision of the block in 1848 created the basic form of the cadastral layout that was still evident in 1988. The research of the diverse sources indicated that generally further subdivisions had occurred during the mid to late 19th century with some aggregation of holdings then occurring when the factories began taking over in the late 19th and early 20th centuries. Provision of access to the land was by way of lanes and rights-of-way that were established concurrently with the original subdivisions and these remained right up until the construction of the Commonwealth Centre.

The locational information related to the development of the block was recorded in a diagram that became known as the 'Space Locator' (see Figure 3.20). The development of this diagram was an evolving process that took months of work and could not have been done without the intensive manual research of the primary sources. This shows each allotment and how it was eventually subdivided. This is linked to Volume 5 of the report which contains all the owners and occupiers information that was gathered for each of these subdivisions. By this means we could overlay the excavation plans showing the location of the rubbish pits and cesspits from which we had extracted artefacts and relate those pits to a specific allotment or allotments that could be linked to the respective owners and occupiers (see Figure 3.9). The importance and value of this diagram cannot be understated and the site locations and designations are still being used in current research and analysis.

A benefit of the rate and valuation books research was that it provided detailed information on the nature of the construction materials of the structures on each allotment. Even without any

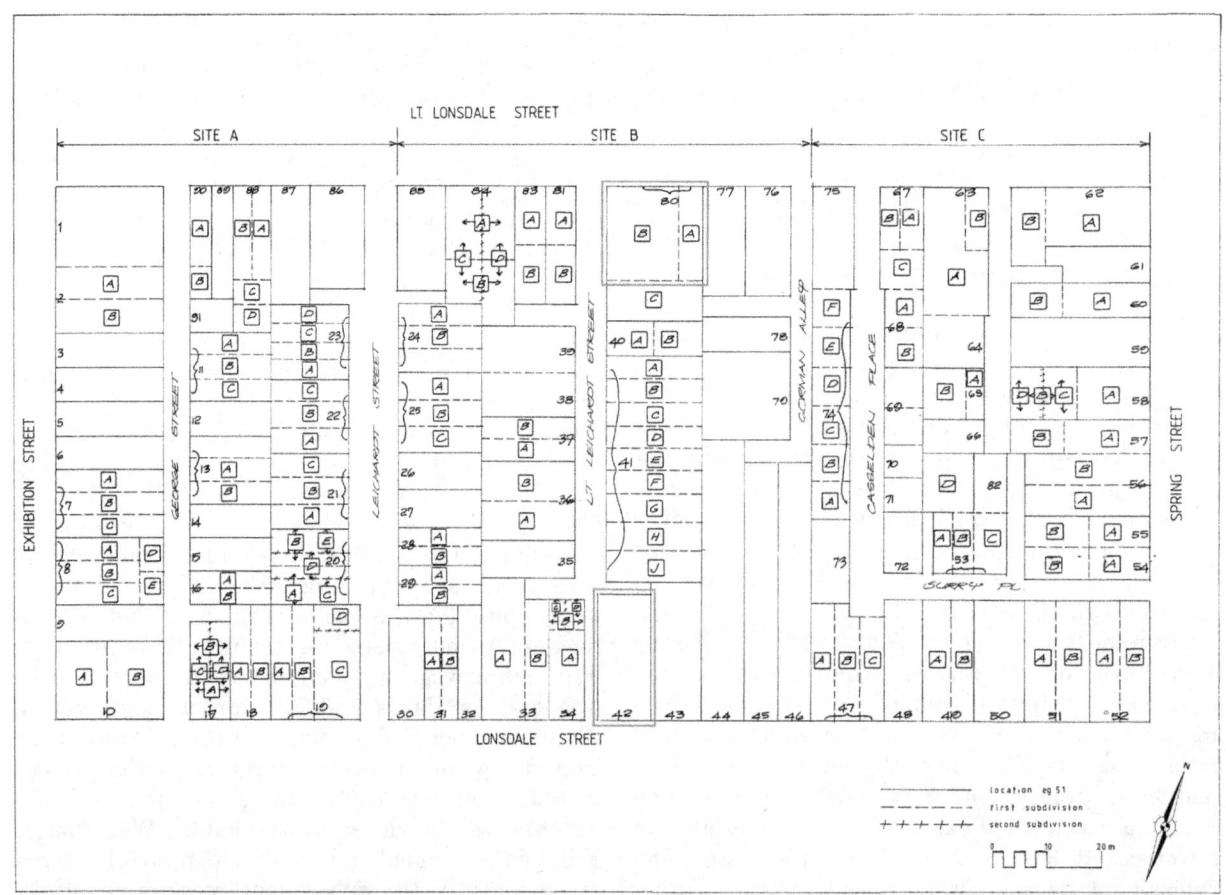

Figure 3.20: 'Space Locator' showing subdivisions of the block with the Black Eagle Hotel (Location 42) and Oddfellows Hotel (Location 80A & B) highlighted.

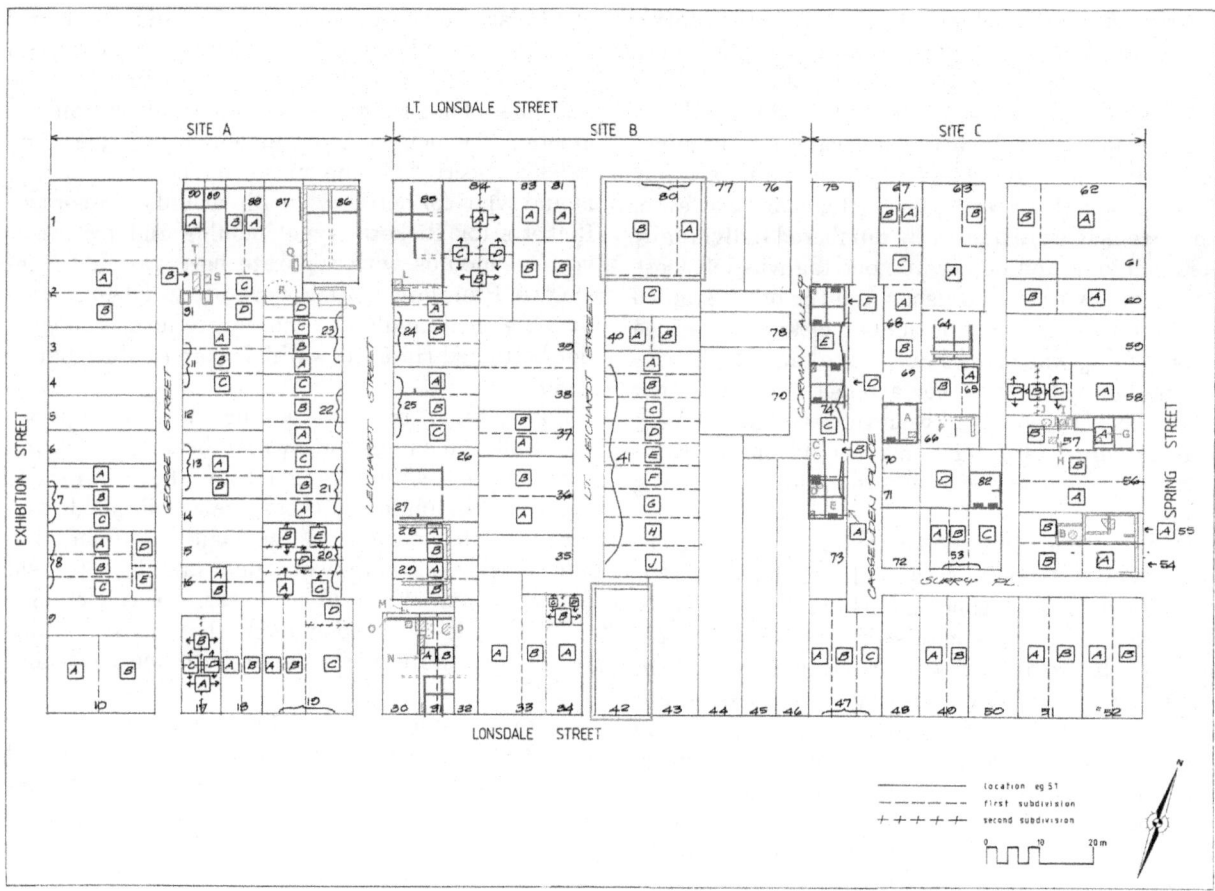

Figure 3.21: 'Space Locator' subdivision plan overlaid with excavated bluestone footings, rubbish pits and cesspits drawn in blue. The positions of the former Black Eagle and Oddfellows hotels (Locations 42 and 80A & B) are also highlighted in red.

physical archaeological evidence of the presence of timber cottages being recovered from any particular lot, from this research we could establish the approximate location of where timber houses had been, how long they had been there, when they were replaced and by what type of structure, and how long that latter structure was there. This proved very useful when we were analysing the artefacts recovered from cesspits in cases where there had been no physical evidence of an early timber cottage during the excavation, but the placement of the pit and the age of its contents seemed to indicate it belonged to an era earlier than the documented and excavated later masonry cottage.

Researching the historical physical development this way produced an information base that not only revealed the names of the people who lived and in many cases worked there, but also gave an idea of their ethnic origin, gender, occupation, duration of their stay in the area, mobility within the area, and the ratio of owners to tenants. While most of this information was not used in the original report as it was way beyond the scope of that project, it has provided a solid basis for the ongoing analysis of the artefactual material and linking it to specific persons where possible. The plethora of academic research that both the artefacts and the historical information have spawned are testament to the validity of the approach, if not the ultimate results of the 1988 project. As the owners and occupiers information had already been compiled for Site B, it provided a ready resource for the 2003 excavation by the Austral Archaeology, Godden Mackay Logan and La Trobe University joint venture – a huge benefit that the original project did not have.

Artefact Analysis and Photography

Artefact sorting and cataloguing was a continuous process throughout the excavation phase with 2 or 3 teams of volunteers washing and cataloguing during the day under the supervision of an archaeologist. Artefact processing also continued after the excavation phase ended and artefact photography was also undertaken by a very talented volunteer, the late Tony Jenner, at this time.

The accession items were generally processed by the volunteers using fabric and function guides from the PA manual. accession items were catalogued using a simple one line entry on a recording form while inventory items and special finds were put aside for the qualified archaeologists or more experienced volunteers to process in a more detailed form.

Artefacts were brought from the site to the central finds area in labelled plastic tubs where they were washed, sorted, counted and catalogued. After sorting and cataloguing, artefacts were bagged and labelled with the trench, unit and catalogue number. A word on the tagging and labelling: great care was taken to double tag every artefact bag as very few of the artefacts were physically numbered individually using chinagraph pen or ink; one tag was left loose in the bag with the artefact/s and the other stapled to the outside as part of the bag closure. The idea was if a bag was opened one of the tags would stay in the bag with any other artefacts and the other could be kept with the removed artefact while it was examined. Information recorded manually on the catalogue sheets was entered into the hyperdig program.

Due to time and economic limitations on the project, only the ceramics and glass inventory items from cesspits and rubbish pits were analysed in any way. While this may seem remiss today, the focus of the excavation was primarily to record the archaeology and recover associated artefacts as part of the urgent salvage process. It was considered that the material could be analysed in detail in the future and that the collection with the accompanying excavation records, would provide an ongoing basis for study for archaeology students well into the future. This has in fact occurred.

In comparison with today there were very limited reference resources available that pertained to imported goods found on Australian colonial sites. The Parks Canada Glass Glossary was used to classify, describe and date the glass containers (generally the last was achieved by reference to their manufacturing technique and registration marks). There was no such Australian resource available for the ceramics in 1988 and so a simple system of classification was devised; other sources were used where available for some item types e.g. clay pipes. Ceramics were mainly dated on the basis of pottery marks found in the standard references (Godden 1974, 1982; Coysh and Henrywood 1982). Reference was also made to contemporary theoretical analytical studies (such as Majewski and O'Brien 1987: 97–208; Worthy 1982: 329–360) although these related to the American context.

The bulk of the ceramic material recovered was mainly of a domestic nature such as tableware and utilitarian items such as water pitchers, washbowls, chamber pots and storage jars; there was also a range of pharmaceutical and personal items including Holloways ointment pots, bear grease pots and lids, as well as rouge pots. Staffordshire figurines were also found. Generally most manufacturer's marks on ceramics recovered from pits dated to between 1840 and 1860. The only Chinese ceramics found were a celadon rice bowl and pieces of a large stoneware crock.

All glass bottles examined in the analysis turned out to be free blown or hand blown in moulds with an applied lip or complete finish. There were no examples of bottles made by semi- or fully automatic machines, which were not invented until 1886 and 1903 respectively. The most commonly occurring mould types for bottles were dip moulds, three-piece Ricketts (or Ricketts type) moulds and two piece vertical moulds with separate base part. All egg-shaped Hamilton bottles were produced in a two-piece vertical mould but there were no examples of flat-bottomed Hamiltons which were produced after 1880.

Bottle types represented included many types of alcohol (champagne, wine, beer, porter and gin); aerated waters, ginger beer (there were also stoneware examples of these); salad oil, pickle and vinegar; pharmaceutical, medicine, perfume; ink and blacking. There were no examples of Codd bottles or similar patent closures in the collection.

Overall it was concluded that most bottles recovered from the pits dated to the period before c.1880.

A few examples of glass tableware were examined; none were complete. Functional groups consisted of press moulded tumblers, wineglasses and sherry glasses.

Results

As mentioned above, the main objective of the project was to undertake a rapid salvage excavation of the site prior to its destruction, determine the level and nature of remains and artefacts and produce a summary report. All documentation and the catalogued artefacts were to be handed over at the conclusion of the excavation, much in the manner of what is currently known in Victoria as a 'Research Archive'. This would allow further future analysis of the artefacts with access to the primary excavation documentation including the stratigraphic records and notes.

The following artefacts and records were duly handed over to the Museum of Victoria in the early part of 1989:

Artefacts:
   482 large boxes (390x300x260mm),
   168 small boxes (390x260x180mm);

Records:
   1 box of accession registers – 4 vols (Nos 1–4),
   1 box of inventory registers – 3 vols (Nos 1–3),
   1 box of inventory registers – 3 vols (Nos 4–6),
   special finds register – 1 vol,
   5 boxes of owners and occupiers records,
   1 box of Melbourne City Council ratebook photocopies,
   part lot plans of Gipps Ward,
   1 box of land title records and directory records.

The following records were handed over to the Victorian Archaeological Survey:
   1 box of stratigraphic records – 4 vols,

1 box of stratigraphic unit sheets (grouped into site phases) and stratigraphic analysis – 2 vols.
Unfortunately, during a couple of subsequent planned relocations by the museum during which the artefacts were moved to several temporary storage locations, many of the records associated with the excavation were mislaid and are now considered lost.

The formal results of the excavation were presented in a five-volume report that was never published and only exists in limited copies. Volume 1 comprised the general Historical and Archaeological Report, while the other four volumes were appendices and comprised:

Volume 2 – Artefact Analysis and Catalogue

Volume 3 – Artefacts Recovered from Site A (Commonwealth Site)

Volume 4 – Artefacts Recovered from Site C (Telecom Site)

Volume 5 – Historical Background Summary and List of Former Owners and Occupiers of Sites A, B and C.

It must be emphasised here that it was never a requirement of the brief nor the intention of VAS, DAS or the archaeological team itself to provide the full analysis of thhe whole assemblage – some 350,000 or so objects – and to write the complete and definitive archaeological report. It was a salvage excavation project in the true sense and sought to capture archaeological information and artefacts that would otherwise have been lost, with the aim of creating a resource that could be further documented and analysed in the future. Unfortunately this point was obviously missed by some and resulted in the project methodology and outcomes later being adversely critiqued by some members of the Melbourne archaeological academic community who had undertaken a subsequent analysis of the artefacts over the period since 1996. Happily this situation was somewhat rectified in 2003 with the further excavation of the last parcel of Little Lon (Site B) when Austral teamed up with La Trobe University and GML in a joint venture and the value of the earlier work became more apparent and better understood.

Section 4.3 of Volume 1 contained summarised results of the individual specific pit investigations. In this section the history of the relevant lots, their stratigraphy and the artefacts recovered from each, were synthesised and some conclusions drawn as to the likely date of deposition, what phase of development they likely belonged to and whom they may have been associated with. While this information has been well and truly superseded by now (see Sarah Hayes and Barbara Minchinton's chapter in this volume and numerous other works on Little Lon), it serves to show how the initial report provided some tantalising glimpses of the possibilities that further historical and archaeological research might provide in the future.

While the report does not include detailed interpretation of the finds within the broader historical or social context, the basic data contained within the archaeology and the artefacts is clearly interesting and informative in itself and suggested many possibilities for further research and analysis. For example the range of pit types excavated covered the gamut of what could have been derived from research of the documentary records of sanitation, but also provided much more than that. Not only was the physical evidence of these documented pit types revealed and recorded, but also hybrid versions of both the officially 'approved' and 'non-approved' cesspits were found. Pits that had been associated with the earliest houses on the block were found even if there was no trace of the house itself. Where there were multiple pits on single or subdivided allotments, their construction order was generally able to be sequenced and associated with an identifiable phase of development (first house, second house etc). The archaeology also revealed the large range of adaptations made to earlier pits to make them comply firstly with the 1861 Central Board of Health requirements for waterproofing and then later to adapt to the municipal requirements for earth closets, pans and finally sewered outhouses in the same locations. The grey soil layer that was encountered across most of the site was a remnant of the overflowing cesspits that saturated the ground under and around the houses and flowed across the site from east to west toward Exhibition Street.

The general conclusions from dating of the artefacts found in the cesspits was that they had probably been deposited as rubbish into the pits in the 1870s and 1880s when the cesspits began to go out of use. After about the mid-1870s, the pits began to be replaced by earth closets or the pan system but this was by no means universal – especially on this site where there was a high number of absentee landlords. Here expenditure on maintenance and repairs is likely to have been minimal as reported in the rate assessors' notes and the police reports. Likewise the range of artefacts recovered from the cesspits begged some interesting questions – some of which have been researched by subsequent historians and archaeologists.

One of the more interesting finds included the large red gum tree stump that was salvaged with some difficulty from under the remnant foundations of buildings in Casselden Place and now rests at the rear of the former Oddfellows Hotel. Another was the extremely intriguing profile of artefacts recovered from one of three pits in the rear yard of a house and shop site on the corner of Leichardt and Lonsdale Streets. What appeared to be a purpose-dug, single use pit (Pit N) contained over 8,000 artefacts, the majority of which were intact bottles and bottle glass – a lot of it high quality imported French wine and spirits – as well as 1242 corks! Just as interesting in this regard is the fact that the pit contained a complete absence of those other ubiquitous bottle types that were recovered from all the other deposits across the site – salad oil, ginger beer, aerated waters and stoneware ink bottles. This pit also included pot lids, figurines, ceramic tableware including large serving platters, a carved bone hairpin, cheap jewelry, smoking pipes, toothbrushes, horse hardware, and some building materials. Of particular interest was the amount and range of clothing and apparel that came from this pit; these included remains of 26 shoes (men's, women's and one child's), and four mens boots; three shirts (one flannel, one finely woven and one unidentified cloth), one shirt or blouse of fine cotton, one finely woven wool jacket, one dark grey knee length wool sock and two pairs of woven wool trousers. There were also a further 92 pieces of unidentified textile and 20 pieces of woollen fabric as well as belt buckles and numerous loose and attached buttons. Some of the loose buttons matched those attached to the clothing items and appeared to have been torn or cut off. Other interesting finds include a number of coins including a Swiss centime, a large amount of bone material from sheep and cow and a cache of 300 very large oyster shells.

This is clearly not a normal domestic assemblage and the report suggested that this was likely to characterise a high class brothel site. There are detailed historical records relating to the land parcel on which this pit was located. A timber house had been built on the site by 1847/48 but this was replaced by a brick house of four rooms and a kitchen by 1854. It may be that this house was first used as a brothel from as early as 1857 when it was run by Louis Amiet as the 'Swiss Boarding House' although according the historical records, there were no registered boarding houses recorded in the study area. At this time cheap, unregistered boarding houses were often used by single women for prostitution. It is also interesting that an 1853 Swiss centime was recovered from this site, perhaps attesting to some connection with the owner. Often shops and back rooms of shops cited as 'tobacconist', 'cigar', 'fruit', 'store' or 'sweet' shops in the ratebooks were disguises for cheap rooms for street prostitutes to use. Likewise the later designations as 'furniture marts' often run by an 'agent' signified their use as brothels. Clearly when a Mrs Bond bought the place in 1876 and used it as a 'store' for a number of years until about 1891, it was being used for prostitution purposes. It may well have continued to be used as a brothel by subsequent owners for another ten years when it was taken over by a Chinese cabinet maker as Chinatown expanded outward from Little Bourke Street. The indicative deposition date of the artefacts from 1870 to 1900 coincides with the ambiguous entries in the rate records and directories. Hayes and Minchinton (this volume) and others have since scrutinised the life and times of Mrs Bond amongst other residents of Little Lon and confirmed that this was in fact a high class brothel. Their case study comparison of the life stories of different women who operated brothels however is telling and reveals the differences in their involvement in this trade and the variance of their origins, situations and outcomes.

To focus on only this aspect of the use of the study area however, is to ignore the bigger picture that the report painted, a claim that was somewhat erroneously levelled at the report in the archaeological literature after the excavation. The overwhelming evidence from the site from both the historical and archaeological sources is that this city block mainly provided a home for a whole range of people from many ethnicities and all walks of life. While many of the poor and dispossessed lived in cheap rented accommodation with a high turnover of tenants, there were equally some middle-class and even higher-status families that lived on the block for relatively long periods.

THE ODDFELLOWS AND BLACK EAGLE HOTELS EXCAVATIONS 1990

These two standing structures are located on Site B, at either end of Little Leichardt Street and its intersections with Little Lonsdale and Lonsdale Streets respectively. The former Black Eagle Hotel is situated on Location 42 and the former Oddfellows Hotel is situated on Locations 80A and B (see Figure 3.8). Parts of them were excavated in May–June 1990 prior to them being leased to private developers for refurbishment and adaptive reuse. While the planned reuses of the structures would generally retain the external walls and most of the standing elements of the buildings themselves, many of the floors and existing surfaces were to be either replaced or disturbed and the introduction of new services throughout was also likely to have below ground impacts.

The Black Eagle was built in 1850 as two conjoined houses with the Oddfellows following in 1853 that also incorporated a house on its eastern side into the design; both places remained in use as hotels until approximately 1910–1920. It was considered that their stratigraphic and artefactual signatures for this period would be (a) extant (as the bulk of this period was generally in the pre-garbage collection era) and (b) fairly similar. Following their closure as hotels as part of the municipal campaign to clean up the area, however, they had quite different uses; the Oddfellows went on to be used primarily as a Chinese furniture factory until 1948 and then had a range of other uses; the Black Eagle had some periods of vacancy but was used as a lodging house from 1909 to 1913 and was then taken over by a Chinese cabinet maker from 1915 to 1917 and was then converted to a printing works in 1919 and run as a family printing business until 1977 when the Commonwealth acquired the site. It was thought

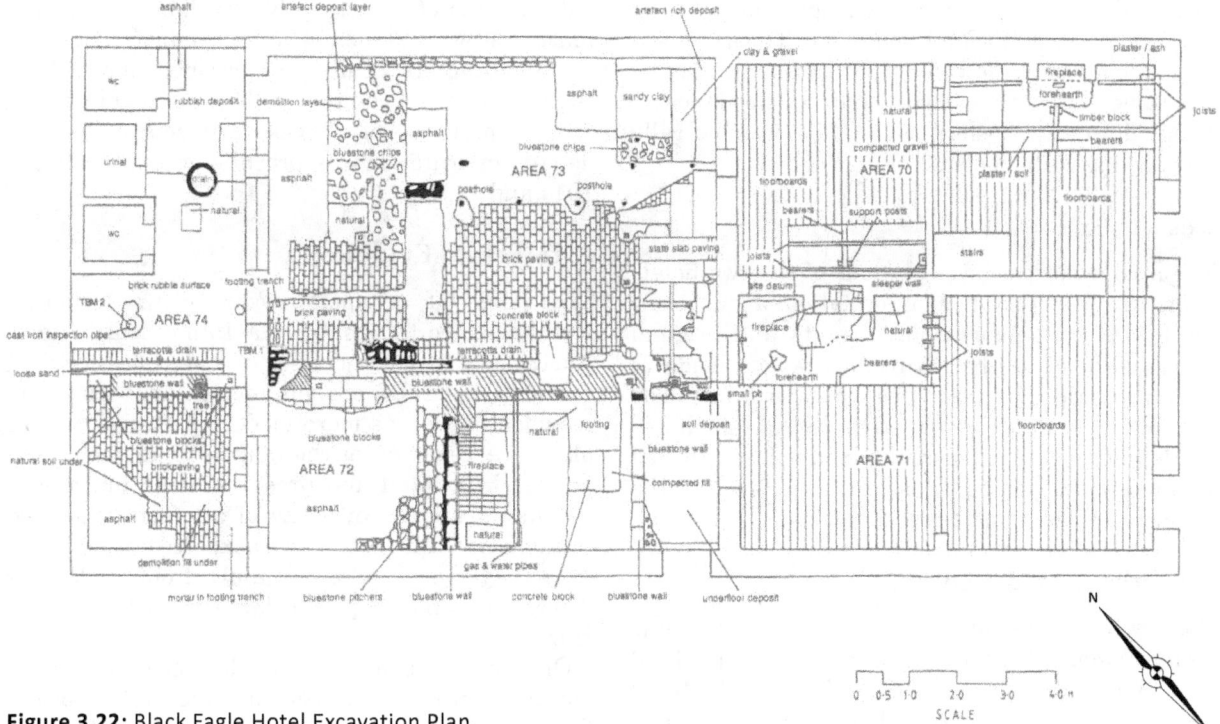

Figure 3.22: Black Eagle Hotel Excavation Plan.

that as well as being able to provide information on the functions and uses of the buildings over their life spans, any artefactual material recovered from the underfloors would also provide a useful comparative dataset to the artefacts recovered from the large-scale excavations undertaken on Sites A and C in 1988. It was recognised that although the use-phase beyond 1910 may have left little archaeological evidence due to the highly developed nature of the sites by that time and the unlikely disposal of material on site, it was an opportunity to see if previously undocumented themes such as Chinese occupation, industrial use or other uses were apparent in the archaeological record.

At the Black Eagle a total of five trenches were excavated within the main building and the areas at the rear (trenches/areas numbered 70 to 74 – see Figure 3.10). These included removal of three sections of the wooden floors in the main building fronting Lonsdale Street (to allow ground access), the entire floor area of the large adjoining shed and part of the rear courtyard.

At the Oddfellows five trenches/areas were excavated in the ground floor rooms and a hallway in the western-most part of the building (trenches/areas numbered 75 to 79 – see Figure 3.11). This comprised about a third of the building – the remainder having been taken over for use by the

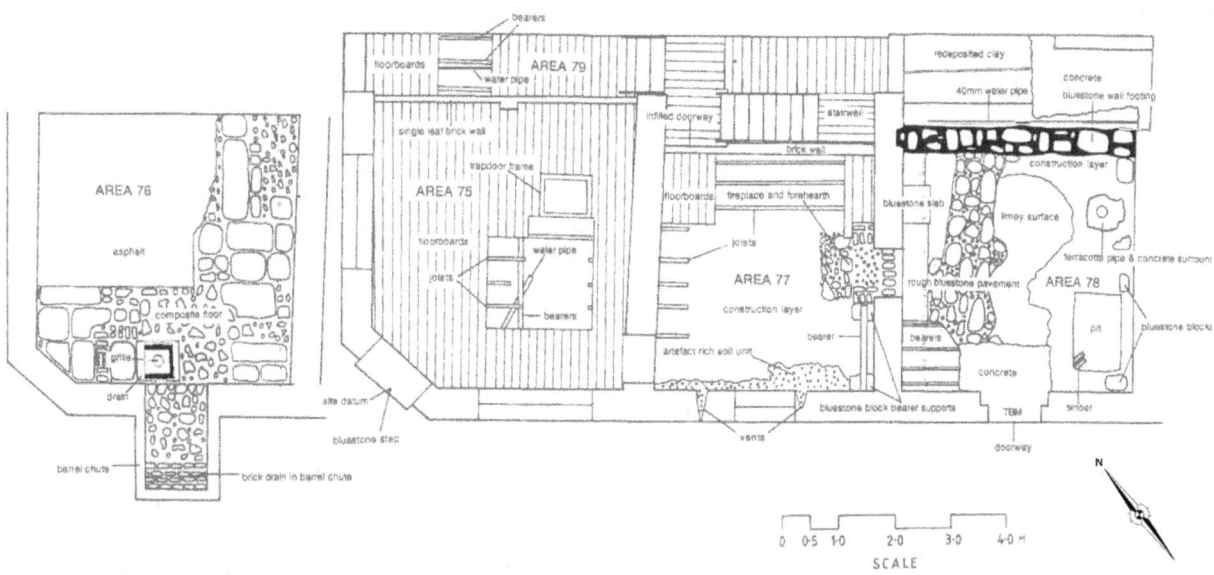

Figure 3.23: Oddfellows Hotel Excavation Plan. Note Area 76 is the cellar and lies below Area 75.

principal building contractor engaged to build the new Commonwealth Offices on Site C. The northernmost room was completely underlain by a cellar of the same size with a barrel chute to the laneway situated in the western wall. This was literally overflowing with modern looking rubbish.

Results

The archaeological investigations of the two hotels primarily revealed new information about their former room configurations, layouts and original fabric, as well as the nature of changes made to accommodate changing uses through time. The artefactual evidence broadly reflected all the phases of the buildings' documented histories but provided some surprises and insights into the lives of the former occupants and users.

Structural Evidence

The archaeology indicated that the Black Eagle Hotel remained virtually as built in late 1850 (and modified almost immediately in early 1851) from that time until the McLelland family took it over as a printery in 1919/1920. They then made extensive modifications including demolition of the rear kitchen and stables, the demolition of some internal walls of the main building to create larger spaces, blocking up of some fireplaces, replacement of the wooden floors, and partitioning of some of the rooms in the upper storey. These extensive changes and alterations seriously compromised the *in situ* conservation of artefact-bearing underfloor deposits which would have been removed or redistributed around the site. Although not a formal part of the work, it was observed that the loft still retained a diverse array of layers of wallpaper that dated back to the 1870s.

The archaeology of the western rooms in the Oddfellows Hotel revealed a cellar in the northern one, an original wooden floor and remains of a fireplace in the central one and evidence of a walled yard that was later converted to a room in the southern one. Like the Black Eagle, the western third of the Oddfellows underwent little structural modification from 1853 until after 1912. The closing of the hotel at that time necessitated a change of use and this was reflected in the structural alterations. Although not archaeologically investigated, it was apparent that in the other two thirds of the building, changes had been extensive and the original interiors were largely gutted.

The only area of the entire excavation of the two hotels that was deemed to have been completely undisturbed was the underfloor deposit in the southern room (Area 78) of the Oddfellows, where an unreinforced concrete floor had been laid over it. The cellar (Area 76) did not contain stratified deposits and was probably in use until the hotel function ceased in 1912. At some point after that it was filled with a mass of bluestone blocks, lime mortar and plaster as well as domestic and industrial refuse. The building materials were possibly sourced from the demolition of the rear wall of the hotel in Area 78; the presence of Chinese artefacts under this deposit indicates it was probably created between 1914 and 1931.

Artefactual Evidence

The range of artefacts recovered was what is now known to be typical of a 19th-century site in Australia. The usual classes of materials including ceramics, glass, bone, shell, metals, and wood were included as well as more modern material such as plastic. A selection of the diagnostic material was analysed in detail and produced some interesting results. While the quantity of artefacts recovered was modest, this was not unexpected considering that they were sourced mainly from underfloor deposits and no cesspits or large rubbish pits were found.

One of the objectives of the research design for this project was to compare the profiles of the finds from the two hotels. The main differences are probably mainly attributable to the greater degree of alterations made to the Black Eagle by the McLelland family about 1920 which compromised the integrity of the deposits investigated there. On the other hand, a small rubbish pit was excavated in the rear courtyard of the Black Eagle which contained some of the oldest glass artefacts recovered in the excavation, whereas no such location was found within the Oddfellows building. These two factors alone account for many of the differences between the assemblages recovered from each hotel.

Of note were the artefacts recovered from the southern room of the Oddfellows. These artefacts came from a wide time span and illustrate many of the uses to which that particular room had been put. The children's toys included a small ceramic doll, a tiny teapot and many playing marbles. These may well have been deposited when the Oddfellows was used as a boarding house immediately after being delicensed in 1912. Also of note were the distinctively Chinese items recovered from the cellar. The building had been used as Chinese furniture factory from 1914 until 1948. The items included food serving items such as a soup ladle, tea cup and plate, a Chinese coin and possibly a Chinese gaming token. The most interesting find however was a notebook written principally in Chinese, but partially in poor English, and with some translations of amorous phrases such as 'give us a ghiss' into Italian. The notebook also appears to contain a record of horse races around Australia with betting ticket numbers and some names and addresses of Chinese people. Research undertaken at the time showed that the races recorded in the notebook were run in November 1930 and January 1931.

Another interesting find was a fragment of a glass tumbler. Just below the rim of the vessel the word 'W. Brandt' is etched in script. William Brandt was the owner of the Black Eagle Hotel in the 1850s but how the fragment found its way into the Oddfellows Hotel situated at the other end of Little Leichardt Street is a mystery.

In terms of function most of the artefacts recovered from both buildings relate to the day-to-day operations of the premises as hotels and/or perhaps illicit boarding houses (as they were never officially registered as such). The bottles and bottle glass, ceramics, glass tableware, silver cutlery, butchered bones, and clay pipes, can obviously be related to the hotel functions.

There was a comparatively large amount of silver plated cutlery recovered in the excavations compared to the earlier Little Lon excavations in 1988/89. All but one piece came from the southern room of the Oddfellows and again this is probably a function of the extensive changes and alterations that occurred at the Black Eagle. The southern room also contained remnants of a chair rail around the walls and this may have been the dining room at some stage with the cutlery being stored, used and ultimately lost through the cracks in the floorboards there.

A majority of the faunal remains were sheep, followed by beef, chicken, fish and shellfish. As per usual, these may not be an accurate guide to dietary preferences as the bones were recovered from underfloors, old yard surfaces as well as demolition and fill deposits.

Conclusion

In this chapter I have tried to present the first Little Lon excavation within its historical context so that it can be better understood and judged by the standards of its time and the constraints which shaped it. Undeniably, the project was a real pioneer for large scale urban archaeology in Australia at a time when inner city development of Sydney and Melbourne were just beginning to stir after the stock market crash of 1987. It was hugely ambitious. It brought together a diverse group representing state and federal government agencies, academic archaeologists, archaeological consultants and the general public to make it happen. It relied on an enormous amount of good will and a passion for archaeology from those involved. And it realised a massive artefact assemblage that provided some information from the initial cursory analysis and has provided ongoing information from subsequent research.

By present day standards however, it was a fairly amateurish archaeological project; it was hastily put together with a ridiculous completion deadline, vast scope, minimal funding that only allowed employment of four archaeologists, and an expectation that an army of untrained community volunteers could do the work. At the time there was very little comparative historical archaeology data available for Melbourne (or for that matter the other Australian cities), as relatively little urban historical archaeological work had been done to that point and nothing of the scale had ever been attempted in Australia previously. The Cumberland Street dig in The Rocks in Sydney was still five years away into the future.

So what was achieved? How did Little Lon ultimately contribute to the future of historical archaeology in Melbourne and Australia?

The greatest benefit without doubt is how it lifted the profile of historical archaeology in particular and archaeology in general within the broader community. The fact that it was literally beneath people's feet in central Melbourne was a huge drawcard and an eye opener to the public. The involvement of hundreds if not thousands of enthusiastic people over four months of excavation and then a more select group for a further six months in assisting with artefact cataloguing and historical research, gave them first hand experience and an appreciation of the highs, lows, excitement and disappointments of archaeology. The high level of media attention and exposure, especially during the excavation, fed the public appetite for information and it became a self-sustaining circle that constantly brought more people to the site and the project.

The role that VAS played in firstly cajoling and bluffing the Commonwealth government into undertaking the project and secondly assisting the consultants with the setup and commencement were critical to its success. The project also subsequently lifted the profile of VAS (and later Heritage Victoria) and its role in promoting and protecting archaeological and built heritage. The fact that a selection of buildings were retained around the periphery of the site and through adaptive reuse incorporated into the development and remain today are partly a legacy of those efforts in protecting and interpreting significant heritage buildings at the site. Walking around the site today it is interesting to see how the buildings are being reused with references to Madam Brussels prominent in the naming of a laneway (originally this was Eagle Alley, later in the 19th century it became Little Leichardt Lane and now Madame Brussels Lane). The subtle interpretation includes a collage of the names and occupations of the past residents, histories of the remaining historic buildings such as the Oddfellows Hotel and a depiction of the pre-European vegetation and topography in the form of the ancient red gum stump; these are all a lasting living legacy of the archaeological project.

Likewise, the subsequent role of Museum Victoria in curating, interpreting, displaying and promoting the artefact collection is a vital aspect of the presentation of the history and development of

Melbourne and is part of that legacy. The museum provides an ongoing presence and reminder of the history of Lonsdale and Little Lonsdale Streets and serves to direct the attention of the public to the physical remains that they can then go and seek out and investigate themselves.

The fact that a quality documentary film of the excavation was made during excavations is also a major achievement of Heritage Victoria and the archaeological team. The film continued to be used in schools as part of an education package for teachers for many years and remains as a record of the project that includes historical, archaeological and social perspectives on the findings of the excavation.

The outcomes of the project produced a wealth of new archaeological information about the development of inner Melbourne in the 1850 to 1920/30 period at both macro and micro levels. The work subsequently refocused the eyes of both historians and archaeologists on the nature of the lives of thousands of people who passed through the city block in that time. And this project brought an awareness of the potential richness of these city sites to the attention of other heritage management agencies around Australia. Major excavations soon followed in other Australian cities in the following years.

The project as a whole (including the excavation, artefact analysis and subsequent detailed historical research about the owners and occupiers) provided a rich resource for further research and analysis. Indeed the land parcel identification system set up manually in 1988 is still in use today. The summary report of the work included a full catalogue of the items recovered and although the analysis was cursory, the assemblage has subsequently proven to be invaluable in providing first hand information about the day to day lives of the residents including diet, lifestyle, the physical conditions, material culture, as well as the mix of socio-economic groups, the presence of long-term and short-term residents and a mix of ethnicities. Indeed the actual production of a five-volume report within a year of completion of the excavation was no mean feat. A number of subsequent excavations around Australia that were smaller and far better funded and resourced have never produced a formal report at all.

But despite these achievements, there were obviously failures and disappointments. It is extremely unfortunate that some of the artefacts and most of the excavation records were lost while the artefacts were in storage with the Museum of Victoria during several of its moves. Similarly unsupervised access to the artefacts for student projects in the mid-1990s resulted in some of the artefacts being lost, rebagged or retagged with the wrong labels and criticism being directed back to the original team. Also the inability to translate the artefact records from Hypercard to another format without a loss of information was extremely frustrating as the team went to great lengths to develop an integrated computer-based cataloguing and recording method at the time but to no avail. When the data got translated so as to be able to be entered into Museum Victoria's EMu database, a lot of recorded information was lost. The lack of positive engagement with the project team by some in the archaeological academic community during the excavation was also disappointing given their initial involvement in the planning day. Seeing as many of the archaeology and history students from the three Melbourne universities attended the site as volunteers and presumably gained valuable, rare, hands-on experience in historical archaeological excavation, field methods and artefact cataloguing, this was somewhat galling.

One of the more tangible benefits of the Little Lon excavation was that it led to a far better organised project for the Stage 2 excavation of the remaining part of the city block (Site B) in 2002. Historical archaeology in Australia had developed and matured a lot in the intervening 14 years. New legislation was in place in Victoria and Heritage Victoria was better experienced and equipped to set the goals and parameters for the Stage 2 project in conjunction with the developer. The combined expertise of the Austral/GML/La Trobe team produced high quality results from the 2002/3 excavations. This project had the luxury of adequate time for planning and execution well ahead of the development construction program and was funded and resourced at a much higher level. The project could not only utilise the MCC ratebook data for the detailed histories of the individual land parcels from the earlier project, but also had comparative archaeological information for the types of sites excavated.

The outcomes of the original Little Lon project produced new archaeological information about the development of inner Melbourne in the 1850 to 1920/30 period. But perhaps more importantly, it revealed the richness of the *potential* of both the material culture and the primary historical records to provide a detailed insight into the early European history of Melbourne. The work subsequently refocused the eyes of both historians and archaeologists on the nature of the lives of thousands of people who passed through the city block in that time. And this project brought an awareness of the archaeological potential of such city sites to the attention of other heritage management agencies around Australia and major excavations soon followed in other Australian cities (if not Melbourne) in the following years. But perhaps the greatest benefit was how it lifted the profile of historical archaeology and created a consciousness of the archaeological resource within the broader community in Melbourne and Australia.

REFERENCES

Unpublished

Austral Archaeology, Godden Mackay Logan and La Trobe University, 2004. Casselden Place, 50 Lonsdale Street, Melbourne: Archaeological Excavation Report. Prepared for the Industry Superannuation Property Trust and Heritage Victoria, Melbourne, Australia.

Australian Construction Services (Archaeology Consultant Justin McCarthy), 1989. Archaeological Investigation – The Commonwealth Block Melbourne Sites A & C, Victoria, Volumes 1–5.

Australian Construction Services (Archaeology Consultant Justin McCarthy), 1990. Archaeological Investigation – The Black Eagle & Oddfellows Hotels (Site B), The Commonwealth Block Melbourne, Victoria.

Department of Housing and Construction, 1979. Historical and Architectural Development of the Commonwealth Centre Site bounded by Spring, Lonsdale, Exhibition and La Trobe Streets Melbourne, 1837–1978. Department of Housing and Construction, Victoria–Tasmania Region, Melbourne.

Published

Coysh, A.W. and R.K. Henrywood, 1982. *The Dictionary of Blue and White Printed Pottery, 1780–1880*. Antique Collectors Club.

Crook, P. and T. Murray, 2006. *Guide to the EAMC Archaeology Database*. Archaeology of the Modern City 1788–1900 Series, Volume 10. Sydney: Historic Houses Trust of New South Wales.

Davison, G. 1978. *The Rise and Fall of Marvellous Melbourne*. Melbourne: Melbourne University Press.

Davison, G., D. Dunstan and C. McConville (eds.), 1985. *The Outcasts of Melbourne*. Sydney: Allen & Unwin.

Godden, G.A. 1974. *British Pottery: An Illustrated Guide*. London: Barrie and Jenkins.

Godden, G.A. 1982. *Encyclopaedia of British Pottery and Porcelain Marks*. London: Barrie and Jenkins.

Hayes, S. and B. Minchinton. Diversity and Change in Little Lon: Ongoing Historical and Archaeological Research (Chapter 9, this volume).

Majewski T.A. and M.J. O'Brien, 1987. The Use and Misuse of Nineteenth Century English and American Ceramics in Archaeological Analysis. *Advances in Archaeological Method and Theory*, Vol II.

Murray, T. and A. Mayne, 2003. (Re)Constructing a Lost Community: Little Lon, Melbourne, Australia. *Historical Archaeology* 37(1): 87–101.

Worthy, L.H. 1982. Classification and Interpretation of Late Nineteenth Century and Early Twentieth Century Ceramics. In Dickens, R.F. (ed.) *The Archaeology of Urban America: A Search for Pattern and Process*. New York: Academic Press.

World Wide Web

Mahlstedt Fire Insurance Plan Map 8a 1923. http://handle.slv.vic.gov.au/10381/128048.

Melbourne Heritage Action, photograph of 27–29 Little Lonsdale Street. https://melbourneheritage.org.au/current-campaigns/save-little-lon-proposed-casselden-place-heritage-precinct/life-as-it-was-lived-in-little-lon/amal-electrix-ltd-early-1980s-slv-little-lonsdale/.

Melbourne and Metropolitan Board of Works Plan 27 East Melbourne. https://digitised-collections.unimelb.edu.au/handle/11343/24037.

Sievers Photograph, Commonwealth Centre Building, corner Spring Street and Victoria Parade, Melbourne 1968 [picture] / Wolfgang Sievers. © National Library of Australia http://nla.gov.au/nla.obj-160560931/view.

4
Assemblage Analysis and Outcomes: Phase 1

Tim Murray

In this chapter I briefly outline two key elements of research at Little Lon conducted by Alan Mayne and myself. The first element derives directly from Mayne's radically different approach to the history of the Commonwealth Block which directly influenced the conduct of the second element (Mayne 1993), the analysis of sections of McCarthy's excavations (1989, 1990) undertaken by Christine Williamson (1998) and of the later work by Sharon Lane at 17 Casselden Place (1995), which was incorporated into that analysis and is discussed in greater detail in Chapter 5.

Mayne and I have published the basis of this new approach to the social history of the Block on several occasions and the essence of those publications is summarised here. Similarly we have also published the outcomes of the analysis of excavated assemblages from phase 1 (and of 17 Casselden Place) (see e.g. Murray and Mayne 2001, 2003; Williamson 1998). My focus in this chapter is on the development of our approach to the analysis of the outcomes of phase 1 of the excavations and its evolution over the late 1990s towards the new research directions enshrined in the research design for the 'Casselden Place' phase 2 excavations (discussed in Chapter 7).

Background

During the early 1990s undergraduate students completed research projects on excavated assemblages drawn from the holdings of the Historic Houses Trust of New South Wales (later Sydney's Living Museums) and from other collections created as a result of the development process. However, by then it was clear that if we were to advance our understanding of the historical archaeology of urban Australia then a great deal more pure research had to be undertaken, both for its own sake as well as to help archaeologists to avoid two serious consequences. The first of these had to do with the perpetuation of approaches to the interpretation of sites, contexts, or artefacts which had not had their efficacy assessed by a thoroughgoing engagement with the material they purported to interpret or explain. The second consequence related to a need to radically increase the interpretative and explanatory output of urban archaeology in order to support arguments that urban sites, contexts, and collections were significant beyond the level of media interest in the public performances of excavation and artefact cataloguing. Those authorities with the primary responsibility for managing the collections from such sites (such as the then Historic Houses Trust of NSW) had begun to point out that lack of interest in the analysis of collections made it more difficult to justify the expense of curating those collections.

The second factor grew from discussions about the theoretical issues that were raised by seeking a more comprehensive integration of archaeological and historical perspectives in doing the archaeology of the modern city. Mayne and Murray were certainly not alone in seeking a more convincingly materialist history of the city. Apart from the significant work of Rebecca Yamin (2001a, 2001b, 2000) – among others in North America, Australian archaeologists – such as Grace Karskens (1997, 1999) and Jane Lydon (1999), had been developing approaches which went beyond simple dichotomies between empirical and theoretical, and which did not dissolve the city, or indeed the neighborhood, as categories of analysis.

With Little Lon we had the chance to analyse a collection which had been to all intents and purposes ignored by historians and archaeologists. We also had the opportunity to re-evaluate McCarthy's seamless synthesis of archaeology and history, which drew so heavily upon what Mayne and I thought were highly problematic notions about slums. In our view even though McCarthy's methodology was right within the mainstream of Australian historical archaeology, it tended to produce conventional historical narratives larded with pots and pipes – histories which carefully avoided the disparities between such diverse sources of information and perspective. In our view those disparities presented significant challenges to historical archaeologists, making it impossible to more thoroughly engage with unexamined assumptions about slums and the lives of the urban poor.

Archaeological and historical (primarily archival) research was first undertaken at Little Lon in 1988, and later in 1990 and 1995 (McCarthy 1989, 1990; Lane 1995). Nonetheless comprehensive analysis of the site documents, artefact collections and documentary databases only really began in 1996 (Mayne and Lawrence 1998; Mayne and Murray 1996, 1999, 2001; Murray and Mayne 2001, 2003). The goal of this later research was to reconstruct life in a 'vanished community', and through this to critically assess the stereotypes of the slum and brothel district which had come to characterize Little Lon (see Davison 1978; Davison et al. 1985). Mayne and Murray considered that this was an unsatisfactory basis for understanding the social and cultural landscapes of this inner-city precinct. Mayne (1993) had already produced a historical critique of 19th and early 20th-century slum stereotypes and Murray and Mayne (2001) discussed an integrated approach whereby historical archaeology can puncture slum stereotypes in order to piece together a more accurate picture of inner-city working-class neighbourhoods around the world. We saw this approach as a development of the work undertaken in The Rocks, Sydney (Godden Mackay and Karskens 1999; Karskens 1996, 1997a, 1997b, 1999; Karskens and Thorp 1992).

This new focus on urban historical archaeology has now been taken up in England, North America and South Africa (see the contributors to Mayne and Murray 2001; but also Tarlow and West 1999; Yamin 1996) and most recently in South America (Schávelzon 2000), and builds on fundamental research into artefacts and systems of interpretation that have guided urban historical archaeology since the late 1980s (Appadurai 1986; Beaudry et al. 1991; De Cunzo and Herman 1996; L'Anglais 1994; Potter 1994; Scott 1994; Staski 1987). We now know that inner-city communities during the 19th and early 20th centuries were more socially and culturally diverse than the previous stereotypes have allowed, and new histories of Melbourne (e.g. Brown-May 1998) are reflecting this.

Melbourne's Little Lon is a central city neighbourhood that existed for a century (from roughly 1850 to 1950) as a place of working-class residence and employment. Intermeshed with these working-class networks was a complicated landscape of small-scale businesses, and a cluster of large factories. Few traces now remain of this diverse community. Its people have long gone, and many of their surface remains have been erased by later occupations. Little Lon is a vanished community. Metropolitan change during the second half of the 20th century and into the twenty-first century has introduced radically different forms and functions to this central city space.

For 40 years social historians in Australia and overseas have sought to understand the social dynamics of inner-city working-class districts such as Little Lon. They have been hampered in this for two reasons. First, because the nature of the documentary data they relied upon meant that the interpretations they developed were general in nature rather than being tied to specific places. Second, because the documents they used reflected the viewpoints of outside observers rather than revealing the experiences of those who actually lived and worked in these neighbourhoods, allowing historians to conflate the imaginary essence of slums with the actual social geography of urban disadvantage. The complexities of neighbourhoods such as Little Lon – their variety of social worlds, and patterns of continuity and change through time – are obscured by the homogenising, universalising, and changeless qualities of the slum myths that have been perpetuated through documentary records and by historical interpretations based upon them.

Archaeologists probe the material evidence specific to these inner-city districts, and thereby have the opportunity to develop research questions that are independent of the assumptions and conclusions that are embedded in the historical record. In the USA, archaeologists Mary Beaudry and Stephen Mrozowski began in the late 1980s to study 19th-century boarding-house sites in the Massachusetts industrial city of Lowell. In Australia, the first phase of archaeological excavation and analysis at Little Lon took place in 1987–1988, and in 1994 the 'Big Dig' began in Sydney's 'Rocks' district.

However, the full potential of archaeological analysis has yet to be realised. In part, archaeological investigation has been held back because time and budget constraints that limited most archaeological activity to monitoring and salvage work rather than intensive analysis. In greater part, new interpretations have been stymied because no adequate historical contextualisation exists for the artefact assemblages from the excavation sites. Because of the paucity of detailed site-specific historical research, archaeologists have tended to fall back upon the same general themes and categories that had been developed by historical mainstream as they attempt to make sense of the material data. They have been caught in a closed loop.

These prevailing historical frameworks were challenged by Mayne and by Karskens and Thorp in the early 1990s. Murray and Mayne subsequently presented an alternative analytical framework that more fully integrates archaeology and history. Their approach (summarised below) was initially applied to the analysis of the Casselden Place cottages in Little Lon. Mayne and Murray went on to showcase the possibilities of this approach on an international scale at the World Archaeology Conference in Cape Town in 1998, and in their edited book *The Archaeology of Urban Landscapes* (Mayne and Murray 2001).

At the beginning of our research on the Commonwealth Block we were interested in finding a way in which they could tell the stories locked up in all those boxes of artefacts from urban sites in Australia. Following the work of the archaeologists in The Rocks, Sydney, we believed that the best way forward was to work towards models integrating archaeological and other historical data in ways that did not sacrifice the integrity of either.

There were two great goals for our analysis of Little Lon. First, to develop an integrated analytical framework – bridging history and historical archaeology – of urban society and its embedded material culture in 19th and early 20th century Australia. Second, to analyse within this framework material culture recovered from Little Lon. In our view at that time this had never been done in Australia, giving rise to a trend within urban archaeology that had served to dissolve 'the city' as a coherent unit of study. The Little Lon project set out to 'read' the cityscape as a cultural landscape, based on what is now a more widely accepted view that texts and artefacts are all documents which are equally open to be read for historical meaning. For Mayne and Murray the task of interpretation did not entail two distinct sets of inquiries, because historians and archaeologists in such cases are interpreting the same interwoven cultural landscape. The documents with which they were dealing were not simply *from* that landscape; they were *of* it, effectively embedded in it. For Mayne and Murray text and artefact therefore had to be studied contextually for their close relationship to the tangible and intangible contours of that cultural landscape.

The basis of an 'ideal' integration in three phases was conventionally well understood, if not always well executed: First, historical research should establish some initial parameters about the site. Second, the site should be excavated. Third, the artefacts and their contexts should be analysed and interpreted. Of course we understood that interdisciplinary dialogue occurs throughout the first two phases. However, we believed that it was in the third phase that the greatest scope for methodological innovation lay, and this became the focus of our project. In order to achieve methodological synthesis specific historical research was required to provide a context for archaeological data, and to help answer questions that resulted from the analyses of excavated information. For example: Why is there this pattern of discard and not another? Why do assemblages vary? What were the conditions of production and consumption of this material culture? How did the people perceive the artefacts?

Mayne and Murray understood that this very specific historical research required historians to approach the archives – to 'read' them – in a different way; not necessarily to support some highly abstract approach to space and culture, but to help answer practical puzzles and problems. They were well aware that this reflexive approach, which is both inductive and data driven, occurs against a complex background of historical discourse. The crucial point for us was that neither this background of deductive strategies, perspectives and assumptions, nor the conventional narratives of the history of the modern city, should dominate. Instead they should be responsive to an active engagement with material culture and archaeological contexts. Of equal importance was an understanding that the job of the historian should not stop with the development of a research design, but that it had to continue though all three phases sometimes dealing with specific issues raised by the archaeologists, and at other times developing interpretive and explanatory options that would propel analysis. Naturally this was all rather more easily said than done.

Returning to the Excavations of Phase 1

The assumption that underwrote our research at Little Lon has been the notion that this new history can only be made through the integration of diverse sources of information in a way which did not ignore such diversity in favour of a seamless unitary account of life at the place. But this integration should be meaningful, and not just an exercise in enhancing the interpretative or explanatory primacy of, for example, the written document, over other sources of information. Thus we explicitly sought to avoid the common outcome where archaeological data function solely as 'illustrations' of accounts derived from written documents or oral histories, and where the richness and diversity of such information as a primary resource for making history is never explored.

On reading McCarthy's comprehensive report (1989) Mayne and Murray noted the most recent discussions of the history of this community had involved the meshing of archaeological data with a selection of written documents, and that this first integrated history had found little to disturb orthodox views of life at Little Lon. But our increasing familiarity with the excavation, gained through a re-excavation of the site records, clearly indicated that due to time and budget limitations very little detailed analysis of the excavated artefacts had occurred, and about the same consideration had been given to understanding the spatial and temporal distribution of such material remains across the site. Thus whatever integration had been achieved was only at the most superficial level, with the archaeological data largely unexplored and in no condition to destabilise the hegemony of the orthodox history of Little Lon.

The re-analysis, focused initially on the object of deriving archaeologically useful information from the excavations, allowed us to detect counter-intuitive patterns in the archaeology of the Casselden Place cottages and elsewhere at Little Lon (Figure 1). Making sense of those patterns, in the context of the clear limits set by the structural properties of the Casselden Place archaeological record as it has been re-constructed by us, has emphasised the need

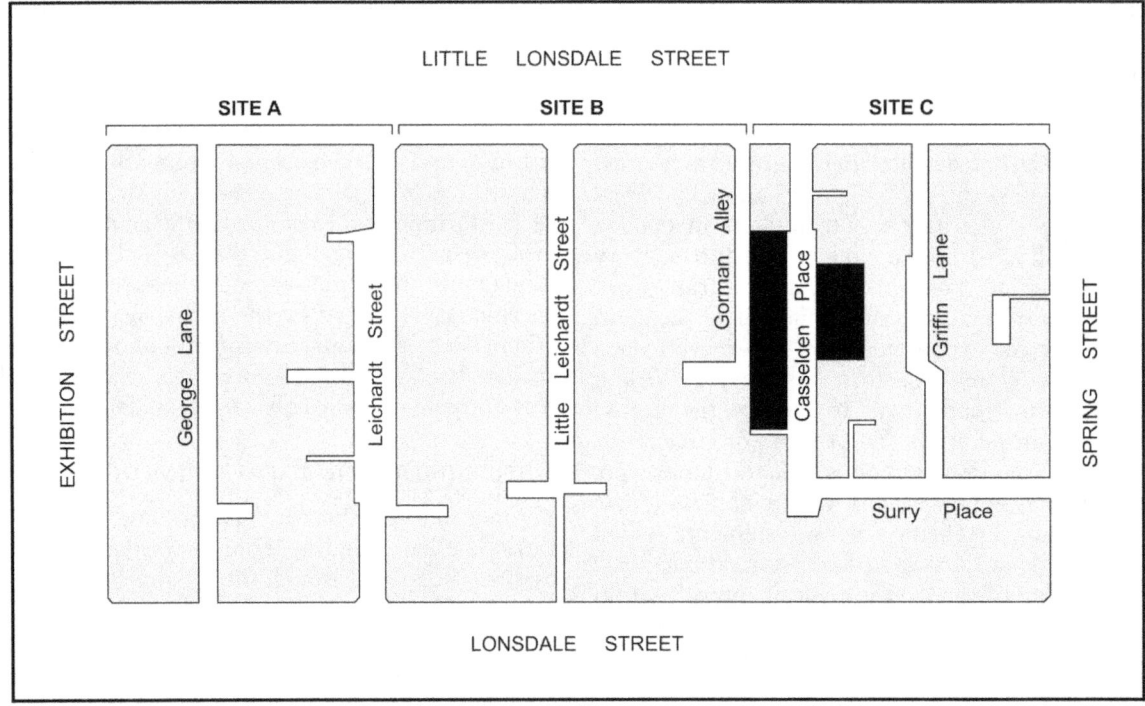

Figure 4.1: The Commonwealth Block showing Sites A, B and C.

to work towards new ways of writing the historical archaeology of the modern city.

McCarthy's report allowed us to identify 19 similar locations along the lane as it evolved between 1850 and 1900, together with some 300 principal tenants (not including spouses, children, and sub-tenants) and 50 owners who were associated with them. Integrated archaeological and documentary data are available for nine of these sites: a collection of cottages along the western side of Casselden Place and, on the opposite side, the Moloney-Neylan site (Location 69) and a house site adjoining it.

In this discussion I will not add data to the comprehensive discussions that have already been published (see Murray and Mayne 2001, 2003). Rather the goal is to outline the consequences of our original analyses for the approach we had developed to define the methodology of our return to the archaeology of phase 1.

Five two-roomed wooden cottages were erected along the western side of Whelan's Lane in 1851. On the basis of municipal documents and maps we inferred that each house had a yard. Probably each had a cesspit as well. We only had clear evidence of cesspits at the house sites of No. 7 and No. 9, but it is possible that others were located in the unexcavated portions of No. 11 and No. 15. At least one of the houses is recorded as having a shed for a workshop. John Casselden, a local newsagent, bought the properties in 1871. He submitted a building application in 1876 to erect six brick cottages on the site of the five wooden cottages and an adjoining unoccupied block (No. 17, at the northern end of his property). By 1878 these had been built: each consisting of three small rooms and a yard. The layout of these houses remained substantially unaltered until they were demolished (with the exception of No. 17) in the 1960s.

The bluestone foundations of these later brick buildings were uncovered by McCarthy's excavation in 1987–1988, and provide the framework within which the material finds have been analysed. The excavators did not identify the foundations of the earlier wooden structures, although two cesspits (which we argue date back to this earlier period) were revealed. Excavations on the row of cottages along the western side of Casselden Place yielded 50,777 individual items. This area was not completely excavated, with three excavation trenches uncovering the complete foundations of cottages No. 7, No. 9 and No. 13, whilst No. 11 and No. 15 remained unexcavated. At the time of excavation most of the area where this row of cottages had stood was covered by bitumen car park. However No. 17, at the northern end of the row, was still standing. In 1995 an excavation of the immediate below-floor surface of two of the rooms in No. 17 was undertaken by the consultants Du Cros and Associates (Lane 1995). The information obtained from this excavation was recorded and analysed as part of our project.

Generally the Casselden Place houses were found to have similar assemblages that exhibited similar spatial patterns. That the structural properties of the deposits from 9 Casselden Place (for example), a house with a very different pattern of occupancy to that of the Moloneys (Location 69), was in essence so similar to the Moloney house, spurred us to begin to re-evaluate a simple correlation between slum dwelling and itinerant lifestyles. The richness of the deposits in places which were understood to be occupied by the poorest elements of Melbourne society opened other pathways for us to explore.

The excavation strategy adopted at Little Lon by McCarthy meant that not all the cottage sites along Casselden Place could be excavated. Nonetheless, we argue that a robust pattern exists across the majority of the cottage sites, including that occupied by the Moloneys. In general terms our reanalysis indicated that these sites have similar assemblages exhibiting similar spatial distributions within the foundations of the later brick cottages.

In the case of the row of cottages on the western side of Casselden Place, these generalisations did not allow us to interpret the assemblages (either from the cesspits or the trenches) at the level of the individual occupants. Although this does not necessarily apply to our interpretation of Location 69 (the Moloney-Neylan site), there is a significant tension between the generalisations of the archaeological analysis and the fine-grained specificity of the historical documents.

The *documentary evidence* about the house sites on both sides of the street confirmed that the cottages in Casselden Place were part of a poor neighborhood. Its houses were small, and municipal rate assessors gave them a low rating. As such they formed the bottom of the rental housing market, places where newly arrived immigrants could find shelter for their families. The cottages were cheap. At a time when 'ordinary houses' were let for 12 to 15 shillings and more per week, two brick cottages of two rooms next door to the Moloney-Neylan house were let at seven shillings per week in 1884, and Casselden's brick row-houses rented at eight shillings each per week in 1888. These small houses were crammed with people. In 1892 the principal tenant of the property next door to Margaret Neylan was fined 'for allowing twelve people to sleep in one room, seven in each bedroom, and three or four in two other rooms'. The occupants were Indians.

But for much of the period between 1850 and 1900 the majority of the lane's residents – such as the Harts, the Cummings, the Taylors, and the Moloneys – were Irish immigrants. Some of the houses were fully occupied by members of the same family; others offered space to single immigrants who were passing through seeking work. Facilities for hygiene, such as running water and waste removal, were basic. Rear yards held over-flowing cesspits, and rubbish was disposed of beneath the floors. Life here was consequently hazardous for infants, and deaths from diseases such as diarrhoea were common.

The cottages in Casselden Place were poor and crowded, but the neighborhood was not a homogenous place of outcasts. The documentary evidence does not support the claims by anti-slum crusaders that violence and criminality were endemic to the lane.

Documentary evidence shows that Casselden Place was populated by people with a wide diversity of manual occupations (both skilled and unskilled). Most were renters. Some – such as the Moloneys – were home owners. A few – such as John Casselden – operated small businesses (in his case a newsagency), and accumulated sufficient capital to purchase multiple real estate in the area. Children from labouring families – if they survived childhood – often moved into skilled trades and the professions. Tenants lived alongside owner occupiers, and landlords lived in the street or close at hand. The documents also show that the children of Casselden Place and adjacent streets married each other, a few staying in the immediate area, the bulk moving into nearby suburbs to pursue their fortunes. Notwithstanding the fact that, with few exceptions such as the Moloneys and John Casselden, the majority of Irish immigrants gradually moved away from the area, a sense of community had been created and was long sustained. Probate papers, inquests, and the correspondence files of the City Council and the Police Department attest to this neighborliness.

The *archaeological record* of Casselden Place is very difficult to integrate into this fine-grained documentary analysis. The key point to emerge from its detailed analysis is the remarkably low level of variability in assemblage structure and composition between houses occupied by the same people (such as the Moloneys at Location 69), and those (such as the Harts, the Cummings, and the Taylors at Location 74B) which experienced a more rapid turnover of occupants. Although the houses were occupied by people of no great means, the archaeology reveals a wide variety of material culture being discarded in such places, ranging from tools of trade to dinner services. They purchased (and discarded) a great many material possessions associated with all aspects of everyday life. The working people of Casselden Place were avid consumers of a wide range of domestic material culture.

Some Preliminary Conclusions

The homogeneity of the total Casselden Place assemblage (and the real possibility that spatial distribution is also homogenous between the houses), in a context which the historical records clearly show to have been occupied by a number of different tenants over the period between 1850 and 1900, raises two obvious questions. How might we account for this counter-intuitive pattern, and how worthwhile was our initial expectation that there should be a strong distinction between the archaeological signatures of short-term and long-term residency?

On the one hand, given the developing scale and power of mass production and mass consumption during the period covered by the Casselden Place objects, it perhaps should not be surprising that there are clear patterns of similarity in assemblage composition which overlie the great diversity of items which were used and deposited by the residents. But it is also true to say that comparative studies from Australian sites which would help us to establish whether there was much value in this analysis are not yet numerous or published in an accessible fashion. On the other hand the identity of Casselden Place as a community must also be understood through analysis of the singular, the different, the heterogeneous. Apart from observing that reconciling these differing perspectives is a task that is still before us, it is also worth noting that significant puzzles and problems thrown up here at Little Lon are common enough in the archaeology of any modern city.

We can identify some of the more obvious puzzles raised by our initial work at Little Lon. Is this homogeneity of assemblage structure a function of the economies of supply in a world shifting at great speed towards mass consumption during the last three decades of the 19th century? If this is so, in such a leveling or conventionalising environment is it possible (or indeed even worthwhile) to seek to establish linkages between place and identity, between uniqueness and specific histories? This is obviously a huge question, but we need to go a little further and understand that homogenisation may well be masking the kinds of heterogenising processes which reflect the establishment of identities which slum reformers in the late 19th and early 20th centuries did so much to stamp out. We need to go deeper past the descriptive statistics which talk of homogeneity, in order to tackle more difficult questions of value and meaning.

That these questions not only exist but have proved difficult to answer convincingly supports our overall goal of demonstrating that we need, as historical archaeologists, to rethink the viability of long-held notions such as the 'slum'. We have had the chance at Little Lon to begin what is going to be a long process of learning to link people, material culture and archaeological contexts at specific sites and within vanished communities. Certainly the documentary record holds out tremendous possibilities for delivering a level of information about the social history of Little Lon which was hitherto considered to be either impossible or meaningless. It is also quite clear that the archaeology is far more equivocal. Selecting the appropriate scale of comparison and generalisation between and among archaeological records (be they the remains of a house, a row of houses such as Casselden Place, portions of a city block such as Little Lon, or even wider still), has proved to be a significant challenge. It seems self-evident that we should want to range from the very specific analysis of place, such as No. 7 Casselden Place and all of its registered occupants, to a consideration of the depositional palimpsest which is the archaeological reality of such a place. Obviously this is situational, but in general we have begun to understand that at its most inclusive, the archaeology of the modern city is the archaeology of the modern world.

It is a natural concern to many that, as one moves away from the specificities of place and the particular nexus between individuals, place and time, the sense and importance of those specificities (the things which make people real flesh and blood human beings in the past) will be lost. It has been argued that in its place a leveling, conventionalising, dehumanising generalisation of human lives will grow up – an outcome which has previously characterised much social history of 'slums'. Acknowledging that there is an inevitable loss of detail and focus as one moves along the pathway of increasing generalisation does not mean that one cannot return to the specificities of place with new perspectives drawn from the wider world. In the case of Little Lon we are only too aware that these important specificities of place, people and time are themselves the products of concepts, categories and units of analysis which are built from acts of comparison and generalisation. Indeed to argue otherwise would be to accept that at all levels of discussion every historical or archaeological observable must be unique. This is an argument that would effectively spell the end of our search for understanding.

At Little Lon we are faced with the pragmatic problem of attempting to integrate the archaeological and historical records of the site in ways which can give us a sense of working-class inner-city neighborhoods during the mid to late 19th century. In the absence of fundamental data about people and things in Melbourne (or for the greater part of Sydney), we cannot yet fully describe the specificities of Casselden Place. To do this we have to compare, generalise and contrast, but our goal of seeking such an intense engagement with people and place will mean that it will be vital for us to move back as well as to move forward in order to write our history of the modern city.

Concluding Remarks

For some time now urban archaeologists have been advocating the need to explore the archaeology of the modern city using several different scales or frames of reference (see for example L'Anglais 1994; Murray and Mayne 2001; Potter 1994; Wall and Rothschild 1996). The most popular (and most basic) of these has been the household but it has also been acknowledged that interpreting the archaeology of households beyond the notion that every household and associated archaeological assemblage is unique, requires archaeologists and historians to compare and contrast, and to establish patterns (see for example Allison 1999; Nelson 1997). These comparisons frequently occur at the level of the area or district in the same city, where archaeologists seek to derive patterns that might be explained as being the result of status, class, ethnicity, or ideology (see for example Cantwell and Wall 2001; Funari et al. 1999; Jones 1997; Lydon 1999; Scott 1994; Staski 1987; Wall 1994; Yamin 1996). Other less frequent comparisons occur at larger scales, for example between cities or countries, acknowledging that the archaeology of the modern western city is also the archaeology of modern global forces of production, consumption, trade, immigration and ideology formation.

Murray and Mayne have argued that patterns of similarity and dissimilarity detected at these larger scales can (and should) become part of our interpretive and explanatory armoury when it comes to understanding patterns and processes at smaller scales. However, we have also stressed that these larger scale enquiries do not by any means exhaust (or diminish the importance of) the site- or household-specific questions that continue to demand adequate answers.

Improving regimes of analysis is obviously one way to promote the difficult business of meaningfully integrating quite disparate data sets using archaeological data to seriously engage with (and possibly revise) conventional readings of social processes or socio-cultural categories over the last 200 years. Another way is to expand our interpretive repertoire, and seek ways to engage with conceptions of the city that move the field of urban archaeology into new areas, extending our engagement with history, sociology and geography beyond the revisionist history of the slum that has been so liberating in recent years.

All this means that we will need to address two very broad themes as we move forward, the first having to do with methods, and the second with questions and systems of interpretation. Of course both themes are properly encompassed by the discourse of theoretical archaeology. The first theme concerns the *how* of integrating the diverse historical and archaeological data sets that characterise modern cities. The search for integration raises questions of data quality, recording, and regimes of analysis, but obviously it is also in a close reflexive relationship with the second theme, which is about the *what* of integration. What is it we want to know about life in cities? How do we convincingly link question and answer? What types of questions are most appropriate for what types of data sets? If we acknowledge that theory often ranges far ahead of data (in archaeology as well as in astrophysics), what kinds of methodologies can we develop that will allow interpretations to grow and evolve in ways that do not become so abstracted from the empirical, that data and their structural properties as archaeological or historical phenomena cease to matter much at all?

I sought to pursue all of these issues in the Exploring the Archaeology of the Modern City Project (EAMC), but instead of achieving neat solutions I think that at this point Penny Crook and I mostly gained a better understanding of the problems (and potentials) encountered at Little Lon. Some of these have already been flagged by Murray and Mayne and by others for general discussion, particularly the serious problems related to the archiving of urban archaeological collections, the building of databases that foster assemblage-based analyses of sites, and the pressing need to look much longer and harder at research design in Australian urban archaeology (see for example Crook et al. 2002; Murray 2002).

But there are also fascinating and vexing matters related to comprehending the formation processes of urban archaeological records, and linking such perceptions to strategies that can help us assess the usefulness or otherwise of the questions we routinely ask, to set the tolerance limits of interpretations, and of course to describe the kinds of integrations between archaeological and historical data that might occur.

Mayne and Murray reflected on the disjunction between the great precision of historical documentation at Little Lon and the much less precise archaeological data from the houses in the Casselden Place section of the original Little Lon site which is now understood to be a common-enough occurrence in this kind of archaeology. Of course it is important to establish how we can pursue our conventional desire to explore domesticity, community, family life, issues of residence and mobility, and still larger issues of how and what people produce and consume in cites, but it is equally important for us to try to understand how data and question can give rise to different agendas. We remain fascinated by issues of resolution – about how the richness of documentary data can create an illusion of archaeological riches, where we find that finer scales of resolution can lead to a pixillation or loss of resolution in archaeological information that does not happen at coarser scales of analysis.

One response that underwrote the expansion of the broad project to Sydney, was the idea that increasing both temporal and spatial scale could bring new patterns into focus that might overcome the disparity in resolving powers Mayne and Murray had noted in the cottages in Casselden Place. We understood that during the course of the 19th century patterns of production, consumption, work and residence changed across the Western world and we recognised the need for comparison between sites in Sydney and Melbourne to gain a clearer understanding of the genesis and development of urban communities. The structure of these comparisons (which occur in local, national and international settings) is described in the following Figure 2.

In our view specific local research questions relating to the nature of archaeological assemblages

GLOBAL MATERIAL CULTURE IN URBAN SETTINGS 1830–1950

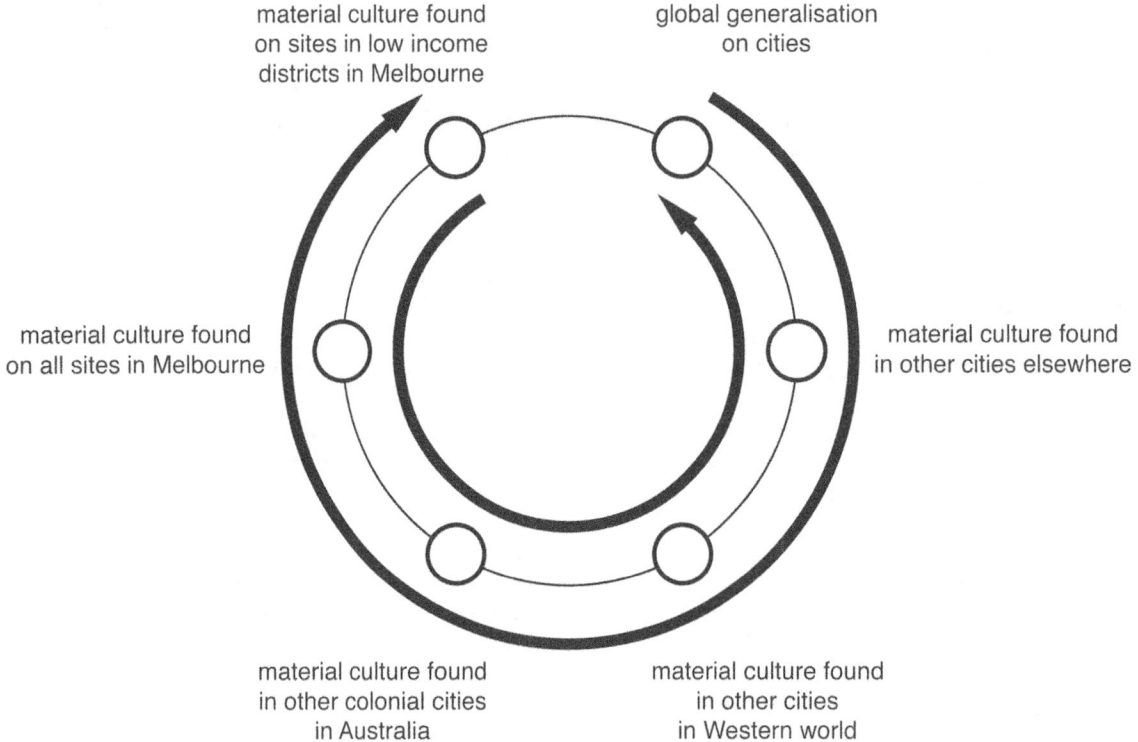

Figure 4.2: Structure of spatial comparison of Australian material culture, form urban settings, in a global context.

in working-class domestic contexts thus have more general application at national and international levels. The consequences of differential patterns of domestic residency for assemblages of material culture recovered from domestic sites are one significant issue. The same applies to questions raised about our interpretation of patterning in those assemblages as being related to gender, ethnicity, and social standing. A concern with understanding the consequences of mass production, improved transport and distribution technologies, and mass consumption unites historical archaeologists across the Western world.

Our analyses in phase 1 allowed an alternative history of Little Lon to take shape around the notion of an integrated history of place and people. This is best exemplified in the transformation of our understanding of what was happening in the cottages at numbers 7–15 Casselden Place, and the perspectives we can gain through a comparison of the archaeological remains at these domestic addresses with those found in a cesspit historically associated with a nearby business enterprise at no. 27 Lonsdale Street. The detailed analysis of the archaeological data, which involved a re-examination of all excavated finds and a careful plotting of the distribution of these remains within the houses, has been strongly supported by the collection of oral histories, and the prospecting of additional written documents (see Murray and Mayne 2001, 2003; Williamson 1989).

In the original integration the primary written sources consisted of rate books and directories, as well as the newspaper accounts and government reports. As our new history is being built around the microscale analysis of places within Little Lon (such as the cottages in Casselden Place) within a macroscale comparative context, the nature of what could be considered to be relevant written documents has also changed. For example, while we did not dispute that Little Lon was primarily occupied by the working classes, there was as yet little knowledge of what material culture might be found in 'poor households' over the last 100 years. This is not a matter which can be resolved using archaeological evidence alone, and our task here was eased by articulating written documents such as mortgage inventories (the existence of which only recently came to light), police records, and the records of social welfare agencies. It is also worth noting that while we began to understand the difficulties of convincingly accounting for a culture of poverty at Little Lon, if such ever existed, we also recognised that we had only the most rudimentary understanding of the material dimensions of domestic life in other Melbourne communities during this period.

Our analysis of the material from the cottages in Casselden Place was directed at assessing whether the orthodox reading of Little Lon – and especially of this alley within it – as the habitation of the worst of Melbourne society is reflected in the archaeological data. Though our results from phase 1 were still preliminary, there was clear evidence that these assemblages represented a very wide range of domestic material culture, and reflected domestic lives which were flourishing and enduring. This pattern provided an alternative to the dominant readings of the supposed behaviour traits identified, and found to be so repugnant, by moral crusaders of the 19th and 20th centuries. But it also posed some obviously questions: Is such a level of variety to be expected in the homes of 'the urban poor', or does it represent some amalgam between genteel domestic lives and criminal behaviour?

Answering these questions required us to face squarely the shortcomings in our understanding of a 'culture of poverty' in Melbourne. Our understanding will be limited and highly provisional until we have analysed the remains of other domestic assemblages from the Commonwealth Block (and in other urban areas as well). But having said this, and bearing in mind that occupation of the cottages at Casselden Place spans the genesis and flowering in Australia of mass production and mass consumption of consumer goods (such as domestic ceramics, bottles, toys and smoking paraphernalia), there is as yet no evidence of any pronounced skewing in the composition of the assemblage from what might be expected in a 'normal' domestic assemblage. Indeed this argument is supported by a comparison between the structure of the Casselden Place assemblages (as a group) with that found at the rear of no. 27 Lonsdale Street, which was a business and boarding house. In this comparison the latter site exhibited a preponderance of recreational artefacts and alcohol bottles and fewer artefacts associated with other aspects of domestic life.

These differences between houses in Little Lon are suggestive, as are the distribution of artefact classes within each of the houses in Casselden Place. Together both sets of information provide the foundations for a history of Little Lon which includes a significant material dimension, and which thus allow for a more nuanced reading of the lives of the urban poor in Melbourne over the last century. But these differences would have gone unnoticed if a re-examination of the archaeological excavations at Little Lon had not been prompted by our desire to write the history of a forgotten community. In doing this we have come to appreciate that although the business of integrating diverse sources of information can be difficult, the sense of expanding possibility is very strong as a wide diversity of potential histories begins to unfold.

Acknowledgements

Alan Mayne was co-author of several of the research papers that the current discussion directly derives from. I thank him for his willingness to engage the 'dark' side of archaeology and to fundamentally alter my goals as an urban archaeologist. Dr Christine Williamson undertook the archaeological analyses at Casselden Place and Ms Kasia Zygmuntowicz undertook the documentary research.

References

Appadurai, A. 1986. *The Cultural Life of Things*. Cambridge: Cambridge University Press.

Beaudry, M. C., L. J. Cook and S. A. Mrozowski, 1991. Artifacts and Active Voices: Material Culture as Social Discourse. In McGuire, R. and R. Paynter (eds.) *The Archaeology of Inequality: Material Culture, Domination and Resistance*, pp. 156–159, Oxford: Blackwell.

Brown-May, A. 1998. *Melbourne Street Life: The Itinerary of Our Days*. Kew, Victoria: Australian Scholarly Publishing.

Davison, G. 1978. *The Rise and Fall of Marvellous Melbourne*. Parkvile, Victoria: Melbourne University Press.

Davison, G., D. Dunstan and C. McConville, 1985. *The Outcasts of Melbourne: Essays in Social History*. Sydney: Allen and Unwin.

Godden Mackay Pty Ltd, 1996. *Cumberland/Gloucester Streets Archaeological Investigation*. Sydney: The Sydney Cove Authority.

Godden Mackay Pty Ltd and G. Karskens, 1999. *The Cumberland/Gloucester Streets Site, The Rocks, Archaeological Investigation Report*, Volumes I–IV. Redfern, N.S.W.: Godden Mackay Logan Pty Ltd Heritage Consultants.

Jones, S. 1997. *The Archaeology of Ethnicity*. London: Routledge.

Lydon, J. 1999. *Many Inventions: The Chinese in The Rocks 1890–1930*. Clayton, Victoria: Monash Publications in History.

Karskens, G. 1996. Crossing Over: Archaeology and History at the Cumberland/Gloucester Street Site, The Rocks, 1994–1996. *Public History Review* 5/6: 30–48.

Karskens, G. 1997a. *The Rocks: Life in Early Sydney*. Parkvile, Victoria: Melbourne University Press.

Karskens, G. 1997b. The Dialogue of Townscape: The Rocks and Sydney 1788–1820. *Australian Historical Studies* 108: 88–112.

Karskens, G. 1999. *Inside The Rocks: The Archaeology of a Neighbourhood*. Sydney: Hale & Iremonger.

Karskens G. and W. Thorp, 1992. History and Archaeology in Sydney: Towards Integration and Interpretation. *Journal of the Royal Australian Historical Society* 78(3–4): 52–75.

McCarthy, J. 1989. *Archaeological Investigation of the Commonwealth Offices and Telecom Corporate Building Sites. The Commonwealth*

Block, Melbourne (5 vols.). Melbourne: Department of Administrative Services and Telecom Australia.

Mayne, A. 1993. *The Imagined Slum*. Leicester: Leicester University Press.

Mayne, A. and S. Lawrence, 1998. An Ethnography of Place: Imagining Little Lon. *Journal of Australian Studies* 57: 93–107.

Mayne, A. and T. Murray, 1999. 'In Little Lon ... Wiv Ginger Mick': Telling the Forgotten History of a Vanished Community. *Journal of Popular Culture* 33(1): 63–77.

Mayne, A. and T. Murray, 2001. Imaginary Landscapes: Reading Melbourne's Little Lon. In Mayne, A. and T. Murray (eds.) *Explorations of Slumland: Archaeologies of Place in the Modern City*, Cambridge: Cambridge University Press.

Mayne, A., T. Murray and S. Lawrence. 2000. Melbourne's Little Lon. *Australian Historical Studies* 31(114): 131–151.

Williamson, C. 1998. Slums and Sluts: Lonsdale Street Project Report. Unpublished report for La Trobe University, Melbourne.

Yamin, R. 1996. Lurid Tales and Homely Stories of New York's Notorious Five Points. *Historical Archaeology* 32(1) : 74–85.

5
Smaller Investigations between Phase 1 and Phase 2

Tim Murray

McCarthy 1990

McCarthy returned to Little Lon in 1990 to excavate the sub-floor and some external deposits of the Black Eagle and Oddfellows Hotels, as mitigation of the impact of the refurbishment and redevelopment of both buildings. The outcomes of this smaller project are discussed in Chapter 3 of this book. In the original report McCarthy reflected at length about his goal of establishing a standard stratigraphic profile that would foster an evaluation of the stratigraphy previously established for Little Lon, and guide his assessment of the profiles derived from the excavation of these new sites. The presence of disturbed deposits (a characteristic feature of Little Lon) and the problems associated with correlating the sections from Area 77 of Oddfellows Hotel with others derived from the site, meant that little progress was made towards the goal of resolving the stratigraphy of the site. Thus it was concluded that the potential of Site B remained undimensioned.

Lane 1995

The refurbishment of 17 Casselden Place, the surviving house in the row excavated by McCarthy (1989) and extensively discussed by Murray and Mayne (2001, 2003) and Williamson (1998) provided the opportunity for excavation of *in situ* sub-floor deposits in the house. Subsequent analysis indicated that this deposit contained a mixture of 19th- and 20th-century artefacts. A 1m x 1m test pit was also excavated in the north-east corner of the house and revealed a shallow stratigraphy over a base of natural clay. All artefacts were analysed by Williamson (1998) and are reported as above.

Andrew Long and Associates 2001

Following the production of an Archaeological Planning Report for phase 3 of the Casselden Place development Andrew Long and Associates were commissioned to undertake a testing program within the existing car park roughly corresponding to McCarthy's Site B. The purpose of the program was to establish 'the distribution, degree of preservation and significance of deposits relating to a 19th- to early 20th-century urban landscape' (Howell-Meurs et al. 2001: 2). The methodology employed was a combination of machine-excavated slip trenches dug in 11 locations and three test pits, the most productive of which was Pit C (a cesspit relating to a house in Leichhardt Street).

Howell-Meurs et al. (2001: 2) concluded that relatively intact deposits existed under the car park surface, and that the nature and significance of these deposits varied across the area.

> The northern part of the site appears to have been significantly disturbed during the construction and development of areas adjacent to the study area. This disturbance appears to have resulted in the planing off of much of the archaeological material, although testing indicates that this was not necessarily uniform across the entire northern half. In contrast the southern section appears to contain more intact deposits with some degree of vertical and horizontal complexity. Structural and artefactual materials recovered to date indicate a broad age range of 1870s to 1920s, although it is probable that earlier remains survive.

Williamson's analysis of the artefacts confirmed a strong similarity with the assemblages recovered from McCarthy's excavation, especially the contents of Pit C.

All artefacts and location details recovered during the testing program have since been added into the relevant site databases. The same applies to those deriving from parts of Site C that overlap with A and which were dug by McCarthy.

McCarthy (1989: 10) also made some specific statements about the research potential of the area he had designated Site B. Some of these were put to the test in a subsequent excavation (1990):

> The excavation of the remainder of the city block would be a fruitful and useful exercise to complete the already valuable information established by the current project. It is known for example that there are likely to be a number of cesspits on Site B. Some of the original houses which straddled sites A and B have been partially excavated in the

current project. Further excavation of the oldest surviving buildings on the block (the Black Eagle Hotel and the Oddfellows Hotel) and deposits associated with these are most likely to yield extensive information.

The results of the archaeological testing program conducted by Andrew Long and Associates (see Howell-Meurs et al. 2001; Long et al. 2001) strengthened our understanding of the history of this part of Little Lon. In an important sense they confirmed the expectations of previous researchers. It is also significant that Long et al. (2001: 7–9) identified that it was extremely difficult to achieve worthwhile comparisons between Little Lon and other sites in the Melbourne central administrative district (such as Queen Street and Cohen Place) when reports of those sites were partial or incomplete. Of course this also supported the observation that our knowledge of the urban archaeological record of Melbourne is highly deficient and, while research to establish the comparability of Melbourne assemblages with those of a similar period in Sydney (and elsewhere) was just getting underway, things were at too early a stage to achieve anything meaningful. Thus Long et al. (2001) identified slums, gender, class and ethnicity (those hardy perennials of urban archaeology) as the broad research themes to be considered.

The results obtained from 11 slip trenches and three test pits are fully described in Howell-Meurs et al. (2001) (and discussed above), particularly the presence of abundant artefacts in Pit C (which appears to be connected with one of the houses we have targeted for close inspection in Leichardt Street) has allowed the development of a model of archaeological potential for the site. It is significant that the Andrew Long and Associates report (Howell-Meurs et al. 2001: 21) identifies features entirely consistent with those already noted by McCarthy:

> Brick, bluestone and concrete building footings, timber post settings and post-holes, a bluestone and gravel road surface, compacted clay and flagged floor surfaces, abandonment deposits containing artefacts and ecofacts, brick and bluestone lined pits cut into the underlying substrate, redundant service infrastructure, residual palaeosols representing remnants of the pre-contact and early contact landscape.

The model of archaeological potential discussed in Howell-Meurs et al. (2001: 21–25) clearly indicated that the complexity of formation processes and post depositional taphonomic processes noted by McCarthy (1989) and Murray and Mayne (e.g. 2001, 2003) was highly likely to apply to this part of Little Lon as well. If this is so, then even within zones of high archaeological potential (such as the southern 'lobe' of the existing car park – corresponding to the area around Leichhardt Street) intact deposits other than cesspits may well have limited vertical and horizontal integrity. Following this point, if (as we suspect) that cesspits were filled as virtually single-event phenomena filled at the time when cesspits were closed or houses abandoned, then our capacity to relate these deposits to those recovered from the interiors of houses would require very precise excavation and recording.

References

Howell-Meurs, J., C. Williamson and P. Davies, 2001. Casselden Place Development Phase 3. Testing Results, 2 vols. Unpublished report to Industry Superannuation Property Trust. Melbourne: Andrew Long and Associates.

Lane, S. 1995. Archaeological Investigation of the Cottage at 17 Casselden Place, Melbourne. Unpublished report to the Heritage and Environment Group, Australian Construction Services.

Long, A., C. Williamson, M. Goulding and J. Howell-Meurs, 2001. Casselden Place Development Phase 3. Archaeological Planning Report. Unpublished report to Industry Superannuation Property Trustees. Melbourne: Andrew long and associates.

McCarthy, J. 1989. Archaeological Investigation of the Commonwealth Offices and Telecom Corporate Building Sites. The Commonwealth Block, Melbourne, 5 vols. Report to Department of Administrative Services and Telecom Australia, Melbourne, VIC.

McCarthy, J. 1990. Archaeological Investigation. Site B, the Black Eagle and Oddfellows Hotels, the Commonwealth Block, Melbourne Victoria, 2 vols. Unpublished report to the Department of Administrative Services.

Murray, T. and A. Mayne, 2001. Imaginary Landscapes: Reading Melbourne's Little Lon. In Mayne, A. and T. Murray (eds.) *The Archaeology of Urban Landscapes: Explorations in Slumland*, pp. 89–105, Cambridge: Cambridge University Press.

Murray, T. and A. Mayne, 2003. (Re)Constructing a Lost Community: 'Little Lon,' Melbourne, Australia. *Historical Archaeology* 37(1): 87–101.

Williamson, C. 1998. Slums and Sluts: Lonsdale Street Project Report. Unpublished report for La Trobe University, Melbourne.

6
The Second Campaign: Casselden Place

Richard Mackay

Today 50 Lonsdale Street Melbourne is occupied by a large high rise building and funky ground level cafes, courtyards and a foyer with unusual artworks, displays of artefacts and engaging interpretation installations which inform passing suits and skirts about a now vanished community.

Before Europeans arrived timbered forests overlooked the bay to the south and while Indigenous people had no doubt traversed the site for millennia, little physical evidence of their passing survived. By the mid-19th century houses had been built and Melbourne's distinctive city grid was being formed. Substantial bluestone and brick buildings and more intensive development followed, as light industry expanded. Intermeshed with these working-class networks were small-scale businesses and a few large factories. By the end of the 19th century, the Little Lon precinct had acquired a nefarious reputation as a crime-laden, degraded slum. But do traditional 'slum' portrayals tell the full story of this central city neighbourhood that existed for a century (circa 1850 to 1950)? Archaeological excavations provide a glimpse into the sometimes murky past of this fascinating inner Melbourne neighbourhood.

The Casselden Place Archaeological Excavations were undertaken in anticipation of a major building development project by the Industry Superannuation Super Trust (ISPT) in 2003–2005. The excavations investigated the middle portion of the Commonwealth Block bounded by Lonsdale, Little Lonsdale, Spring and Exhibition Streets (Plate 6.1). The excavations were carried out in two stages from May to July 2002 (Stage 1) and from November to December 2002 (Stage 2), by Godden Mackay Logan Pty Ltd, Austral Archaeology Pty Ltd and the Archaeology Program, La Trobe University. The project managers for ISPT were Clifton Coney Group (Vic) Pty Ltd. The excavations were carried out with the support and assistance of Heritage Victoria, who in addition to their role as principal consent authority, provided the conservation personnel and facilities.

THE CONTEXT

Austral Archaeology Pty Ltd had undertaken a previous phase of archaeological excavations in the precinct, during 1988, at the Commonwealth Block to the west of the Casselden Place excavations. Prior to the results from that first phase of Little Lon, it had been argued that historical research into this precinct was effectively complete (Murray 2005: 170). However, the first phase of onsite work at Little Lon and some small projects that followed (e.g. Long et al. 2001) showed that a rich archaeological resource remained and that further evidence of Melbourne's 19th-century history beckoned. In particular there had been a growing awareness, both in Australia and internationally, of the value in interactive synthesis of historical and archaeological data in urban contexts.

Over the years preceding the Casselden Place project, Dr Alan Mayne from Melbourne University and Prof Tim Murray from La Trobe University had been analysing and publishing information from the Little Lon project and associated research (Mayne and Murray 2001). Their work underpinned the merits in extending the onsite investigations across the entire block. Their collaborative study of the historical and archaeological data generated by the earlier work and was part of a larger international corpus of study into urban communities which progressively demonstrated the value of large-scale historical archaeology. In Australia large inner-city archaeological excavations such as 'The Big Dig' in Sydney's Rocks (Godden Mackay Pty Ltd 1996), paralleled international projects, such as Rebecca Yamin's excavations at New York's Five Points (Yamin 2001). Through such projects historical archaeology demonstrated its relevance to historical inquiry and knowledge and showed how important data may not be available from documentary sources, but rather found on site (see Mayne 2003). In Australia, these new approaches provided opportunities for private-sector archaeologists to make meaningful contributions to academic discourse, encouraged cross-disciplinary studies and spawned new narratives about major historical themes, including convicts, slums and governance (see Godden Mackay Logan Pty Ltd et al. 2004 and Karskens 1997 and

1999). Major cultural resource management projects, including archaeological salvage, also provided opportunities for an eager and interested public to engage with history and archaeology in a hands-on, almost visceral, manner.

By contrast with the preceding Little Lon project the Casselden Place archaeological excavations were instigated at a time when Australian historians, archaeologists, government agencies, academics and some industry sectors had become aligned in recognising the value and imperative of urban archaeology as a precursor to major city development; an alignment which fortuitously coincided with strong statutory controls that enabled regulatory bodies to require developers to conduct large-scale urban archaeological programs.

From the outset, Heritage Victoria had made the proponents for the 50 Lonsdale Street development aware that compliance with the *Victorian Heritage Act* 1995 would require systematic investigation and removal of all archaeological features within the site prior to the commencement of construction works. Excavation of the site revealed a buried urban residential/light industrial streetscape dating to the mid-19th and early-20th centuries that closely matched the assemblage of features and artefacts revealed in the earlier Little Lon excavation. The excavation of the Casselden Place site (Plate 6.2) became an important stage in the progressive archaeological investigation of the Commonwealth Block, adding important new information about the history of the Little Lon precinct.

THE RESEARCH DESIGN

Using the context provided by years of prior analysis and research of the Little Lonsdale Street precinct, a detailed archaeological research design was prepared to frame and guide the new phase of archaeological excavation (Murray and Mayne 2002). For much of its history, the Casselden Place area was characterised as a notorious centre for crime, prostitution, and poverty – and an urban 'slum'. The Casselden Place project strove to challenge these generalised perceptions and associations. Writing his 'Songs of the Sentimental Bloke' in 1915 C.J. Dennis had described the folk of Little Lon as 'low degraded broots' (Dennis 1915). But was this an accurate portrayal?

An important goal of the project was to reconstruct life in this 'vanished community', and to assess and critique the stereotypes of the brothel district which had come to characterise the area. The archaeological research design aimed to test and to extend existing knowledge of Melbourne's late-19th and early-20th century history, with particular focus on the lifestyles and social mores of the people.

An underlying principle of the research design was synthesis of historical research and the data generated by archaeological excavation. The research design specifically addressed archaeological features that are typical of urban historical archaeological sites – and therefore subjected to specific taphonomic processes. For example, at Casselden Place major investigative and analytical opportunities were offered by the sealed deposits within cesspits from known addresses, whose occupants could be identified by historical research.

The research design briefly traversed the role of problem-oriented research into practice of archaeology and the archaeological activity at Little Lon since the 1980s, as well as summarising the core history of major allotments, based on Mayne's research. This contextual narrative framed the ensuing research principles which were structured around three elements: concepts, methods and application (Murray and Mayne 2002: 24–32).

Conceptually, the research framework was an ethnographic integration of history, archaeology and anthropology, grounded in the fine-grain of the lives of particular people from particular times and places. The ability to correlate physical and documentary evidence was therefore fundamental to interpretation. Methodologically, the framework provided that material evidence must drive interpretation rather than simply providing additional data. This approach required firstly that documentary data be re-interrogated in the light of physical evidence and secondly that hypotheses were tested by reference to earlier phases of excavation and to other sites. In light of the assessed research potential of the site, being the likelihood of presence of intact archaeological features, the research design prescribed three groups of research questions linked to both data sets and methodologies.

The Group 1 questions were directly focused on the need to determine the structural properties of the archaeological record itself:
- Is the stratigraphic sequence previously noted at Little Lon repeated in this adjacent area?
- Are there sealed deposits such as cesspits that have clear vertical stratigraphic integrity?
- Are there deposits that exhibit either horizontal or vertical stratigraphic integrity? (Murray and Mayne 2002: 43)

The Group 2 questions, reflected the need to determine the relationship between structures and deposits of material culture that are found in and around them. They were particularly directed at assemblages in particular locations, distinguishing between 'domestic' and 'industrial' assemblages:
- Is it possible to discriminate between the assemblages created by earlier houses and those of later brick structures?
- Is it possible to discriminate between assemblages created by itinerant occupants of these houses as distinct from more settled patterns of occupation noticed elsewhere on the site?
- Is it possible to confirm hypotheses concerning specific activity areas within each of the houses,

that were noted in some houses in Casselden Place? (Murray and Mayne 2002: 44)

The Group 3 questions, which were generally of a higher order, required more complex post-excavation analysis, reflected the need to gain additional information about specific locations. Historical research had identified a number of ethnic groups in the Little Lon area (including Irish, Syrians, and Chinese) and sometimes at specific addresses. The Casselden Place excavation presented an excellent opportunity to correlate material culture and known patterns of settlement. The resulting research questions were therefore directed at the themes of poverty, marginality and ethnicity:

- Is it possible to gain a clearer understanding of the relationship between domestic dwellings and 'industrial' buildings on the site during the mid-to-late 19th century?
- Can the dwelling places in these areas of the site be related to previously excavated structures so that we can gain a more general understanding of life in this neighbourhood during the target period?
- Is it possible to offer a more detailed characterisation of ethnicity based on material culture?
- Is it possible to gain a clearer understanding of what constitutes a domestic assemblage in inner-city contexts in Melbourne so that it might be compared with assemblages from sites of similar antiquity and location in Sydney and in other major cities of the Western world? (Murray and Mayne 2002: 44–45)

The project analysed these and other questions, yielding data and conclusions of great value to inter-site comparative studies, and which have contributed to ongoing scholarly pursuits in urban archaeology.

For the archaeology project team, the most significant challenge was to transform the task of site-clearance and mitigation such that the historical and cultural capital of the people of Melbourne could be enhanced, rather than reduced, by destruction of what was left from the period before 1950. In this sense, the goal was both the acquisition of information about the place and the creation of knowledge. In this way, the research potential of Little Lon, which had been progressively revealed since the first phase of excavation in the late 1980s, could be further realised.

HISTORICAL RESEARCH PROGRAM

A major difference between the first phase of archaeological investigations at Little Lon in 1987–1989 and the Casselden Place program in 2002–2003 involved the manner in which historical research was integrated with the archaeology. In the first phase, much of the historical research occurred after the onsite investigations and was focused on enabling the archaeological team to reference and contextualise the archaeological data they were discovering. This process reflected the timing and budgetary pressures of the development context and was typical for urban 'rescue' archaeology at the time. The dig itself had not been fully informed by detailed prior analysis of key resources such as rate books, directories, or land title information, although some preliminary research had allowed the identification of the Little Lon allotments from first subdivision in 1848 until the 1920s and 1930s. These numbered 'lots' became the framework for defining trenches and site units for all subsequent investigations into the area including the 2002 Casselden Place project, with the result, firstly, that the data have been consistently gathered and can be directly compared and, secondly, that historical and archaeological information related to each allotment can be correlated.

Mayne's previous research of the history of Little Lon positioned the Casselden Place investigations favourably from the outset. He was able to guide historians Laura Donati and Sara Martin, towards directly relevant detailed documentary analysis in support of the archaeological team. Donati researched rate books, electoral rolls, and post office directories in order to expand the 1988 database, thereby providing a cohesive and ordered set of information about the owners and occupiers of the Casselden Place site from the middle of the 19th century to the middle of the 20th century. Martin extended this core base of data through analysis of contemporary maps, plans, and property title records.

Following the onsite phases, the interactive collaboration between historians and archaeologists continued. A workshop was convened for the research team in December 2003, at which preliminary excavation results were tabled and locations of particular archaeological interest were identified for further, more intensive historical research, using additional sources such as birth, marriage and death records. Following a second interactive workshop in April 2004 the historical investigation was broadened to cover other sites along Leichardt and Little Leichardt streets, and to pursue general research questions within the Little Lon neighbourhood that had been raised by the excavation and subsequent analysis of the archaeologists. Throughout, the historians were mindful of the need to use a consistent approach to research, analysis and presentation to the historical research used in the earlier analysis of the Little Lon site, so that the Commonwealth Block could be examined as a single neighbourhood entity.

THE EXCAVATION PROCESS

Stage 1 (May–July 2002) of the onsite investigations involved excavation of an area of approximately 3,360m^2 comprising a bitumen-sealed car park. Stage 2 (November–December 2002) focused on a modern walled garden featuring deep deposits of recent fill, an area beneath three buildings fronting Little Lonsdale Street, and part of properties fronting Lonsdale Street, totalling approximately 960m² (Figure 6.1).

In Stage 1 the site was divided into three areas, each comprising several allotments. Each allotment was treated as a 'trench' for excavation and reporting purposes. The size of the areas reflected the degree of survival of archaeologically sensitive deposits and features. Area 1, in the northwest part of the site, extended between the rear of the Little Lonsdale Street properties in the north, the line of Little Leichardt Street in the east, the re-formed Leichardt Street/Telstra Corporate Centre property boundary in the west and by the lot 35/36A boundary in the south. Area 2, in the southwest corner, extended from Lonsdale Street to the boundary with Area 1. Area 3 comprised Little Leichardt Street and all properties located to its east. The three Areas comprised the following allotments:

- Area 1 – lots 24A/B, 25A/C, 26, 27, 28A, 36A/B, 37A/B, 38, 39, and rear lot 84
- Area 2 – lots 32, 33A/B, 34A, 34B/C, 34B/D, 35 and Eagle Alley
- Area 3 – lots 40A/B, 41A–H, 41J, 80C and Little Leichardt Street.

In Stage 2, where the total area to be excavated was smaller, a decision was taken to divide those parts of the Casselden Place site into eight smaller Areas (4 to 12), most of which constituted a single allotment:

- Area 4/4A – lots 78 and 79
- Area 5 – lot 42
- Area 6 – lots 84A/D and 84B/D
- Area 7 – lots 83A/B
- Area 8 – lot 43
- Area 9 – lot 44
- Area 10 – lot 45
- Area 11 – lot 46
- Area 12 – Eagle Alley

In each area a single team operating under the direction of a trench supervisor and trench assistant was responsible for removing soil, artefact recovery and sieving, recording and liaison with the photographer and records manager. All features, deposits and structures were removed down to culturally sterile subsoil, except for removal of substantial remains which were recorded *in situ*. Deposits were removed stratigraphically, allotment by allotment. Features and deposits in each area were numbered independently, being provided with a 1, 2 or 3 prefix by area. This number was also attached to recovered artefacts. Excavation

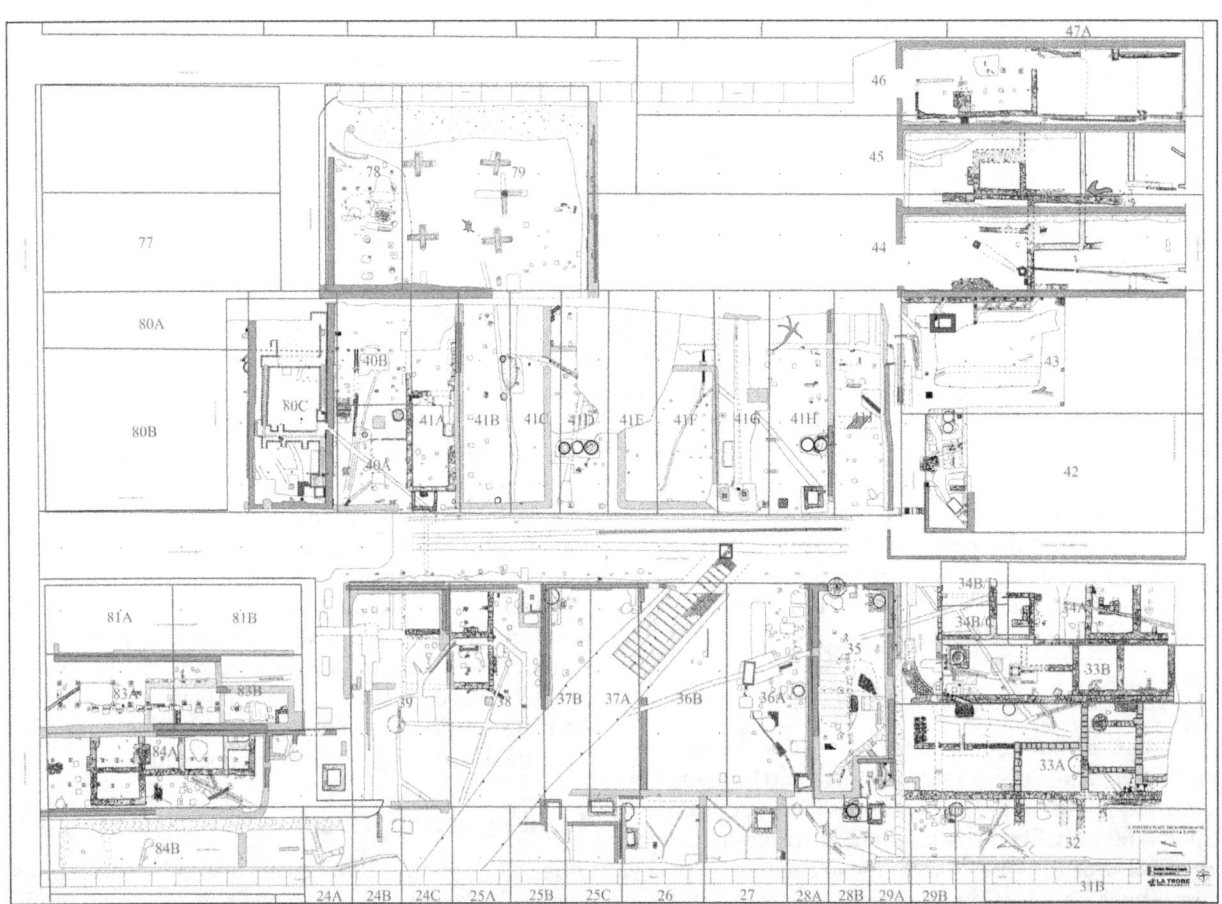

Figure 6.1: The Casselden Place Site, with excavated features shown and allotments superimposed (Reproduced from Godden Mackay Logan et al. 2004: Volume 2).

Figure 6.2: Archaeological excavation in progress: trench supervisor and community participants (Photo: Tony Jenner for Godden Mackay Logan, Austral Archaeology and La Trobe University).

areas were recorded in trench diaries and on context sheets. All excavation areas were recorded in words, photographs and plans. Intact occupation deposits were carefully excavated in squares and spits allowing three-dimensional co-ordinates to be attached to the artefact assemblages.

Most excavation was undertaken by hand, except in locations where substantial structural remains or deep fill deposits were encountered. In these situations, mechanical excavators were employed to remove these features under archaeological supervision. Artefacts were collected from deposits by the excavators and deposits were sieved. Total artefact recovery occurred for most archaeological contexts, insofar as possible, in order to gather comprehensive information about the artefact assemblage, with the remainder being sampled. The exceptions were contexts with recent filling episodes or contamination. These contexts were sampled primarily for information that would assist in developing a chronological framework for the site. Samples were also taken of building materials such as stone, brick, cement and mortar, and of all the cesspit fills. Environmental evidence, such as pollen samples, was also collected. On occasion, the Excavation Director modified the proposed course of excavation when circumstances required, such as the presence of contaminated, or temporarily unworkable deposits, spoil removal, machine work and priorities, to interpret features and deposits to assist future planning and accelerate progress.

Visible artefacts were manually collected from deposits, but a large number of features required wet-sieving to recover smaller finds, or to separate contaminated or waterlogged matrix from the objects. All cesspit fills and occupation deposits were treated in this manner. Similarly discrete deposits that had become damp as a result of rain were wet-sieved. The treatment of each deposit was determined by the trench supervisors, based

Figure 6.3: Excavation of allotments 33 and 34 (Photo: Tony Jenner for Godden Mackay Logan, Austral Archaeology and La Trobe University).

on an assessment of the ability of each deposit to contribute worthwhile data, bearing in mind the likely results, relative to the amount of effort required to undertake recovery.

When elements of the natural soil profile were encountered, the horizons were shaved using flattened, sharpened shovels, until undisturbed culturally sterile subsoil/clay was encountered. This process allowed the surfaces to be reduced incrementally, enabling artefacts to be recovered and changes in the deposits to be observed. This approach was primarily adopted in order to identify any potential Aboriginal cultural material from both Contact and pre-Contact periods.

Excavation of the cesspit features, of which there were 20, required the use of a variety of techniques. Buried barrel cesspits were excavated by hand and whenever variations in the cesspit fill were encountered new context numbers were assigned (Figure 6.4). Where no variation was noted the fill was excavated as a single unit. Following the clearing of the barrels, the features were recorded in plan and by photograph, and elevations and half-sections were drawn. The remnant timber base of the cesspits were then lifted to determine whether a cesspit was located beneath. Bluestone-lined cesspits were excavated by hand only where the matrix was sufficiently solid to allow the excavators to work within the pit in safety. Where the cesspit fill comprised coarse rubble, or was saturated or contaminated, a backhoe with a narrow bucket emptied the fill onto plastic sheeting, which was then hand sorted and/or wet-sieved. Composite cesspits, where barrels had been set in earlier bluestone cesspits, were all excavated manually.

Refuse pits, which varied in size from less than 1m in diameter and 500mm deep to up to 2m in diameter and 1.5m deep, were manually excavated. In most instances, the matrix was wet-sieved, but in Area 2 a large rectangular pit of unknown function, filled with clay and rubble, was partly cleared by machine and then excavated by hand.

Figure 6.4: Excavated 'barrel' cesspit (Photo: Tony Jenner for Godden Mackay Logan, Austral Archaeology and La Trobe University).

At the conclusion of the excavation, the site was made safe by in-filling all deep pits and features, covering and securing contaminated soil heaps, and cleaning and securing all work areas.

Managing the Artefacts

At Casselden Place extensive data recording and preliminary analysis occurred during the onsite excavation. Most artefacts were cleaned and processed on site during the excavation phases. Archaeological contexts occurred across 39 allotments and two road reserves. Many of these were structural deposits and produced no finds, but others, including cesspit fills, dumps and occupation deposits, produced vast quantities of artefacts. Conservators from Heritage Victoria undertook initial conservation work during the excavation phases of the project. There were substantive advantages in this approach, because the artefact analysts were able to familiarise themselves with the locations where important artefacts were found, to speak directly with excavators and to establish or clarify possible relationships between artefacts and contexts. The onsite presence of a wide range of specialists (some working in other non-artefact roles) offered synergies when artefact analysts could compare notes and utilize the knowledge of those around them. By the time that digging concluded, the artefact catalogue was virtually complete, many artefacts had already been conserved, or at least stabilised, and analysis of the results could commence immediately.

Approximately 300,000 artefacts were recovered from the Casselden Place site. Artefacts were labelled according to trench and context, then cleaned, dried, sorted and bagged for cataloguing and analysis. The excavation team identified significant items which required specialised conservation treatment, or special attention, especially the organic remains (bone, shell, timber, cloth). Some objects were then transferred offsite for treatment but considerable care was taken to keep track of their location so that they could be reunited with the rest of the assemblage prior to analysis.

The methodology for cataloguing artefacts paralleled the system used for documentation and analysis of the assemblage from the adjacent Little Lon site, and the collection from the earlier Casselden Place development phase 3 testing excavations. All material recovered from the Commonwealth Block sites (Little Lon and Casselden Place) has therefore been consistently recorded and can be analysed as a single assemblage. The database records information about artefact location, type, dimension, quantity, integrity, modification, decorative pattern, manufacturer and time period with simple interpretive fields indicating the potential social role played by each artefact. The recording system was designed to facilitate comment on the overall character of the assemblage, as well

Figure 6.5: Onsite processing of artefacts by specialists and community participants (Photo: Tony Jenner for Godden Mackay Logan, Austral Archaeology and La Trobe University).

as to enable the placement of individual artefacts and broader components of the assemblage within their temporal, spatial and social contexts.

ARCHAEOLOGY AND SITE PHASES

Analysis of ethnographic and historical documents created soon after Europeans arrived in Victoria indicate that the central Melbourne area was within the territory of the Wurundjeri-willam clan of the Woiworung (also referred to as the Wurundjeri) people, who were one of the five tribes comprising the Kulin Nation (Barwick 1984). The site chosen for the settlement of Melbourne was a popular meeting place for the local Kulin nation groups, who continued to visit the area in the early years following European settlement (Presland 1983).

During the archaeological excavations a handful of stone artefacts, initially thought to be of possible Aboriginal origin, were recovered. However, representatives from Aboriginal Affairs Victoria (AAV) inspected the pieces and did not identify any as being of definite Aboriginal origin. Sadly the very absence of Aboriginal cultural material from the site speaks eloquently of the impact of the arrival of European settlers on the first peoples of the area.

The archaeological excavation exposed more than 2,800 archaeological 'contexts', including structural features, cesspit fills, dumps and occupation deposits that produced the artefacts. The site's archaeology was dominated by post-colonial settlement remains, including artefacts dating from the earliest phases of Melbourne's occupation by Europeans. Light industry was also present from an early stage and had become firmly established in the area by the early 20th century.

For Casselden Place the site phasing process grouped the information derived from the analysis of deposits and features, and from the examination of the artefact assemblages found in association with these deposits and features, within discrete periods of time. The phase system, despite its reliance upon absolute dates, and the obvious limits of gaps in the physical stratigraphy on site, restricted chronological latitude, thereby allowing deposits or artefacts to undergo specific time-bound analysis where, under other circumstances, only general comments might be made.

Some deposit types do not readily identify within the absolute nature of the phase system. Deposits derived from continuous deposition, such as underfloor occupation deposits may have accumulated gradually over several phases. Former topsoil deposits that were later used as yard surfaces may also contain artefact assemblages that extend over multiple phases of use, as later material is incorporated and mixed indiscriminately with earlier deposits. In such cases phase ranges were used.

For the Casselden Place project, site phases were determined through examination of the available documented history of the place with meaningful historical events or landmarks defining the beginning and end of each phase. Remains of structures from all of the identified historical periods were exposed. Seven site phases were identified:

- **Phase 1:** the period before 1837, rather than having a start date is marked by an end date of 1837. This is an extremely long phase and covers the period of potential Indigenous occupation of the site and ends with the official European settlement of the Port Phillip district. In regard to the European history of the place, this phase includes the period of first contact and possible unofficial or ephemeral occupation.
- **Phase 2:** was a short phase, extending from 1837 to 1848, and is marked by the establishment of Melbourne and extends to the year in which the site was surveyed and subdivided making it available for development. In terms of occupation of the site, evidence of temporary or unofficial occupation of the place might survive.
- **Phase 3:** covered the period 1849–1890 and marks the period of intensive (primarily domestic) occupation and subdivision. The end-date of 1890 marks a point in Australian history at which economic growth slowed to an economic depression in the following phase.
- **Phase 4:** the period 1891–1920 marks a change in the character of the site with an increasing degree of mixed occupation including both commercial and industrial enterprises becoming more apparent in a formerly domestic enclave. This phase also covers the period of the First World War, the results of which were profound in their social influence. This phase also includes the increasing presence of Chinese and other non-Anglo-Celtic occupants.
- **Phase 5:** the years 1921–1959 saw the district develop into an almost exclusively light and heavy industrial zone. It was a period that saw 'slum clearance' programs brought into being and was the period that also saw the Great Depression and the Second World War.
- **Phase 6:** began in 1960 and ended in 1988. The site underwent a significant change, as various sections of the block were acquired by the Commonwealth in preparation for redevelopment. The result was widespread demolition and the removal of many of the industrial enterprises occupying the site. During this phase, the Casselden Place site had effectively become part of Melbourne's expanding CBD fringe.
- **Phase 7:** extended from 1989 to 2003. The start date coincides with the period following the development of the adjoining Telstra block and provides a post Little Lon phase in terms of the region's archaeology.

(Godden Mackay Logan et al. 2004: 47–48)

These seven phases provide a chronological framework within which the deposits, structures and artefact assemblages exposed by archaeological excavation could be meaningfully analysed. Through the process of excavation, a relative chronology for each excavation area was recognised and displayed in the form of a 'Harris matrix'. The matrix assists with organising the site's stratigraphy in a logical manner based on the physical relationship between each of the excavated deposits and features. These were arranged by allotment, so that the story of each occupation unit could be separately examined. The phasing system allows examination of separate allotments and at a grouped community level.

The relative chronology formulated during the excavation was therefore interpreted to become an absolute chronology in which each deposit and feature can be attributed to a particular period. This absolute chronology enabled particular excavated features to be connected with documented evidence related to their creation or removal. Most of this evidence was derived from construction data for buildings and the appearance (or non-appearance) of structural elements on dated maps, plans and illustrations. Rate books and directory entries provided precise dates for the appearance of some new structures or the disappearance of old structures, and in some cases offered details of materials used in construction and dimensions, both of which were apparent in the archaeological record.

This process of forming an absolute chronology was refined by reference to the artefact assemblages associated with these structures and deposits. Some artefact types provide a readily recognisable *terminus post quem* for their associated assemblages, and therefore for the deposits from which they were recovered. At Casselden Place such items included artefacts that actually bore a date (such as coins) or particular artefact types that have a recorded date of introduction. By evaluating the whole assemblage from each deposit, the date of deposition could be estimated, thereby refining possible end dates for particular archaeological features and their associated events.

Of course, not all deposits could be associated with a single phase, particularly in areas where there are no datable deposits or features, or where artefact assemblages were small or equivocal. In these instances, a date range was applied to the archaeological contexts, typically extending across two or sometimes three phases. Deposits associated with phases 3 and 4 (the period 1849–1890) yielded the most significant information regarding the manner in which the site was occupied and developed. These phases saw the high concentrations of dwellings and large numbers of people occupying the site. Among the excavated deposits, 21% were attributed to phase 3, 5% to phase 4 and a further 5% to either phase 3 or 4. A further 30% of the contexts could not be dated more precisely than a range of phase 3 to 5. The number of pre-phase 3 deposits was relatively small. Phase 1 was represented by 47 contexts (1%) and consisted primarily of subsoil deposits. Only 11 deposits were attributed to phase 2 (less than 0.5%), while 93 contexts fell within the range of phase 1 to phase 3 (3%). Thirteen per cent of the contexts were clearly related to phases 5 to 7, during the period after 1921. The spread of contexts by phase across the site varied from allotment to allotment. This appeared to be a function of site formation processes in some parts of the site during phases 5 to 7 (1921–2003) that saw the wholesale removal of phase 1 to phase 4 contexts down to subsoil. (Godden Mackay Logan et al. 2004: 49).

Analysing the Artefacts

Detailed artefact analysis commenced following the completion of the catalogue, after onsite investigations and recording had concluded. At first, analysis concentrated on deriving information about site chronology, which would assist in stratigraphic phasing. This initial focus assisted with understanding the nature of the deposits, for example, to gauge the degree of site disturbance. The artefacts were then analysed, having regard to the questions posed in the research design, as well as other questions raised by the nature of the artefacts themselves. The artefacts provided information that was not recorded in historical sources, such as what people were eating, the things they used and discarded, the nature of the houses they lived in, and whether different ethnic groups living at Casselden Place had ethnically distinct material culture. Other research goals, such as interpreting the archaeology of 19th-century working class communities in ways that would contribute to investigations into gender, the nature of childhood, and the world of work, also guided the analysis.

For each artefact class, analysis commenced with a detailed description of what artefacts were found and where, enabling the team to create maps showing the distribution of artefacts across the site, and to establish which allotments had greater relative artefact density. Differences in distribution were also investigated to establish whether such differences arose from the type or age of the artefacts, or were they a function of context, for example whether the place was a house, a street or a factory. Places where archaeological deposits retained integrity and where historical research indicated a closer analysis would help answer research questions, were allocated higher priority and became the focus of very detailed archaeological and historical research. The first phase of analysis, involving description, pattern generation and comparison, provided baseline information to support more complex investigations foreshadowed in the research design. In this sense, answering the initial 'what', 'when' and 'where' questions through integrated research and documentation of the physical evidence allowed archaeologists to pursue more complex 'how' and 'why' questions.

Interpreting the Artefacts

Faunal remains indicated that people mostly ate mutton and some beef, supplemented by lots of fish and oysters, as well as mussels, pork, lamb, veal, rabbit, chicken, turkey and goose. The meat cuts suggests that residents could afford good quality cuts of mutton and beef. Botanical remains include 18 types of plant foods, deposited over a 70-year period. These may have been home grown, obtained by foraging, or purchased from nearby markets or hawkers. Although representing only a fraction of the total diet of the community across a century, these remains show that a wide range of foods was consumed and that, by contrast with the slum stereotype, the inhabitants of the precinct were generally well fed and had access to a diversity of foodstuffs from local markets or door-to-door vendors (Simons and Maitri 2006).

The glass and stoneware assemblage provides information about patterns of trade and levels of industrialisation at the site (Davies 2006). The primary sources of these artefacts were inner-urban Melbourne, as well as Europe and the United Kingdom. The Chinese presence at Casselden Place may be apparent in artefacts such as wide-shouldered stoneware food jars used to store preserved Asian comestibles such as tofu, sweet bean paste, pickled cabbage or shrimp paste (Williamson 2006).

Ceramics from the excavation include vases, figurines and tableware items such as serving platters and bowls, decanters and egg cups. The majority of the domestic ceramic assemblage was manufactured in England, predominantly in Staffordshire. A smaller proportion derived from French and Asian (predominantly Chinese) manufacturers. Decorative styles were not limited to the cheapest types. Tablewares seem to have been purchased as individual pieces rather than

Figure 6.6: Faunal remains included mutton beef, pork and lamb (Photo: Tony Jenner for Godden Mackay Logan, Austral Archaeology and La Trobe University).

in large sets. Mismatched sets, and sets of items transfer printed in more than one colour, can be interpreted as evidence of decisions being made by the inhabitants about consumption and that choices were being made and money was found for 'extras'.

Analysis of the ceramic assemblage also revealed some unexpected taphonomic evidence. Because of their potentially long use-lives, ceramics are often assumed to be deposited many years after their date of manufacture and purchase. By contrast, clay smoking pipes, which tend to have very short use, are presumed to be deposited quickly. Over half the identifiable domestic ceramics from the Casselden Place site were manufactured prior to 1870. Evidence, such as the dating of the Copeland/Spode maker's marks, the absence of the Staffordshire knot and the words 'Ltd' and 'trademark' on maker's marks, suggests that the assemblage was manufactured between the late 1850s and late 1880s. Four of the five clay pipe manufacturers were only in production for short periods of time, and had ceased operation by 1865. On the basis of these results, it appears that there is no significant difference between the dates of manufacture of the domestic ceramic and pipe smoking related artefact assemblages, with the majority of both dating to the period between 1850 and 1870 (Williamson 2006). The temporal data for both ceramics and clay smoking pipes therefore suggests that there was no substantive time lag between the date of manufacture of the ceramics and their incorporation into the archaeological record. This finding has consequences, not only for dating archaeological deposits at the site, but also in considerations of socioeconomic status during its occupation and behavioural implications regarding access to goods and consumerism generally.

The miscellaneous artefacts included a broad range of items associated with work, recreation, education, fashion, food consumption, health, and other facets of everyday life and illustrates how people living during the second half of the 19th century, in the inner city of Melbourne, had access to a diverse array of products (Plate 6.3). It is also apparent that consumer choices were not bound by frugality or necessity. The occupants of the Casselden Place allotments owned items that reflected pride in their personal appearance, and their homes. Children enjoyed manufactured toys which, while not necessarily expensive, do provide evidence of capacity for discretionary spending. The pictures that emerge of the community, diverge from contemporary popular images of Little Lon as a slum district, burdened with filth, characterised by neglect, and subject to poverty and hardship (Porter and Ferrier 2006).

In short, examination of the artefact assemblage suggests that, while the inhabitants of Casselden Place were hardly wealthy, they were able to purchase many of life's little luxuries that had become more widely available during the 19th century. Jewellery, dolls and figurines were not uncommon, neither were items closely associated with hygiene and grooming. The site's artefacts provide evidence of diversity in employment, the ages of the residents, and their relative economic circumstances. This array of diverse material culture, from what was perceived at the time a poor area of the city, offers insights into working-class communities and suggests that indicators of status or class contained in the material archaeological record enable alternative perspectives and narratives about Australian society, culture and identity.

REPORTING AND RECORDS

Consistent with the requirements of the consent for the project issued by Heritage Victoria, a detailed Research Archive Report was assembled as the permanent archival record of the excavation project data. An introductory volume included a succinct synthesis in 'plain English' which addressed the questions posed in the research design prepared by Murray and Mayne.

The Research Archive Report is presented in four volumes (comprising six separate documents):
- **Volume 1** (introduction and background) outlines the history and location of the site, with summary histories for a number of the more archaeologically productive allotments at the site, together with the 'plain English' account of the excavation and results.
- **Volume 2** presents the trench reports, prepared by the trench supervisors responsible for the excavation of the site. The trench reports describe and interpret the archaeological remains, with reference to the artefacts recovered and the histories researched for the site.
- **Volumes 3i and 3ii** comprise the artefact reports. These present the results of the analysis of the artefacts recovered during excavation. They are generally divided according to fabric and function, and rely on the artefact catalogue.
- **Volumes 4i and 4ii** (appendices) present the raw data that underlie much of the analysis and interpretation in volumes 2, 3i and 3ii. Historical research, Harris matrices, tables and graphs are all presented in Volume 4i and 4ii, together with the artefact catalogue and a summary of media coverage generated by the excavations.

An innovative and important achievements of the Research Archive Report is the integration of historical research with the data generated by physical archaeological investigation and artefact recovery. The Casselden Place precinct at Little Lon may has been more thoroughly understood and in a deeper context than the shallow perspectives of contemporary commentators – although ample evidence for poverty and squalor existed at the site, the excavation and ensuing synthesis also revealed another more 'respectable' side of early inner city Melbourne.

In the years since, the physical and documentary resources generated by the Casselden Place Archaeological Excavations have provided the basis for both graduate and undergraduate research and interpretation projects and have been more extensively analysed, integrated, discussed and published in a dedicated volume of the *International Journal of Historical Archaeology* (Murray 2006b).

COMMUNITY ENGAGEMENT

The Casselden Place Archaeological Excavations generated considerable public interest, which was incorporated within the project as a means of engaging with the emerging 'social value' of the site and project. In Australia, traditional approaches to understanding the heritage significance of archaeological sites had focused on their scientific or research value. Emphasis had been placed on research frameworks which ensured that as archaeological sites were investigated (and often destroyed in the process), the information that they contained could be recovered and could contribute to an understanding of history or the place itself.

The Casselden Place Archaeological Excavations were part of a wider trend that not only addressed the scientific values of archaeological sites but also their broader values in a social context. In recent years, archaeology has increasingly been seen as a means of connecting people with their history and their heritage. As a result, community involvement in excavations, through initiatives such as hands-on digging, school projects, tours and media coverage, has become an important feature of urban archaeology. If such processes and events are recognised as a social 'good', the understanding of archaeological sites in a social context and their interpretation is as critical a conservation action as the more specialist, scientific pursuit of research outcomes (Mackay 2005).

The excavations provided an opportunity to develop avenues for community archaeology in an urban context on a large scale. With the active encouragement and assistance of Heritage Victoria, the program included: a major media launch and extensive coverage, a structured schools program undertaken in conjunction with the Museum of Victoria, organised tours and presentation of community information through signs, a brochure and website, community participation in the excavation itself and a customised learning and participation program for undergraduate archaeology students.

During the excavation itself, the general community was able to enjoy site tours coordinated by Heritage Victoria. An onsite platform facilitated informal visits and close access. Information about

Figure 6.7: Casselden Place Archaeological Excavation Project media launch May 2002 (Photo: Tony Jenner for Godden Mackay Logan, Austral Archaeology and La Trobe University).

the site and progress of the excavation was regularly posted on the Heritage Victoria website.

Community participants who wished to become actively involved in the excavation were accommodated, taking into consideration their varying degrees of archaeological experience and physical ability. Around 400 community participants and students participated. They helped to dig, wash artefacts, and process finds. University students across a range of disciplines contributed on a voluntary basis.

Local media coverage included all of the major daily newspapers, (comprising 17 newspaper articles), commercial and non-commercial television (through 18 television reports), and a number of radio stations (in all 37 radio mentions: 13 interviews and 24 news grabs). A number of these news items were re-broadcast or re-issued as news releases in other states and overseas. Television items were released through South-East Asia by ABC Asia-Pacific and in the UK through the BBC.

The Casselden Place Project thereby became more than an exercise in data gathering and testing scientific hypotheses. It became an 'event' that used the archaeological place, relics, and the processes of archaeology itself to relate tales in a way that connected people with history, across a wide spectrum of society. The 'tales' that the excavation generated were not always ones that might have been predicted by the archaeologists. Murray (2005) has observed that the project generated a number of competing histories that varied in content and accuracy depending on the authors. Some media outlets were interested principally in contraceptive devices and the remains of brothels. Others became fascinated by a skeleton, supposedly found during the dig, allegedly of a murdered prostitute (although no such skeleton was ever found).

Notwithstanding the distractions of alluring alternative histories, participation by both media and community proved highly successful. The profile of Australian historical archaeology was raised, invaluable excavation experience was provided to a host of archaeology students, and ISPT raised its own profile as a good corporate citizen and incorporated the site, its history and the archaeological project as a core branding theme in the public areas of the new development. The involvement of university students also reflected highly effective collaboration between two private consulting firms (Godden Mackay Logan and Austral Archaeology) and a university (the Archaeology Program, La Trobe University).

Conclusion

Understanding the archaeology of the modern city poses significant challenges to archaeologists and historians, and to those responsible for managing urban archaeological sites. The Casselden Place Project provides but one window into the urban past offered by the collaborative integration of academic and commercial archaeology and history in a development context.

The archaeological investigation of the Casselden Place site widened the window into Melbourne's urban past which had been opened by the initial Little Lon excavation, more than a decade before. Leveraging off growing recognition by government and the private sector of the value of urban archaeological resources, and fostered by an open innovative collaboration between a major city developer, two archaeological consulting firms and La Trobe University, the project demonstrated that with the support of consent authorities and the co-operation of the development industry, collaborations between the academic world and heritage consultants could be highly successful. The Casselden Place Project made a significant contribution to the 'slum debate' in Australia and has shined a light on the lives of the inhabitants of the Little Lon district from the earliest years of Melbourne's settlement to its radical modification by demolition and changing uses in the mid- to late-20th century. The artefacts, photographs, illustrations and Research Archive Report comprise an invaluable database for future research into Melbourne's history, for the interpretation of the history of this precinct and for multidisciplinary studies of urbanism and the modern city archaeological remains of the area in future development.

Acknowledgments

This chapter draws heavily from Volume 10 No. 4 (2006) of the *International Journal of Historical Archaeology*, which was devoted to the Casselden Place Archaeological Excavation and also incorporates content directly from the 'Plain English Report' within Volume 1 of the 2004 Research Archive Report and other related reports prepared by Godden Mackay Logan Pty Ltd, Austral Archaeology and the Archaeology Program at La Trobe University for the Industry Superannuation Property Trust (ISPT) and Heritage Victoria. These reports embody and include the synthesising and research efforts of Alan Mayne (Melbourne University) and Tim Murray (La Trobe University), as well as the historians, archaeologists and other members of the Casselden Place team, particularly Site Manager Justin McCarthy, Excavation Director Graham Wilson, historians Laura Donati and Sara Martin and trench supervisors and other members of the team involved in onsite work and post-excavation analysis and reporting: Ilya Berelov, Peter Davies, Åsa Ferrier, Kevin Hickson, Anne Mackay, Maddy Maitri, Lyndon Patterson, Jenny Porter, Allison Simons, Andrew Sneddon, Zvonka Stanin, Cathy Tucker and Christine Williamson. The excavation project was commissioned by ISPT through

Cessation of Transportation Medal

One of the most significant finds at Casselden Place was a medal struck to commemorate the Cessation of Convict Transportation, dated 1853. The medal is regarded as the most important medal struck in Tasmania, for it commemorates not only the victory of the Anti-transportation Movement but also the Jubilee of the Founding of Tasmania. The medal's design was approved by the Anti-transportation League committee in 1853 before being struck in England. As a result, the medals did not actually arrive for distribution in Australia until 1855. The medal features James Wyon's portrait of Queen Victoria on one side, with the reverse showing the armorial bearings for Tasmania in a shield. The shield is quartered by the Southern Cross and bears pastoral, commercial and agricultural emblems supported by the emu and kangaroo, surmounted by a rising sun motif.

James Wyon was a member of the Wyon dynasty of engravers and was cousin to the distinguished William Wyon who was Second Engraver to the Royal Mint (1816–1828) and later Chief Engraver (1828–1851). James Wyon had been employed since 1825 first as an assistant to his cousin and later, after the death of William, as Resident Engraver, and is best known for engraving the dies for sovereigns and half-sovereigns at the new Sydney branch of the Royal Mint.

The medal was cast in three different metals depending on their numerical distribution. One single medal was struck in gold for presentation to Queen Victoria, 100 were struck in bronze for committee members and 9000 were struck in white metal for general distribution. The medal recovered from Casselden Place appears to be a bronze issue. Many of the white metal medals went to Tasmanian schoolchildren who, at the cessation celebrations, had each been issued with a piece of Demonstration Cake and a ticket enabling them to receive a medal when they arrived in the colony. When the medals arrived in Launceston on 3 August 1855, 4000 were immediately dispatched to Hobart, 3000 were held in Launceston and 2000 were sent to country districts of Green Ponds, Norfolk Plains, Ross, Evandale, Longford and other districts.

Reproduced from Godden Mackay Logan, Austral Archaeology and La Trobe University 2004: Vol 1: 39–40.

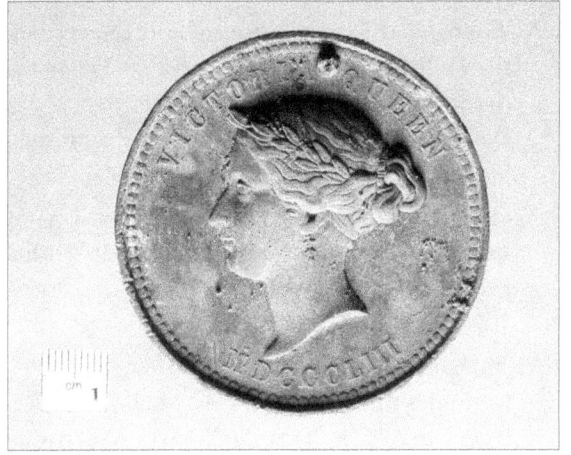 

Figure 6.8: Cessation of Transportation Medal: obverse and reverse (Photos: Tony Jenner for Godden Mackay Logan, Austral Archaeology and La Trobe University).

Marcus Fakhry. The project managers were Clifton Coney Group (Vic) Pty Ltd, particularly Claudio Cardillo, Philip Flynn and Andrew Stevenson. The excavations were carried out with the support and assistance of archaeologists Jeremy Smith and Leah McKenzie, and conservators Karina Acton, Annie Muir, Penny Byrne, Giselle Banks, Jennifer Dickens and David Graves from Heritage Victoria.

REFERENCES

Barwick, D. 1984. Mapping the Past: An Atlas of Victorian Clans 1835–1904. *Aboriginal History* 8: 124–126.

Davies, P. 2006. Mapping Commodities at Casselden Place, Melbourne. *International Journal of Historical Archaeology* 10(4): 343–355.

Dennis, C.J. 1915. *The Songs of the Sentimental Bloke*. Sydney: Angus and Robertson.

Godden Mackay (eds.), 1996. Cumberland/Gloucester Streets Site Archaeological Investigation, 6 vols. Unpublished report prepared by Godden Mackay Logan. On file at State Library, NSW.

Godden Mackay Logan, Austral Archaeology and La Trobe University, 2004. Casselden Place 50 Lonsdale St Melbourne Archaeological Excavations, Research Archive Report prepared for ISPT and Heritage Victoria, Volumes 1–4, Godden Mackay Logan Pty Ltd, Redfern. On file with Heritage Victoria.

Karskens, G. 1997. *The Rocks: Life in Early Sydney*. Melbourne: Melbourne University Press.

Karskens, G. 1999. *Inside The Rocks, the Archaeology of a Neighbourhood*. Alexandria, NSW: Hale and Iremonger.

Long, A., C. Williamson, M. Goulding and J. Howell-Meurs, J. 2001. Casselden Place Development Phase 3, Archaeological Planning Report. Unpublished Report to Industry Superannuation Property Trustees. Prepared by Andrew Long and Associates, Melbourne. On file with Heritage Victoria.

Mackay, R. 2003. Whose Archaeology is It, Anyway? In Murray, T. (ed.), *Exploring the Modern City. Recent Approaches to Urban History and Archaeology*, pp. 169–173, Sydney: Historic Houses Trust of NSW.

Mackay, R. 2005. Archaeology: Stories and Contemporary Social Context. *Historic Environment* 18(3): 27–30.

Mackay, R., J. McCarthy, A. Sneddon and G. Wilson, 2006. Down Little Lon: An Introduction to the Casselden Place Archaeological Excavations, Melbourne. *International Journal of Historical Archaeology* 10(4): 305–316.

Mayne, A. 2003. A Road to Nowhere? In Murray, T. (ed.), *Exploring the Modern City: Recent Approaches to Urban History and Archaeology*, pp. 65–87, Sydney: Historic Houses Trust of NSW.

Mayne, A. 2006. Big Notes from a Little Street: Historical Research at Melbourne's 'Little Lon'. *International Journal of Historical Archaeology* 10(4): 317–328.

Mayne, A., and T. Murray (eds.), 2001. *The Archaeology of Urban Landscapes: Explorations in Slumland*. Cambridge: Cambridge University Press.

Murray, T. 2005. Images of Little Lon: Making History, Changing Perceptions. In Lydon, J. and T. Ireland (eds.), *Object Lessons: Archaeology and Heritage in Australia*, pp. 167–185, Melbourne: Australian Scholarly Publishing.

Murray, T. 2006a. Integrating Archaeology and History at the Commonwealth Block: 'Little Lon' and Casselden Place. *International Journal of Historical Archaeology* 10(4): 395–413.

Murray, T. 2006b. Introduction (to Casselden Place Volume). *International Journal of Historical Archaeology* 10(4): 297–304.

Murray, T. and A. Mayne, 2002. Casselden Place Development Archaeological Investigation Works Phases 1 and 2, Full Research Design, prepared for Godden Mackay Logan, in association with Archaeology Program La Trobe University and Austral Archaeology. On file with Heritage Victoria.

Murray, T. and A. Mayne, 2003. (Re)Constructing a Lost Community: Little Lon, Melbourne, Australia. *Historical Archaeology* 37(1): 87–101.

Porter, J. and A. Ferrier 2006. Miscellaneous Artifacts from Casselden Place, Melbourne. *International Journal of Historical Archaeology* 10(4): 375–393.

Presland, G. 1983. An Archaeological Survey of the Melbourne Metropolitan Area. *Victoria Archaeological Survey Occasional Report No. 15*, Department of Conservation and Environment, Melbourne, p. 26.

Simons, A. and M. Maitri, 2006. The Food Remains from Casselden Place, Melbourne, Australia. *International Journal of Historical Archaeology* 10(4): 357–373.

Williamson, C. 2006. Dating the Domestic Ceramics and Pipe Smoking Related Artifacts from Casselden Place, Melbourne, Australia. *International Journal of Historical Archaeology* 10(4): 329–341.

Yamin, R. 2001. Alternative Narratives: Respectability at New York's Five Points. In Mayne, A. and T. Murray (eds.), *The Archaeology of Urban Landscapes: Explorations in Slumland*, pp. 154–170, Cambridge: Cambridge University Press.

7
Assemblage Analysis and Outcomes: Phase 2

Tim Murray

This chapter discusses and essentially represents the unpublished research design written by Murray and Mayne (2002) for the Casselden Place excavations, which comprised phase 2 of the major excavation work on the Commonwealth Block site. There is an obvious connection between the thinking behind our earlier work on the cottages in Casselden Place discussed in Chapter 4, and the more evolved consideration I represent here. Perhaps most important is the very clear connection between our experiences of that research and the evolution of the research design for phase 2 in light of developments in urban archaeology that had occurred in Australia and elsewhere. It is also worth noting that over a decade spanned McCarthy's original excavations and those that were to be published in 2004 by the consortium of GML, Austral Archaeology and La Trobe University. The design and conduct of research on the Commonwealth Block was very much an iterative process, one that continues right through to the present. The most complete discussion of the analysis and outcomes of this work can be found in published form in the papers published in the *International Journal of Historical Archaeology* (volume 10 number 4) that were directly based on the constituent reports that made up the major site record (GML et al. 2004). There is no need to recapitulate those data or those discussions.

In the research design Murray and Mayne spent some time reflecting on the role of research designs in heritage archaeology (as distinct from those produced within the academic context as we had in our grant application to the Australian Research Council to support the analysis of the McCarthy excavations discussed in Chapter 4). This discussion accurately reflects the kind of thinking that was necessary to encompass the evolution of a project that at various stages was dominated by heritage concerns, and at other times approached the kind of 'blue sky' context of pure academic interests.

THE RESEARCH DESIGN FOR THE PHASE 2 EXCAVATIONS

The overt discussion of the role of research design in the practice of archaeology has spawned a vast, diffuse, and often contradictory literature. Flowing from the principle that the questions asked of a site or assemblage should relate meaningfully to methods of data recovery and analysis (mediated by methodology, or 'middle range theory') it has been generally agreed that good research design is the key to resolving several significant tensions that inevitably arise from the archaeological process.

Chief among these tensions is the notion that excavation (still a fundamental means by which archaeologists recover information) involves the destruction of sites and contexts. Of course it is true that much archaeological research can be (and continues to be) done from the desktop, in the laboratory, or through the use of non-invasive and non-destructive technologies such as Ground Penetrating Radar (GPR). Nonetheless the characterisation of the archaeological record as a 'non-renewable resource' that underwrote much early work on research design in the 1960s and 1970s, is still accepted in both the academic and heritage management spheres of contemporary archaeological practice. Whatever the sphere of practice, two fundamental arguments logically follow from this acceptance:

- that destruction of significant sites or features should only be sanctioned if it can be demonstrated that an excavation will materially contribute to our knowledge of the site and its social and cultural context however broadly or narrowly defined
- that formal means of demonstration need to be established, whether these be broadly accepted standards of data recovery, recording and analysis, or through clear methodological links between data and the construction of knowledge about the place (middle range theory).

Naturally these two arguments, which together encapsulate the significance of research design, have different impacts depending upon the context of excavation.

In the case of pure academic research (which represents a minute percentage of excavation events throughout most Western countries) the task of raising funds and gaining permission from heritage managers is very difficult. Raising funds for research projects requires competition with other projects and other investigators drawn from disciplines across the humanities and social sciences. Evaluation of projects is extremely stringent and geared to the requirement that such research (and the researchers who undertake it) are of international quality, and that the research has the capacity to create new knowledge. In recent years the major source of funds in Australia (The Australian Research Council) has only been able to fund approximately 22% of all applications. The success rate for historical archaeology falls roughly within this average. Typically research projects might last for a minimum of three years, many a great deal longer. Notwithstanding issues related to funding, the approval process adopted by heritage managers of academic projects requiring excavation has to balance the benefits that might flow to society from the project against the fact that the sites to be excavated are usually not under threat of development.

Excavation in a heritage management context has obvious differences. Funding is supplied by developers, the quantum being established through negotiation between the developer, the archaeologist and the responsible management authority. The purpose of the excavation is to salvage historical and archaeological information from a site that is (in the bulk of cases) to be destroyed as a result of development. The selection of the site, the time frame of the work, and indeed the kinds of archaeological activities to be undertaken (excavation, cataloguing, analysis, reporting) are ultimately either determined or constrained by others. Of course there are ethical and professional standards that apply to the work of archaeologists in the heritage context (as there are in the academic situation). It is widely appreciated that the simple retrieval of information does not present the best outcome for a society whose heritage is to have a component of its social and cultural value 'cashed up' as a development site.

GML Pty Ltd in a landmark report *Parramatta Historical Archaeological Landscape Management Study* (PHALMS) (2000) summarised this situation well:

> most Australian archaeologists – historical and prehistorical alike – recognize that the research design is a useful tool in the best-practice recovery and interpretation of archaeology in Australia. It is a tool for ensuring that, as the record is destroyed, the data retrieved will make a meaningful contribution to understanding the past. The best place to start is with questions that make a meaningful contribution to current and relevant research topics (2001: 20).

The PHALMS approach, with its emphasis on establishing research frameworks that integrate a diversity of historical disciplines while addressing questions that range from the purely local to regional, national and international contexts, provides a model for creating research designs in heritage archaeology. But creating research designs is one thing, evaluating them is quite another.

In the academic context research designs are evaluated in the grant application process and through the publication of peer-reviewed research. In circumstance of peer-review of publication, the growth of knowledge is fostered through criticism and fearless analysis, and there is no doubt that such evaluations actually occur. However a close analysis of the discourse of contemporary archaeological theory demonstrates that this process of formal evaluation through the publication and open discussion of research findings is happening with much less frequency. There are many reasons for this, but perhaps the one of greatest concern is a view (now quite popular among adherents to a variety relativist epistemologies) that the value of theories and perspectives should not be judged on their capacity to be verified or even assessed with respect to a body of empirical data. Thus an argument that a certain distribution of material culture is indicative of a certain social process or structuring principle might well persist in certain parts of the profession even when it might be logically invalid or not supported by empirical data. The impact of relativism has exacerbated a declining commitment to intense analyses of artefact assemblages in academic archaeology, because the high cost and long timeframe of such analyses has been thought to decrease chances of success with applications to grant bodies.

These are matters of serious concern in academic circles, but they flow through into the realm of archaeological heritage management as well. Here research designs are rarely, if ever, evaluated because the capacity for empirical evaluation frequently does not exist. Naturally this does not mean that archaeologists working in this context lack the skill or the knowledge to do so. What they lack is money and time. In practice the very large sums of money required to undertake detailed analyses of major urban assemblages are rarely available, and heritage managers appear to be content with a report and a catalogue that may or may not have its quality assessed. Neither of these deliverables is in any way a sufficient basis on which to evaluate the quality of research designs, nor are they (particularly in the case of large and complex sites) a sufficient mitigation of the impact of development.

On this basis it would not be too great an exaggeration to contend that in archaeological heritage management the purpose of research design is to sometimes create a space where descriptive research can be undertaken in a way that leaves the theoretical underpinnings of the research untouched by an encounter with the empirical. Allied with this is the often implicit (but occasionally explicit) belief that 'future researchers' can undertake the task of analysis and, by extension, evaluation. The fact that if (by some miracle) this were to happen then the costs of such research are not borne by those who made money from the developments, or by those agencies who seem to insist that good heritage archaeology must take place within a research framework. Leaving aside work undertaken by self-funded students, the costs will have to be borne by the Australian tax payer, who might be rightly forgiven for asking whether quality research be undertaken in the absence of analysis and explicit systems of evaluation.

Thus the increasing problems noted with respect to the abstractions of theoretical archaeology apply with even greater force in archaeological heritage management. We are now used to research designs asking questions that reflect what is thought to be the cutting-edge of theoretical archaeology. Close analysis of those research designs demonstrates that in many cases little or no chance of answering such questions exist, either because the appropriate methodologies are absent or they are so contested.

This is an entirely unhealthy situation. While documents such as the PHALMS report espouse the virtues of research design and regional research frameworks, and even innovate by developing structures that build evaluation into the archaeological process, the funding and management of such evaluations is still an open question. Collaborative research between academic and heritage management archaeologists of the kind that has happened on the Commonwealth Block is one way of demonstrating the benefits that might flow from using detailed archaeological and historical analysis to close the circle from research design, excavation, and the production of a catalogue. This can only be useful, but in the end the commitment to quality heritage archaeology must lead managers as well as practitioners to develop funding and management strategies that will address the very serious issues that confront us. Fixing the same problem in the academic context is a challenge outside our present purpose.

Recent archaeological testing on previously unexcavated sections of the Commonwealth Block (Howell-Meurs et al. 2001) has confirmed the existence of deposits of similar complexity and importance to those originally revealed by McCarthy (1989). The excavation of these remaining deposits (and the related investigation into the relevant documentary sources) has the clear potential to make a major contribution to urban historical archaeology at the local, national and international scales. However its most fundamental contribution will be towards developing a clearer statement of the social, cultural and scientific significance of the place, and through this to enhance its understanding by the people of Melbourne. There is already good evidence for the power of historical archaeology to do this. As a result of research at Little Lon the Museum of Melbourne was able to develop a major interpretive display based on the site that forms an integral part of a major exhibition *The Melbourne Story*. Thus a related research goal at Little Lon was to leverage these forms of interpretation and communication into a more comprehensive program for managing urban archaeological heritage in Melbourne and other places (see AlSayyad 2001; Ashworth and Tunbridge 2000; Orbasli 2000).

Thus far Murray and Mayne had published only that research specifically relating to patterns of residence and assemblage composition in the Casselden Place area of the site. Undertaking the re-analysis of Little Lon was a particularly arduous task. It took nearly three years of painstaking analysis to give Murray and Mayne the opportunity (which was denied McCarthy) to change our understanding of the distribution of material culture across the site. Nowhere has this been more dramatic than in Casselden Place.

These data had allowed Murray and Mayne to detect counter-intuitive patterns in the historical archaeology of Little Lon. Making sense of those patterns, in the context of clear limits being set by the structural properties of the Casselden Place record as it has been re-constructed by them, is an ongoing issue. One of the great surprises of the detailed analysis was the homogeneity of specific domestic assemblages (and the real possibility that spatial distribution is also homogenous between the houses in Casselden Place), in a context which the records quite clearly show as having been occupied by a number of different tenants over the period between 1851 and 1880. Defining the meanings of the assemblage homogeneity raises significant questions about consumption and production of domestic material culture in the 19th century.

An Overview of Land Use in the Casselden Place Development

Little Lonsdale Street

On the eastern side of Leichhardt Street, at 53–55 Little Lonsdale Street [McCarthy Location 85] an apparently late 19th-century two-storey red brick building stands on the site of an earlier hotel. Opened as the Governor Bourke Hotel in 1848, it was renamed the British Hotel in 1883 and changed again to the Auckland Hotel, before ceasing trading in the middle of the decade. The building was occupied thereafter as two separate properties until combined into the one business in 1924 as Samuel Grinblat's furniture factory. Both premises had been used from the mid-1880s by a succession of Chinese cabinetmakers. Number 53 Little Lonsdale Street was used as a Chinese restaurant between 1907 and 1918. Number 55 Little Lonsdale Street functioned as a Chinese general store from 1911 until 1923.

The last Chinese occupiers were the cabinet makers Wah Way & Co in 1930. The property stood vacant during the Great Depression, was occupied by H. Burge Bros (furniture manufacturers) in 1934, by C.R. Mackenzie (an upholstering company) in 1935–1939, by Hanson & Bricknell (pattern makers) between 1940 and 1947, and by Brownrigg & Henderson (upholsterers) in 1950.

Next door, at 49–51 Little Lonsdale Street [McCarthy Location 84], a furniture factory was built c.1905 on the site of several 1850s brick houses. It was occupied until 1941 by Chinese cabinet makers, and was used thereafter as a sheet metal works. Alongside, at 47 Little Lonsdale Street [McCarthy Location 83] a store yard operated throughout the 19th and well into the 20th centuries. A cabinet making workshop was built here during the mid-1920s, and was replaced by a municipal electrical sub station in the late 1940s. At 41 Little Lonsdale Street next door, on corner of Little Lonsdale and Little Leichhardt Streets [McCarthy Location 81], two brick houses can be traced back to the 1850s. The rear house [McCarthy Location 81B], listed as 29 Little Leichhardt Street, was occupied until 1936.

The former Oddfellows Hotel, standing at the corner of Little Lonsdale Street and Little Leichhardt Street [McCarthy Location 80], is amongst the oldest surviving hotels in Melbourne. It is one of only a handful of early city hotels whose exteriors have not been substantially modified by later renovations. The former hotel, with its slanting entrance doorway at the Little Leichhardt Street corner, in fact only occupies part of the property. The building's easternmost section was constructed and occupied in 1849 by a carpenter, Henry Charles Wills, and initially consisted of a two-roomed house with a carpenter's yard. Wills duplicated the house in 1850 to form a single-storey rowhouse pair of two-roomed houses. The pair has been cited as the oldest example of its type in Central Activities District. Second-storey additions were built in 1852. The second of the pair was absorbed into the Oddfellows Hotel, but the original dwelling – although structurally indistinct from the hotel – remained functionally separate (and was listed as such in post office directories until 1910). It was used for a time as a boarding house, and from the late 1890s onwards was tenanted by Chinese cabinet makers. Wills extended his original property west to Little Leichhardt Street in 1853, erecting a large two-storey stuccoed building which was licensed in September 1853 as the Oddfellows Hotel. The hotel was delicensed in 1912 and the entire property sold to a well-known merchant, Cheok Hong Cheong. The buildings were used thereafter as a Chinese cabinet making business until 1929. They lay vacant as the Great Depression worsened, reopened as a café in 1931, and were again empty during 1935. This volatility was to persist. The premises reopened as a Chinese furniture factory in 1936, but again stood vacant at the end of the decade. It operated as a café in 1940, and is listed as 'confectioner' in the following year. It was again empty in 1943. The property was acquired by the Commonwealth in 1948.

Three former factory buildings occupy the remainder of Little Lonsdale Street to the intersection with Spring Street. The first of these [McCarthy Locations 76–77] adjoins the Oddfellows Hotel, and extends to Gorman Alley. This red-brick factory building, now renovated as a childcare centre, was part of Lugton and Sons' engineering business, which expanded south across the entire block to Lonsdale Street between the 1860s and the First World War. Alexander Lugton, an engineer, bought the western portion of the present property in the early 1860s. It consisted of an early 1850s brick house and bakery. Lugton initially leased this property, and in 1865 bought the adjoining corner property siding Gorman Alley. This consisted of another gold-era brick house, corner shop, and slaughterhouse with sheds. Lugton remodelled it into an engineering workshop and forge in 1866. After purchasing the adjoining rear properties in Gorman Alley during the 1880s, the Lugton family company remodelled the two Little Lonsdale Street properties into one large engineering and boilermaking factory in the early 1890s. The family did not live in the neighbourhood they were so markedly changing, but in pleasant suburban Fairfield. The company extended their business through to Lonsdale Street shortly before the First World War, when it bought the vacant brothels of the late Madame Brussels at 32–34 Lonsdale Street and at the rear of Casselden Place. The Lugton family wound up their engineering business in the mid-1920s, and the Little Lonsdale Street factory was thereafter occupied by Chinese furniture manufacturers until the early 1930s. It stood vacant during the height of the Great Depression, and was used as a marble sheeting works from 1934 until 1940, when it became Gloria Knitting & Underwear Mills. This clothing business still occupied the building when it was resumed by the Commonwealth.

Next door to the former Lugton factory, and extending between Gorman Alley and Casselden Place, is another 19th-century factory building [McCarthy Location 75]. A small brick house was built here in 1854 and became a butcher's premises late in the decade. Alexander Lugton established his engineering works here from 1860 until 1866, when he moved to the other side of Gorman Alley. The property was then occupied by a tinsmith business, and from 1870 was rented to Joseph Porta, who set up a bellowmaking factory. Porta had migrated from Birmingham, lured by the gold rush, in 1851, and during the later 1850s and 1860s tried his hand at farming. As the bellowmaking business expanded, Porta constructed the present two-storey brick and stucco building across the full width of the block during the latter 1870s. He became a close friend of Alexander Lugton, and in the early 1880s resettled his family from the inner suburb of Fitzroy to leafier Alphington near his friend Lugton.

Joseph and his two sons relocated their business to still larger premises on the other side of Casselden Place in the mid-1880s. They sublet the vacated building, which became a chemical factory for the remainder of the decade. Chinese cabinetmakers occupied it from the mid-1890s until 1936. Thereafter it was used by a motor accessories manufacturer until the mid-1940s, and became an engineering works from 1946 until its resumption by the Commonwealth. It was subsequently leased by Amal Electrix Company.

The third industrial building – a single-storey red-brick factory [McCarthy Locations 63, 67] that extends along Little Lonsdale Street between Casselden Place and the former Griffin Lane (which now provides car access to parking beneath the new Commonwealth office block at 2 Lonsdale Street) – was built in 1922 as W.H. Blakley's engineering works. A blacksmith's works had occupied the easternmost portion of the property from the late 1870s, and in 1883 Porta and Sons built a new workshop on the site. Joseph Porta senior died in 1898, but his sons continued the bellowmaking business here until 1920. The western portion of the property, extending down to Casselden Place, had been occupied since the mid-1850s by a small brick house and a stone-built corner shop. They comprised the most valuable property in the immediate neighbourhood when first built, but their social status gradually deteriorated. Chinese tenants moved in early in the 20th century. The buildings were torn down when Blackley's engineering factory was built in 1922–1923. This large scale and sophisticated factory continued to operate here until the property was resumed by the Commonwealth.

Spring Street

Standing on the corner of Little Lonsdale and Spring Streets is the former Elms Family Hotel [McCarthy Location 62]. The present building, a two-storey red-brick hotel, was built by Emma Elms in 1907. It was the only neighbourhood hotel to survive the strict licensing laws passed early in century and still be operating after the First World War. The present hotel building stands on the site of much earlier structures. On the very corner, a hotel was built in 1849 and licensed in following year as the Old Governor Bourke Hotel. George Elms took over the licence in 1881, and after buying the property, changed its name to the Elms Family Hotel in 1887. As the Elms Family Hotel expanded, it incorporated the adjoining properties south along Spring Street and west to Griffin Lane at the rear.

Next door to the Elms Family Hotel stands the former convent and mission hall of the Sisters of the Community of the Holy Name [McCarthy Location 59]. Whereas Casselden Place has been misrepresented as symbolising the outcast lives of Melbourne's slum denizens, the Spring Street Mission has been cited – more accurately – as a symbol of the bourgeois social reform movement which sought to civilize away the imagined infamies of Little Lon. A brick house had stood at 261 Spring Street since the early 1850s. It was remodeled as a hall in 1876, and became a dancing academy. The hall was used in the late 1880s as a cigar factory, but fell vacant during the Great Depression of the early 1890s. In 1894, as the activities of the Mission to the Streets and Lanes expanded in Little Lonsdale Street, the Sisters rented the former Spring Street dancing academy as a Mission Hall. The Church of England bought the Spring Street hall in 1904, and in 1913 incorporated it into a new three-storey mission convent designed by architects Bates, Peebles and Smart, which was one of Melbourne's oldest and most successful architecture firms. An imposing new red-brick facade was built, and to the original hall was added a chapel, offices, bedrooms, dining room, and sanctuary. The additions extended the Mission north along Spring Street – incorporating the adjoining property at 265 Spring Street – to the Elms Family Hotel.

The new Mission was a centre for church outreach, hosting bible and Sunday school classes (and in so doing became the founding place of both the Greek Orthodox and Syrian Orthodox Churches). It also became a community focus for the surrounding neighbourhoods. In addition to running the St George's elementary school, the Sisters operated a dispensary and ran mothers meetings at Spring Street, and allowed the hall to be used as a meeting place for boys' and girls' clubs, scouts, a choir and brass band. The Sisters established a new Mission in nearby Fitzroy in 1957, following the Commonwealth's acquisition of the Spring Street building in 1948.

Lonsdale Street

Nos 32–36 Lonsdale [McCarthy Location 44–46] are the site of Madame Brussels' principal brothel. Brussels was described in the *Truth* newspaper during 1906 as 'the worst and wickedest woman in Melbourne'. Her main business premises were at 32–36 Lonsdale Street, on the site of the existing triple-fronted brick terrace alongside the towering Casselden Place Commonwealth office block. Lonsdale Street, and Brussels' properties in particular, were the centre of Melbourne's highclass prostitution market. She bought 32 Lonsdale Street in 1880 and leased and eventually purchased its neighbours, retaining them till her death in July 1908.

Born Caroline Baum in Germany in 1851, she was variously described as Mrs Hodgson – after her first husband – and as Mrs Caroline Pohl, after her 1895 marriage to Jacob Pohl, a German engineer.

Brussels was targeted in 1889 by moral crusaders led by evangelist Henry Varley and the Salvation Army's Colonel James Barker, who were intent on driving prostitution out of the city. However, in a crowded court room battle it was Brussels who triumphed. She and neighbouring brothel owners were again brought to court in 1898, but again Brussels survived. She was prosecuted once more in 1906. Strict new legislation the following year paved the way for a final crack down on the Lonsdale Street prostitution trade in 1908. But by July, in any case, Brussels was dead. Her Lonsdale Street property was bought and rebuilt c. 1918 by the engineering company Lugton and Sons. It was retained by the Lugton family until resumed by the Commonwealth, and was used as a printing works by the National Press and Keating Wood P/L.

The adjoining two-storey building at 38–40 Lonsdale Street [McCarthy Location 43] stands on the site of a wood and coal yard that operated until the late 1870s. It was replaced by a factory, which was recycled from the mid-1880s until the early 1890s as the Scots Church Society District Hall. It was occupied in 1893 by the Central Methodist Mission's Relief Department, as a clearing house for the destitute during the Great Depression of the 1890s. After the Mission relocated to George Lane, the building was occupied until 1916 by Chinese cabinetmakers. An upholstering business occupied the building until the mid-1920s, a tyre repairer until the early 1930s, and a rubber manufacturer until 1941. Between 1943 and 1950 the building was used as the office of the distinguished architectural firm of L.M. Perrot & Partners.

The former Black Eagle Hotel stands next door at 42–44 Lonsdale Street [McCarthy Location 42], on what was once the eastern corner of Little Leichhardt Street. It comprises a pair of gabled row houses built in 1850. It has been described as the most intact pre-gold rush hotel in Melbourne, and as perhaps the oldest surviving hotel in the Central Activities District. The pair were built by William Kennon, a stonemason, who purchased the site in the first land sales late in 1847. He lived here from 1848 in one of earliest buildings to be erected in the area. Kennon's two surviving row houses were licensed as the Black Eagle Hotel in April 1850. The hotel was closed at the end of 1908 as a result of the campaign to reduce the number of hotels in Melbourne. It was used thereafter as a lodging house until 1914, as a Chinese furniture factory until 1919–1920, and thereafter until 1977 as a printing works.

The remainder of the Lonsdale Street boundary to the study area has been cleared of buildings. Number 46 Lonsdale Street, which stood on the western corner of Little Leichhardt and Lonsdale Streets [McCarthy Location 34], was occupied by a brick shop and house that had been built in the 1850s. The property was used as a grocery until early 1880s, and was thereafter occupied by a tailor until the late 1890s. The property was then used by Chinese cabinetmakers until 1916, and again from 1922 until 1932. They were replaced by a Chinese timber merchant who ran a business here until 1938. It was taken over by Plywoods & Furniture Timbers P/L, which continued to operate here until the Commonwealth property resumptions.

Number 48 Lonsdale Street [McCarthy Location 33B] comprised another brick shop and house, also built in the 1850s. A butcher operated here from the late 1850s to the early 1870s, and was followed by a series of short-term small businesses until Chinese cabinetmakers moved in during the mid-1880s and remained until 1930. A leadlight manufacturer operated here 1934–1950. Next door, at 50–52 Lonsdale Street [McCarthy Location 33A], a bowling alley operated during the mid-1850s. In 1872 a brick butcher's shop was built to replace the older butcher's premises next door, and operated until 1927–1928. The building was then occupied by a Chinese cabinetmaker until 1935, and from 1936 to 1946 by a Chinese herbalist. During the late 1940s the building was occupied by an engineering business and then textile manufacturers. Another early 1850s brick house and shop stood alongside at 54 Lonsdale Street [McCarthy Location 32]. It had originally been occupied by a shoemaker, and during the 1860s by a draper. A German tobacconist and importer occupied the property from the late 1880s until 1909, and until the First World War it was used by an Italian underwear manufacturer. It was listed thereafter in post office directories as 'confectioner'.

Number 56 Lonsdale Street [McCarthy Location 31B] comprised a small brick two-storey row shop with residence above. It had been built c. 1872, together with the adjoining property at 58 Lonsdale Street, replacing a timber yard that had operated since the 1850s. Lebanese shopkeepers lived here during the 1890s and early 1900s. It is listed as 'confectioner' in 1912–1920 and again from 1936–1937 until the Commonwealth resumption. Chinese cabinetmakers had occupied it between 1922 and 1928, and during the early 1930s it was occupied first by an electrical engineer and then by a soap manufacturer. The identical property next door at 58 Lonsdale Street [McCarthy Location 31A] housed a tobacconist until the late 1880s, and thereafter a succession of small businesses. Lebanese migrant bootmaker Joseph Malouf, his wife Sadie, and their eight children lived here from 1902 to 1937. It was then used by a printer between 1939 and 1946, and by a rubber manufacturer during the late 1940s. Number 60 Lonsdale Street [McCarthy Location 30], on the eastern corner of Leichhardt Street, is the site of a wooden cottage that was built during the late 1840s. It was replaced in the mid-1850s by a brick and stone house and shop. It functioned as a boarding house during the late 1850s, and was used by a general dealer during the 1860s, and by a draper during the 1870s. A furniture mart operated here during the early 1880s, and a grocery later in the decade. Lebanese immigrants settled here during the early 1890s. They ran a fruiterers' business until 1916, and a drapery and importing business until 1924. Post office directories list the property as 'confectioner' in 1925–1929, and again in 1935–1947. It was identified as a Chinese Club in 1930, and labeled 'Italians' in 1931.

Leichhardt Street

No trace remains above ground of either street or the buildings that lined it. The 19th-century houses that once stood along the western side of Leichhardt Street were replaced during the early 20th century by George Warrington's expanding factory complex, which was in turn obliterated by construction of the Telstra headquarters late in the century. On the eastern side, three small brick cottages [McCarthy Locations 24A–24C] were built in the early 1850s behind the Oddfellows' Hotel. Chinese cabinetmakers moved into these dwellings at the turn of century. Two of them, 28–30 Leichhardt Street, still stood in 1950. To their south, a group of smaller brick cottages [McCarthy Locations 25–27] had been built during the mid-1850s, and were also tenanted by Chinese cabinetmakers from the end of the 19th century. Numbers 18–20 Leichhardt Street, single-storey buildings, continued to be occupied by Chinese cabinetmakers until the 1930s, and were thereafter used by a metal works, electrical manufacturers, and manufacturing chemists up to the 1950s. Numbers 8–14 Leichhardt Street, a row of four tiny two-storied brick houses at the end of the street [McCarthy Locations 28 & 29], were built c. 1854. These houses, occupied by Chinese cabinetmakers since the turn of the 20th century, still stood when the area was resumed by the Commonwealth.

Little Leichhardt Street (Tucker's Lane, Eagle Alley)

No buildings now stand along this former laneway, which ran between the Oddfellows' Hotel and the Black Eagle Hotel. Several small wooden houses were built on the lane's eastern side in the late 1840s, and survived until the early 1870s. Small brick houses also stood along this side of the lane. By the early 20th century, however, these had all been replaced by store yards and Chinese cabinetmaking factories. On the western side, a small single-story brick house was built [McCarthy Location 39] in the late 1840s. The McIlwaine family bought it in 1880 and lived there continuously until 1931. The building was then occupied by Chinese tenants, until it was absorbed by the adjoining wood carving business (R.J. Hutchens & Sons) in 1939, which was still operating here when the area was resumed by the Commonwealth a decade later. Further south along the lane, small wooden and brick homes that had been built in the late 1840s and early 1850s were all converted by the end of the century into Chinese cabinetmaking works. Three of these structures (Numbers 9, 13, 15) still stood in 1950.

McCarthy Locations 35–38 and 40–41 also appear to have had buildings standing on them for the majority of the target time period, but insufficient documentary research has been undertaken to establish patterns of occupancy. This will be a fundamental goal of the new round of documentary research spawned by the project.

Gorman Alley

Several wooden houses were built along Gorman Alley during the 1850s, and were absorbed into Lugton's expanding engineering works as the century progressed [McCarthy Locations 78–79]. The rear entrance to Brussels' brothel stood at the end of the alley.

RESEARCH PRINCIPLES

Our research design rested on three elements which are briefly described: concept, method and application. The specific research questions that are listed below were one means by which Murray and Mayne could provide a clear link between the ideas we had about the value and significance of Little Lon, and the information archaeologists are likely to recover from the excavation of the site and the analysis of its artefact assemblage.

Concept

The task at Little Lon is to imaginatively reconstruct a vanished community. This is not an act of reconstruction. Our task, rather, is to use avaialible archaeaological and documentary in an attempt to understand a world which has vanished from view. Historical archaeologists cannot do so by arbitrarily imposing our own meanings and scales of significance, in order to achieve intelligibility on our terms and thereby claim 'this is really how it was'. Instead they must begin with the ambiguities and discontinuities of the evidence that is available to us, and puzzle over the historical contexts into which such evidence once fitted. This conceptual approach has been termed ethnographic by Mayne. It integrates history, archaeology, and anthropology.

Ethnography is grounded in fine-grained descriptions of particular people in particular times and places. For Mayne and Lawrence (1998) an ethnography of place, by integrating the interpretation of material data from particular home sites with family reconstitution analysis of their occupants, provides a matrix of household case studies upon which interpretation of the broader archaeological record from the entire excavation can proceed. The life stories provide pegs to sustain an engaging narrative that draws associations between particular lives and the broader archaeological record for which such individual matching is not possible. Equally important, they act as controls against which to check that the contextualisations historical archaeologists fashion at a more general level of analysis for material data of indeterminate ownership are in accord with this matrix of known lives. Our arguments thus proceed from particular interpretations to broader scales of analysis, the particular continually mediating (and in turn being tested by) our identification of broader associations and patterns in the full historical record.

Method

Material evidence must drive interpretation, rather than simply providing another set of data that is subjected to, rather than reformulating, prevailing historical questions and emphases. This requires a re-examination of familiar historical sources in the light of new research questions that are suggested from studying archaeological evidence. It also requires detailed interrogation of additional documentary data which are unfathomable without the specific clues and queries that are brought to them from analysis of the material evidence. These intersections between archaeology and history must be played out both during the excavation phase and post-excavation analysis.

Hypotheses and conclusions must be tested comparatively. How do findings from the study area compare with those from other sites at Little Lon such as Casselden Place and Cumberland Place? How do they compare with those from the range of Sydney sites being reinvestigated by Murray in the Archaeology of the Modern City project, and overseas? What synergies thereby emerge about the material and cultural landscapes of poor neighbourhoods and households in big cities? Interpretation thus proceeds from the particular to the general, rather than by starting with universalist and totalising perspectives about urban poverty which are then imposed upon particular places. By asking questions about context and comparison as one studies particular sites one is able to pose and answer bigger questions about social class, gender, and ethnicity in poor neighbourhoods.

Application

Little Lon is not an 'innocent' research assignment. There are six influential overlays which together have fundamentally conditioned both the nature of the site today and historical understanding of it. In order to reach a balanced historical understanding of the study area it is essential that one questions and possibly contradicts these overlays and the clichés embedded in them. However their influence is too entrenched for them altogether to be displaced, so one must work through and beyond them in order to develop alternative research questions that reveal the more complicated actualities of Little Lon.

• 'A Bridge to the Past'

Archaeology fascinates the general public. It seems to connect the present day to how it 'really was' in the past. Previous urban archaeology projects in Australia, such as the 1987–1988 excavations at Little Lon, Paddy's Markets in Sydney 1990, the 1994 'Big Dig' in 'The Rocks', or the 2000 Camp Street excavations at Ballarat, all generated enormous community interest and involvement. These digs were largely underwritten by public statute and by the good will of public authorities. Levels of public interest and support are conditional. They carry a legitimate expectation that the results of these projects will be built into accessible and credible histories. The problem to date is that archaeology (with a notable exception being the Cumberland and Gloucester Street excavations) has rarely fed into public history outcomes. The challenge facing our project is to demonstrate that the seamless application of archaeology and history can take us beyond such historical stereotypes, and reveal the vanished community that was Little Lon.

• 'Earlier is Better'

Little Lon is an artefact of the late-19th and early-20th centuries. Although the uncovering of material evidence about pre-European and early colonial settlement would be welcome, it is unlikely and should not drive excavation strategies and laboratory analysis. Over a century and a half of intense European land use have eroded the physical evidence of Aboriginal occupation. The continuous operations of the land and property market are likely also to have erased most European inscriptions upon the land before the gold rushes. Historical archaeologists should be alert for the unexpected, but they must also conduct analysis in ways that will answer research questions that we know can be addressed through the archaeological and historical data linked directly to this site. Analysis should therefore concentrate upon the third quarter of the 19th century (when this city district was first intensively settled, and to which most archaeological evidence to date relates); the final quarter of the century (when the first generation of residents were replaced by newcomers, and when some historians suggest a stable working-class community was replaced by a culture of poverty); and the first third of the 20th century (during which time multicultural diversity became more pronounced, and the precinct unravelled as a residential community).

• 'At the Bottom of the Pile'

In public understanding, Little Lon was a community 'at the bottom of the pile'. It was a slum. This perception conditioned public policy, and thereby drove the slum clearance programs which bulldozed much of the study area and dispersed its people. Little Lons' reputation as a slum continues to condition historical understanding of the precinct. Little Lonsdale Street was represented in middle-class discourse since the late 19th century as 'the heart of slumdom'. C. J. Dennis tapped this convention, and further entrenched it, when – in his best-selling *The Songs of a Sentimental Bloke* (1915) and *The Moods of Ginger Mick* (1916) – his verses allowed readers to imagine Little Lon as a marker of the chasm which supposedly separated the lawns and newly built bungalows of the suburban Australian mainstream from 'the slums o' town'. Dennis' Little Lon was a shadowy and foreign territory of simmering violence where low-life brutes 'deals it out wiv bricks an' boots'. A 'slum war', often characterised by its promoters as a crusade to assert modernism and moralism, drove residence from central city. Starting in the 1880s, it gathered momentum before the First World War. In State Parliament, a Select Committee into Housing was appointed in 1913, and in 1914 was succeeded by a Royal Commission on the Housing of the People in the Metropolis. Meanwhile the City Council responded to awakening community concerns by enforcing its by-laws against houses 'unfit for human habitation'.

The anti-slum drive resumed with renewed strength after the First World War. F. Oswald Barnett led a new slum crusade in the early 1930s, leading to the establishment of the Victorian Housing Commission at the end of the decade with Barnett as one of its commissioners. By then, however, the crusaders' focus was shifting away from the central city – where the battle had essentially been won – to the adjoining ring of working-class inner suburbs. It was therefore as something of a mopping-up operation that the *Sun* newspaper, in 1943, unveiled plans for a 'slum penetrating' scheme – featuring a grand new civic centre and wide new streets – which would finally obliterate Little Lon. The *Sun* restated its ambition in 1947, promoting 'a Vision Splendid' of towering government offices, shopping precincts, and an underground railway in the city's north-eastern core. In 1948 the Commonwealth Government compulsorily acquired the blocks on either side of Little Lonsdale Street, from Latrobe Street in the north to Lonsdale Street in the south, and from Spring Street in the east to Exhibition Street in the west. Most of the northern block was bulldozed in the late 1950s and 1960s to make way for an government office tower. The rest of the block was cleared in the 1970s for a Telstra telephone exchange building. To the south of Little Lonsdale Street, demolition and redevelopment carved a similar swathe. This process was capped by the construction in the 1990s of huge tower blocks at Little Lon's eastern and western ends: Casselden Place Commonwealth Government Offices, and the Telstra headquarters.

In Sydney, archaeologists and historians have overturned conventional historical representations of the 'Rocks ... as a pestilential "slum"' in which poverty, disease, filth and immorality went hand-in-hand. Archaeological excavation at Foley Square, in New York City's lower Manhattan, has likewise presented vignettes of working-class households which fly in the face of Dickensian characterisations of Five Points as a notorious slum. In West Oakland, California, once marginalised as an immigrant slum, a rich neighbourhood history is being pieced together that combines oral history, architectural studies, archaeology, and archives research. Combining archaeological analysis and historical methods of family reconstitution, Murray and Mayne reached similar conclusions from intensively studying Casselden Place in the Little Lon area.

The Little Lon study area has provided an opportunity to test and elaborate upon these findings. What was the urban fabric of this place like, and how did it change through time? What patterns of occupation and property ownership are evident across time? To what extent was this precinct really singled out by municipal sanitary inspectors and the police? Do arguments about the emergence of an entrenched 'underclass' and 'culture of poverty' in Melbourne match the evidence from this site? Are the clues to homeliness, neighbourliness, and 'community' that were identified at Casselden Place and Cumberland Place matched or contradicted here?

- **'Brotheldom'**

Little Lon is remembered not only a notorious slum but as a debauched 'red light' district. This misrepresentation was pioneered by 19th-century evangelists. The Church of England's Mission to the Streets and Lanes began in Little Lon during 1885, with the establishment of a mission house run by lay sisters in Little Lonsdale Street. This was the genesis of the mission convent of the Sisters of the Community of the Holy Name. The Roman Catholic Church was also active in the neighbourhood. Sister Mary McKillop started a slum mission in Latrobe Street in 1891, and opened the St Joseph's elementary school nearby on Little Lonsdale Street in 1897. A St Vincent de Paul Home also operated in Little Lonsdale Street. From 1927, the headquarters of the Melbourne City Mission were located on the corner of Little Lonsdale and Exhibition Streets. On the opposite corner, the Salvation Army had since 1897 run Hope Hall as a women's shelter and – as a large sign on the pavement outside announced – the 'Headquarters of Army Slum Work'. In 1910 the Army opened a Home for Women in Little Lonsdale Street, as a citadel from which its 'Slum Sisters' could mobilise their rescue missions to slumland's fallen women.

The Little Lon slum stereotype thus overlapped with the precinct's developing reputation as Melbourne's chief red-light district. That notoriety was cemented at the turn of the century as moral crusaders led by evangelist Henry Varley and Colonel James Barker of the Salvation Army targeted Madame Brussels, a brothel owner in the neighbourhood since 1876. Brussels' name was thereby established in popular consciousness by the time of her death in 1908 as 'one of the most notorious harlot-house keepers that Australia has ever seen or heard of'. The conflation of slum and brothel in common-sense understandings of Little Lon owed much to the sensationalism of city newsmakers. Not only was Little Lon the heartland of slumdom, it was also besmirched by the mass-circulation *Truth* newspaper as the 'Brotheldom of Melbourne'. The *Truth* styled Brussels the 'queen' of brotheldom, and linked her 'notorious' Lonsdale Street 'Bawdy House' to the 1891 disappearance of the Parliamentary ceremonial mace, which was rumoured to be have been displayed to brothel patrons in lewd caricatures of parliamentary procedures. By the early 1930s, as moral purity campaigns and slum abolitionism gathered pace, the *Truth* used Little Lon to highlight a police 'war' on vice that was launched by the First World War hero (and now Police Chief Commissioner) General Blamey. The newspaper tagged Little Lon 'the Street of Evil', and trumpeted that the *Truth*'s campaign for the wiping out of the city plague spot that has endured for so many years under the institutional name of '"Little Lon" has caused a sensation in the city.' The *Truth* thundered that 'Little Lonsdale St., Melbourne's Red Light district, is doomed.'

Historical hyperbole about the seamy side of Little Lon is entrenched. However it tells us nothing about the everyday lives of the majority of people who lived or worked in the district. It is therefore important that excavation and analysis of Brussels' brothel site in Lonsdale Street be undertaken with a sense of historical perspective rather than with an eye to shallow sensationalism. Brussels' long association with the study area is a significant element in the overall history of the neighbourhood, but there are many other elements equally as important which have not been emphasised by either archaeologists or historians. The Brussels site has a longer association with the printing industry than it does with prostitution, and its purchase by the Lugton business empire carried far greater social and economic consequences than did bourgeois bonking in the beds of Brussel's bawdy house. Two overlooked research questions relating to prostitution require attention. First, how absolute were the borders of discontinuity between the different social worlds that made up Little Lon? Second, how widespread and enduring an activity was brothel-based prostitution in the neighbourhood after establishments such as Brussels' had been closed? The over-representation of 'confectioners' (supposedly a pseudonym for brothel) in Lonsdale and Little Lonsdale Streets merits careful study.

• **Ethnic Ghetto**

Little Lon was described to the Royal Commission on the Housing of the People in the Metropolis as an enclave 'occupied by Assyrians, Italians, Indians and Chinese; there are no Europeans there'. It has been suggested that by the early 20th century, Little Lon had become amongst the most cosmopolitan neighbourhoods in Australia. This suggestion needs to be rigorously tested. Lebanese and, to a lesser extent, Italians did settle in the neighbourhood from the late 19th century. It is also now generally accepted that a significant Chinese presence was evident from the late 1890s. The incomplete archaeological records that survive from the first stage of excavations at Little Lon do not permit elaboration of this interesting theme. However analysis of post office directories suggests an overwhelming Chinese presence in the study area which persisted from c. 1900 into the 1930s. Is there an archaeological imprint of this Chinese presence? There is some basis for questioning this as remains are not numerous. As McCarthy (1990) observed in the Oddfellows Hotel, yard surfaces were paved, refuse was collected regularly for disposal off-site, and cesspits closed up when the sewerage was installed. Nonetheless it is important for us to ask how permeable were cultural and racial boundaries within the neighbourhood? Did Chinese cabinetmakers use Little Lon only as a workplace, or did they live here as well? To what extent did they participate in the reciprocal relationships of neighbourliness which characterised this community?

• **Marginality**

A slum is supposedly a marginal place; it is a place of inertia, obsolescence and decay. A slum is supposedly the antithesis both of the residential suburbs where responsible workers lived, and of the business inventiveness that underwrote city growth. Clear evidence of homeliness and neighbourliness at Casselden Place has already dented these characterisations. Indications that an extensive and enduring (if volatile) collection of small businesses existed in Little Lon further erodes the slum stereotypes, and need to be tested further. John Leckey (2005) has demonstrated that the study area also housed innovative, large-scale, and successful industrial businesses: for example Warringtons in Leichhardt Street, and the Lugton, Porta, and Blakley factories in Little Lonsdale Street. What are the implications of this finding? Does business entrepreneurialism at Little Lon disprove the slum stereotypes? Or does it highlight the fragmented, fractured, and discontinuous worlds that perhaps characterised the district? Was industry an outside phenomenon that intruded upon and unravelled the residential essence of Little Lon, or had it always been a core component of the district?

A Review of Archaeological Potential

Four separate excavation campaigns (briefly described in Chapters 3, 4 and 5 of this book) make it clear that Little Lon has very high (albeit quite uneven) archaeological potential.

Historical research, considered in conjunction with the McCarthy database and the findings by Andrew Long and Associates, suggests that the following locations should be the focus of careful stratigraphic recording (preferably 3D if the horizontal and vertical integrity of the deposits warrant it). The primary purpose of this will be to establish the structural properties of the archaeological record in areas of highest archaeological potential. From this determination will flow an understanding of the tolerance limits that can be placed on archaeological records that require a high degree of horizontal or vertical stratigraphic integrity, particularly those associated with linking particular occupants to particular archaeological records.

Leichhardt Street East Side
[McCarthy Locations 24–29]

Historical evidence suggests that most of the small brick cottages that were built along this side of the laneway during the 1850s survived to the mid 20th century. It is unclear, however, when houses were recycled as business premises, and to what extent the physical fabric of these properties was altered. Unambiguously, however, the entire area was occupied by Chinese cabinetmakers from the 1890s until the 1930s and beyond. Historical evidence suggests that the row of four two-storied brick houses at the end of Leichhardt Street [Locations 28 and 29] provides the most promising archaeological site along the laneway. They were built c. 1854 and survived into the 1950s.

Little Leichhardt Street

Several small wooden cottages were built along the lane's eastern side in the late 1840s, and small brick houses were added later. It appears that most or all of these structures had been replaced by Chinese furniture factories by the late 19th century. On the western side, the most promising site appears to be McCarthy Location 39, where a small single-story brick house was built in the late 1840s. The McIlwaine family bought it in 1880 and lived there continuously until 1931. Properties to the south of the McIlwaine site also hold archaeological potential; domestic structures of both wood and brick were built here during the 1840s and 1850s, and became Chinese cabinetmaking businesses late in the century. An intact (but to what extent modified?) streetscape survived here into the 1920s, and three of these structures still stood in the 1950s. As is the case at Little Leichhardt Street, this local neighbourhood had a heavy Chinese presence from the late 19th century into the 1930s.

Lonsdale Street
[McCarthy Locations 30–34]

It is unfortunate that high contamination levels compromise the archaeological potential of some of these locations, as this local neighbourhood has high historical significance. Most of its buildings survived from the 1850s into the 1950s, and witnessed an interesting sequence of domestic, business, and ethnic, and gender-specific imprints. There is a strong likelihood that prostitution took place over an extended period in several of these properties.

Lonsdale Street
[McCarthy Location 44–46]

This was the site of Madame Brussels, principal brothel, but it was also associated with a number of other significant occupiers, and Brussel's property was rebuilt at about the time of the First World War. This site is not to be dug but has been included here so that its archaeological and historical potential can be formally noted.

Little Lonsdale Street
[McCarthy Locations 81–85]

An interesting sequence of buildings and activities are evident in this block, but it is unclear from the historical record how disturbed the site is as a consequence of rebuilding.

Some Methodological Issues

Our basic analytical method will be to move through microscale analysis of particular sites and contexts, towards macroscale comparisons between places, be they communities or cities. This is not a linear process. Perspectives gained from comparison may also be applied at the particular level. At the core of the process lies the analysis of assemblages of artefacts rather than a more traditional focus on the historical potential of individual artefacts as objects of illustration.

Excavated collections of artefacts from the site will be analysed parallel to archival research into specific locations, which will become the basic units of analysis (as they were during research at the Cumberland and Gloucester Street site in Sydney). Our analytical strategies are founded on the creation of relational databases which contain precise information about artefacts and their contexts. Historical data, drawn from registers of births, deaths, marriages, wills, probates, inquests,

Post Office Directories, rate books, citizens lists and rolls, electoral rolls and land titles should make it possible to relate people, the material things they used and discarded, and the places they lived and worked. If it transpires (as it did in the re-analysis of the Casselden Place cottages by Murray and Mayne) that the structural properties of the archaeological records of these locations make it unlikely that we can make a convincing case to create such specific relationships, then less fine-grained comparisons of the kind reported by Murray and Mayne (2001, 2003) will be attempted.

Once analysis of the locations and their assemblages is complete, and the historical data (described below) have been collected, Murray and Mayne will integrate these data to produce an interpretive synthesis of location and its assemblage, and a synthesis of all the historical archaeology that has been undertaken at Little Lon will be a key deliverable of the project.

A Review of Historical Potential

Archival research undertaken in connection with the first phase of excavation at Little Lon (see McCarthy 1989), and subsequently extended and in some case corrected in the project run by Mayne and Murray (see e.g. 1999, 2001) and related research by Mayne and Lawrence (1998), demonstrates the wealth of archives directly related to Little Lon and the people who lived and worked there.

Significantly, for most of the questions that lie at the core of this research design to be answered a new round of detailed archival research will be required. There are two specific groups of tasks. First, to expand Mayne's family reconstitution database from Casselden Place, and targeted sites in Spring Street and Lonsdale Street. This will involve:
- review, validation and correction of Justin McCarthy's 19th-century database; Mayne's database on post office directories for the entire study area is complete for the period 1900–1950
- analysis of 20th century MCC ratebook records
- expansion of Mayne's records from MCC Citizens Rolls
- expansion of Mayne's records from Commonwealth electoral rolls
- expansion of Mayne's records from registrations of births, deaths and marriages
- expansion of Mayne's records from probate data.

The second group of tasks will be to consolidate research by Mayne on:
- VPRS police files
- MCC property condemnation files
- Citizen's Welfare Bureau (former Charity Organisation Society)
- Parliamentary Papers
- newspapers.

Specific Research Questions in Hierarchical Order

The very worrying situation where claims made in research designs about hypotheses and methodologies, and their links to the concerns of contemporary archaeological theory, either have not been or cannot be evaluated has already been discussed. Although the focus of our discussion was on the situation in archaeology conducted under the rubric of heritage management, Murray and Mayne were careful to point out that many of the same problems exist in the academic context – which might generally be presumed to be the primary source of interpretive perspectives for archaeology undertaken in *both* contexts.

The questions offered here and the interpretive perspectives discussed above are firmly grounded in an understanding that historical archaeology still has a very long way to go before it can (with confidence) demonstrate the veracity of many of its interpretive and methodological instruments. But what makes this current work at Little Lon unique in Australian historical archaeology is the opportunity of directly testing conclusions that Murray and Mayne have drawn from the re-analysis of another part of the same site. Thus while we cannot claim that all aspects of our research at Little Lon can be evaluated at this point, we do want to try to cast the net as broadly as possible.

Adopting a hierarchical approach to a statement of research objectives, as advocated in the PHALMS document (Godden Mackay Logan 2001), has an additional benefit in the present project. Here three types of questions can be readily distinguished:
- those that can be resolved directly through excavation
- those that can be resolved by a combination of excavation, the analysis of assemblages, the integration of previously analysed assemblages from Little Lon, and the integration of specific written documentary data
- those that will be primarily resolved through a combination of the analysis of assemblages, the integration of previously analysed assemblages from Little Lon, and the integration of written documentary data, both specific and generalised.

While it is not strictly true that this division represents a hierarchy of questions from simple to complex, there is a reasonable degree of fit.

The need for potentially higher levels of recording (the point proveniencing of artefacts on excavated surfaces within houses or in cesspits that are considered to have high levels of stratigraphic integrity) has already been discussed. Indeed the resolution of stratigraphic issues that have been such a constant feature of work at Little Lon might well require such an approach to be taken in areas of highest archaeological potential.

The fact that artefact analysis will proceed at the assemblage level based on a recording form that will allow direct comparison with the re-analysed database from Little Lon (deriving from the Mayne and Murray project), and that being developed by Penny Crook for the Archaeology of the Modern City Project has also been discussed.

The reconstruction of a vanished community remains the core goal of both archaeological and historical research. In order to achieve this, work should concentrate on two key periods: First, the 1850s–1870s. Historical research to date on family reconstitution at Little Lon, and archaeological analysis of cottage sites in Casselden Place, have provided a compelling picture of family formation and neighborliness during this time period. This research suggests that the neighborhood was largely residential, and comprised many young working-class Irish families. Many rented, but a significant number were home owners. Their surviving material culture does not reflect a 'culture of poverty' but a resilient working-class culture that was already actively accumulating mass consumption household and personal items. These findings have been echoed by studies elsewhere in Australia and overseas. Research on homesites in the neighbouring streets of Little Lon will further extend, test, and consolidate these findings.

Second, the 1880s–1890s. It is sometimes suggested by historians that suburbanisation during the 1880s, and economic depression during the 1890s, together with industrial encroachment throughout this time period, transformed Little Lon from a stable working-class community into an underworld of paupers, criminals, and deviants. The research findings by Mayne and Murray contradict these arguments. Research on the cottage and industrial sites along Leichhardt Street, Little Leichhardt Street, and Gorman Alley will clarify these issues. It will also test the suggestions made by Mayne and Murray about generational and ethnic succession in the district. Who replaced the Irish couples who had settled here during the 1850s and 1860s? Did their children, as young adults, form families of their own in the area, or did they move elsewhere? If, as Mayne and Murray suggest, they tended to move elsewhere, who replaced them? To what extent were homes replaced by factories (for example, Wharrington's, Lugton's, Porta's), and to what extent did Chinese, Lebanese, and Italians settle in the district during the 1880s and 1890s?

It is generally understood that during the course of the 19th-century patterns of production, consumption, work and residence changed across the Western world. Karskens has provided a detailed and nuanced analysis of life in 'The Rocks' area of Sydney that (as a result of the Cumberland and Gloucester Street excavations of the Sydney consultancy Godden and Mackay) remains a benchmark for understanding processes of change in urban settings in 19th-century Australia. Murray (1999) and Murray and Mayne (2000) have explicitly recognised the need for comparison between sites in Sydney and Melbourne to gain a clearer understanding of the genesis and development of urban communities.

Specific local research questions addressed in this excavation relating to the nature of archaeological assemblages in working-class domestic contexts thus have more general application at national and international levels. The consequences of differential patterns of domestic residency for assemblages of material culture recovered from domestic sites is one significant issue. The same applies to questions raised about our interpretation of patterning in those assemblages as being related to gender, ethnicity, and social standing. A concern with understanding the consequences of mass production, improved transport and distribution technologies, and mass consumption unites historical archaeologists across the Western world.

Further archaeological and historical research on the adjoining areas of Leichhardt Street, Little Leichhardt Street, and Gorman Alley will provide a more reliable account of these processes to be developed for Little Lon that can then be more readily compared and contrasted with databases and contexts from Sydney, Cape Town, London and cities of comparable size and age in North America.

Linking Research Questions to Datasets and Methods

All questions are linked to the creation of a site database through the detailed recording of locations and contexts, the creation of a catalogue, the prosecution of archival research, the comparison with previously excavated and analysed assemblages from other parts of Little Lon. Our focus is on the period 1860–1920, a period during which there were considerable changes in the vectors of site formation – cesspits giving way to sewerage, the establishment of regular refuse collections, demolition of houses to be replaced by factories, major changes in the ethnic composition of the community, and challenges to the legitimacy of life at Little Lon through the work of religious groups, social reformers, and governments.

Group 1: Questions Answered by Excavation.

- Is the stratigraphic sequence previously noted at Little Lon repeated in this adjacent area?
- Are there sealed deposits such as cesspits that have clear vertical stratigraphic integrity?
- Are there deposits that exhibit either horizontal or vertical stratigraphic integrity?

This group of questions specifically relate to the need to determine the structural properties of the archaeological record of Little Lon. What is the level of disturbance? How does disturbance limit or constrain our capacity to interpret the archaeological record in terms of higher order questions (Groups 2 and 3)? Relevant data can potentially be obtained from any part of the site, but the primary goal of this group of questions is to establish the tolerance limits of interpretation. If there is evidence of severe disturbance on the site (as has been noted in previous excavations) then excavators need to establish whether the cultural layers at Little Lon need to be treated as a palimpsest (as a single analytical unit) or whether other strategies are possible.

Group 2: Specific questions answered by a combination of excavation, the analysis of assemblages, and the integration of written documentary data, all with respect to specific locations.

- Is it possible to discriminate between the assemblages created by earlier houses and those of later brick structures?
- Is it possible to discriminate between assemblages created by itinerant occupants of these houses as distinct from more settled patters of occupation noticed elsewhere on the site?
- Is it possible to confirm hypotheses concerning specific activity areas within each of the houses, that were noted in some houses in Casselden Place?

This group of questions specifically reflects the need to determine the relationship between structures and deposits of material culture that are found in and around them. Excavation should first establish the stratigraphic integrity of deposits and in those areas of high integrity, 3D recording should be adopted. Documentary research into specific locations will provide critical contextual data. Our hypothesis from the analysis of Casselden Place is that there is considerable stratigraphic ambiguity in the earliest (wooden house) phase of construction. At Casselden Place in the bulk of instances (excepting cesspits) to differentiate between assemblages on the basis of temporality. Murray and Mayne were also unable, counter-intuitively, to discriminate between assemblages located in houses occupied by itinerants and those by people, such as the Maloney's, who were longer-term residents. These hypotheses are best addressed in the excavation of McCarthy Locations 24–29 and 39, where patterns of occupancy very similar to those of Casselden Place appear likely from the documentary record. Information gained through answering this group of questions will allow us to address (during the analysis phase) the themes of poverty, marginality and ethnicity discussed above.

Group 3: General questions answered by a combination of the analysis of assemblages, and the integration of written documentary data, both specific and generalised.

- Is it possible to gain a clearer understanding of the relationships between domestic dwellings and 'industrial' buildings on the site during the mid-to-late 19th century?
- Can the dwelling places in these areas of the site be related to previously excavated structures so that we can gain a more general understanding of life in this neighborhood during the target period?
- Is it possible to offer a more detailed characterisation of ethnicity based on material culture (see Jones 1997; Lydon 1999)?
- Is it possible to gain a clearer understanding of what constitutes a domestic assemblages in inner-city contexts in Melbourne so that it might be compared with assemblages from sites of similar antiquity and location in Sydney and in other major cities of the Western world?

This group of questions reflect the need to gain additional information about specific locations at Little Lon through structured comparisons with other locations or areas on the site, other relevant sites in Melbourne, and other relevant sites in Australia and overseas. These are higher-order questions that will be effectively addressed in the analysis phase of the project. Comparisons can be made on the basis of assemblage structure, the presence of particular artefacts, the databases of residence and occupancy derived for Little Lon and other sites generally. They can assist us in addressing the themes of poverty, marginality and ethnicity and relevant data should be recovered from McCarthy Locations 24–29 and 39. If a way can be found of excavating and cataloguing the materials to be found in McCarthy Locations 30–34, excavators might also gain direct access to data relevant to a discussion of the evolution of Little Lon from a place of residence to one of work and limited residence.

Our expectation is that the analysis of assemblages derived from these new locations should provide data that will allow us to establish whether the patterns of residence, occupancy, ethnicity and community life Murray and Mayne had observed in other parts of Little Lon. If these patterns are confirmed then we believe that we will have a firmer basis for comparing Little Lon with other similar sites in other Western cities over the same time period. In this way we will gain a perspective on both the specificities of life in Little Lon and more general understandings of life in the modern city during the period 1860–1920.

CLOSING REMARKS

Understanding the archaeology of the modern city, whether it be in Australia or elsewhere, poses significant intellectual and financial challenges to archaeologists, and to those whose job is to manage the physical remains of this complex and ambiguous theatre of human action. For us the most significant challenge is to transform a task of site-clearance into a creative act, where the historical and cultural capital of the people of Melbourne is enhanced rather than reduced through the destruction of what is left to us from the period before 1950. In this sense our goal has to be both the acquisition of information about the place and the creation of knowledge through an intersection of new data with our existing frameworks of understanding. In this way the historical potential of Little Lon, which has been unfolding since the first excavations began very late in 1987, will be further realised.

Murray and Mayne began this discussion with some remarks about the need to develop structures and practices that should allow us to evaluate research designs and the many questions that archaeologists ask in them. Little Lon provides us with a rare opportunity to do this because historical archaeologists have the chance to follow up on issues raised by a re-analysis of the original McCarthy excavations undertaken by Mayne and Murray. That re-analysis was dogged by problems flowing from the post-excavation history of the excavation records and the assemblage. Clearly all of our efforts related to evaluating the performance of research designs will come to nothing if the integrity of those records and artefacts is not maintained well into the future.

ACKNOWLEDGEMENTS

I thank my co-autjor Alan Mayne for his significant input into the research design which is here re-presented in a slightly edited form.

REFERENCES

AlSayyad, N. (ed.), 2001. *Consuming Tradition, Manufacturing Heritage: Global Norms and Urban Forms in the Age of Tourism*. New York: Routledge.

Appadurai, A. 1986. *The Cultural Life of Things*. Cambridge: Cambridge University Press.

Ashworth, G. J. and J. E. Tunbridge, 2000. *The Tourist-Historic City: Retrospect and Prospect of Managing the Heritage City*. Oxford and New York: Pergamon.

Beaudry, M. C., L. J. Cook and S. A. Mrozowski, 1991. Artifacts and Active Voices: Material Culture as Social Discourse. In McGuire, R. H. and R. Paynter (eds.) *The Archaeology of Inequality: Material Culture, Domination and Resistance*, pp. 156–159, Oxford: Blackwell.

Brown-May, A. 1998. *Melbourne Street Life: The Itinerary of Our Days*. Melbourne: Australian Scholarly Publishing.

Davison, G. 1978. *The Rise and Fall of Marvellous Melbourne*. Melbourne: Melbourne University Press.

Davison, G., D. Dunstan and C. Mcconville (eds.), 1985. *The Outcasts of Melbourne: Essays in Social History*. Sydney: Allen and Unwin.

DeCunzo, L. and B. L. Herman (eds.), 1996. *Historical Archaeology and the Study of American Culture*. Winterthur, Delaware: Winterthur Museum.

Godden Mackay Pty Ltd and G. Karskens, 1999. *The Cumberland/Gloucester Streets Site, The Rocks, Archaeological Investigation Report*, 6 vols. Sydney: Godden Mackay Logan.

Godden Mackay Logan Pty Ltd, 2001. *Parramatta Historical Archaeological Landscape Management Study*. Report prepared for the NSW Heritage Office. Sydney: Godden Mackay Logan.

Godden Mackay Logan, La Trobe University and Austral Archaeology, 2004. Casselden Place, 50 Lonsdale Street, Melbourne: Archaeological Excavations – Research Archive. HV report collection no. 3916.

Howell-Meurs, J., C. Williamson and P. Davies, 2001. Casselden Place Development Phase 3. Testing Results, 2 vols. Unpublished report to Industry Superannuation Property Trust. Melbourne: Andrew Long and Associates.

Jones, S. 1997. *The Archaeology of Ethnicity*. London: Routledge.

Karskens, G. 1996. Crossing Over: Archaeology and History at the Cumberland/Gloucester Street Site, The Rocks, 1994–1996. *Public History Review* 5/6: 30–48.

Karskens, G. 1997a. *The Rocks: Life in Early Sydney*. Melbourne: Melbourne University Press.

Karskens, G. 1997b. The Dialogue of Townscape: The Rocks and Sydney 1788–1820. *Australian Historical Studies* 108: 88–112.

Karskens, G. 1999. *Inside The Rocks: The Archaeology of a Neighbourhood*. Sydney: Hale and Iremonger.

Karskens, G. and W. Thorp, 1992. History and Archaeology in Sydney: Towards Integration and Interpretation. *Journal of the Royal Australian Historical Society* 78(3–4): 52–75.

L'Anglais, P.-G. 1994. *La recherche archéologique en milieu urbain: d'une archéolgie dans la ville une archéolgie de la ville*. Québec: CELAT.

Lane, S. 1995. Archaeological Investigation of the Cottage at 17 Casselden Place, Melbourne. Unpublished report to the Heritage and

Environment Group, Australian Construction Services.

Leckey, J. 2005. *Low, Degraded Broots? Industry and Entrepreneurialism in Melbourne's Little Lon, 1860–1950*. Melbourne: Australian Scholarly Publishing.

Long, A., C. Williamson, M. Goulding and J. Howell-Meurs, 2001. Casselden Place Development Phase 3. Archaeological Planning Report. Unpublished report to Industry Superannuation Property Trustees. Melbourne: Andrew Long and Associates.

Lydon, J. 1999. *Many Inventions. The Chinese in The Rocks 1890–1930*. Melbourne: Monash Publications in History.

McCarthy, J. 1989. *Archaeological Investigation of the Commonwealth Offices and Telecom Corporate Building Sites. The Commonwealth Block, Melbourne*, 5 vols. Report to Department of Administrative Services and Telecom Australia, Melbourne, VIC.

McCarthy, J. 1990. Archaeological Investigation. Site B, the Black Eagle and Oddfellows Hotels, the Commonwealth Block, Melbourne Victoria, 2 vols. Unpublished report to the Department of Administrative Services.

Mayne, A. 1993. *The Imagined Slum*. Leicester: Leicester University Press.

Mayne, A. and S. Lawrence, 1998. An Ethnography of Place: Imagining Little Lon. *Journal of Australian Studies* 57: 93–107.

Mayne, A. and T. Murray, 1996. *Reading a Cultural Landscape: An Historical Archaeology of Melbourne*. Department of History, University of Melbourne and School of Archaeology, La Trobe University.

Mayne, A. and T. Murray, 1999. 'In Little Lon ... Wiv Ginger Mick': Telling the Forgotten History of a Vanished Community. *Journal of Popular Culture* 33(1): 63–77.

Mayne, A. and T. Murray, 2001. The Archaeology of Urban Landscapes: Explorations in Slumland. In Mayne, A. and T. Murray (eds.) *The Archaeology of Urban Landscapes: Explorations in Slumland*, pp. 1–7, Cambridge: Cambridge University Press.

Mayne, A., T. Murray and S. Lawrence, 2000. Historic Sites: Melbourne's Little Lon. *Australian Historical Studies* 31(114): 131–151.

Murray, T. 1999. *The Archaeology of the Modern City. Reanalysing Core Collections in Historic Sydney*. Department of Archaeology, La Trobe University.

Murray, T. and A. Mayne, 2001. Imaginary Landscapes: Reading Melbourne's Little Lon. In Mayne, A. and T. Murray (eds.) *The Archaeology of Urban Landscapes: Explorations in Slumland*, pp. 89–105, Cambridge: Cambridge University Press.

Murray, T. and A. Mayne, 2002. Casselden Place Development, Phases 1 and 2. Research Design. Unpublished report to Industry Superannuation Property Trust, Melbourne.

Murray, T. and A. Mayne, 2003. (Re)Constructing a Lost Community: Little Lon, Melbourne, Australia. *Historical Archaeology* 37(1): 87–101.

Orbasli, A. 2000. *Tourists in Historic Towns: Urban Conservation and Heritage Management*. London and New York: E. & F.N. Spon.

Potter, P. B. 1994. *Public Archaeology in Annapolis: A Critical Approach to History in Maryland's Ancient City*. Washington: Smithsonian Institution Press.

Schávelzon, D. 2000. *The Historical Archaeology of Buenos Aires: A City at the End of the World*. New York: Kluwer Academic.

Scott, E. M. (ed.), 1994. *Those of Little Note: Gender, Race and Class in Historical Archaeology*. Tucson: University of Arizona Press.

Staski, E. (ed.), 1987. *Living in Cities: Current Research in Urban Archaeology*. Pleasant Hill, California: Society for Historical archaeology.

Tarlow, S. and S. West (eds.), 1999. *The Familiar Past? Archaeologies of Later Historical Britain*. London: Routledge.

Yamin, R. 1996. Lurid Tales and Homely Stories of New York's Notorious Five Points. *Historical Archaeology* 32(1): 74–85.

Further Reading

Aston, M. and J. Bond, 2000. *The Landscape of Towns*. Alan Sutton.

Birmingham, J. 1990. A Decade of Digging: Deconstructing Urban Archaeology. *Australian Journal of Historical Archaeology* 8: 13–22.

Cantwell, A-M. and D. diZerega Wall, 2001. *Unearthing Gotham: The Archaeology of New York City*. Yale University Press.

Council of Europe, 1999. *Report on the Situation of Urban Archaeology in Europe*. Strasbourg: Council of Europe.

Funari, P., M. Hall and S. Jones (eds.), 1999. *Historical Archaeology: Back From the Edge*. London: Routledge.

Staski, E. (ed.), 1987. *Living in Cities: Current Research in Urban Archaeology*. Society for Historical Archaeology Special Publication No. 5.

Wall, D.D. 1994. *The Archaeology of Gender: Separating the Spheres in Urban America*. New York: Plenum Press.

Wall, D.D. and N. Rothschild, 1996. History and Archaeology of New York. In *Unearthed Cities: Edo, Nagasaki, Amsterdam, London, New York*. Tokyo Metropolitan Edo-Tokyo Museum.

Young, A.L. (ed.), 2000. *Archaeology of Southern Urban Landscapes*. Tucson: University of Arizona Press.

SOME WEBSITES OF INTEREST

The Five Points Site – a best-practice interpretation of the historical archaeology of a New York neighbourhood: r2.gsa.gov/fivept/fphome.htm

Río Nuevo Project (Tucson, Arizona) – the most exciting urban archaeology project in the south west: www.rio-nuevo.org/rionuevo

The City of Reno (Nevada) ReTRAC project – an excellent example of community projects in urban archaeology: www.usmayors.org/uscm/us_mayor_newspaper/documents/08_13_01/reno.asp see also www.retrac.org

The Archaeology of the National Constitution Center (Philadelphia PA) – see also the National Parks Service (USA) website: www.constitutioncenter.org/sections/news/releases/treasures.asp

City of York Urban Archaeology Database: www.york.ac.uk/depts/arch/yccweb/admin/uad/uad.htm

8
Little Lon and Museum Victoria: A Tale of Benign Neglect, Restoration and a Bright Future

Charlotte Smith

As custodian of the Little Lon[1] assemblage, Museum Victoria has always understood its capacity as a resource for storytelling. A selection of artefacts has informed two key displays at the institution's flagship site, Melbourne Museum, since its opening in 2001. 'Stories from a City: Little Lon' was a key display in the Australia Gallery, Melbourne Museum's first social history exhibition (Plate 8.1). 'Stories from a City: Little Lon' combined: excavated archaeological material; a recreated archaeological core; archaeological tools of trade; audio recordings of contemporary newspaper accounts, contemporary fiction and oral testimonies; and archival and contemporary images.

Evaluation conducted by Museum Victoria staff in 2005 showed that 'Stories from a City: Little Lon' was one of Melbourne Museum's most popular displays.[2] Visitors enjoyed learning about the unusual, interesting and colourful aspects of Melbourne's history. Many liked the sense of the city's 'dark side' as portrayed through personal stories: 'they appreciated the selection of archaeological material, the inclusion of drawers under cabinets that enabled them to see more finds from the excavations, and the insight into archaeologists' work. The combination of original stories, photographs and objects, with the physical representation of historical-archaeology methodology', was particularly well received (Smith and Tout-Smith 2010: 39).

In 2008 a new social history gallery, 'The Melbourne Story', opened at Melbourne Museum. 'Stories from a City: Little Lon' was replaced by a (re)creation of two cottages representative of those that populated the lanes of Little Lon in the 19th century (Plate 8.2) The weatherboard cottages' small, crowded, poorly lit rooms are dressed with a mixture of props and collection objects (i.e. archaeological artefacts). Additional archaeological material is displayed on the periphery of the space in archetypal museum cabinets.

The artefacts displayed were selected to illustrate the type and variety of material excavated from the area over the 15-year period 1988–2003. They are interpreted and arranged by theme: alcohol and drinking, childhood, cultural diversity, food and cooking, health and hygiene, home wares, jewellery and ornamentation, leisure, smoking, social reform, and work.

These themes are contextualised through the personal stories of five characters who lived, worked and studied in Little Lon: Anne Cunningham (1835–1904), an Irish immigrant, widow and a mother of three; John Maloney (1825–1882), an unmarried labourer born in Ireland who made enough money in Victoria's goldfields to buy a modest home in Little Lon; Carlo Bracchi (c. 1850s–1932), an Italian immigrant who started life in Melbourne hawking ice-cream from the streets and lanes, then built a two-story house and factory in Little Lon that thrived; Sister Esther (1858–1931), an English-born Anglican nun who worked for the Mission to the Streets and Lanes, which had its headquarters in Little Lon; and Marie Hayes (1920–2010), a third-generation Australian and Little Lon resident, who lived in the home her great-grandfather had built in the 1850s. The curatorial intent behind the artefact selection and mode of display is to contextualise the cultural, social and political complexities of life in 19th- and early 20th-century Little Lon.

---

[1] The first season of excavation within the Commonwealth Block was in an area referred to in the popular press as Little Lon. This term has since become synonymous with all material excavated from the area, and is used by museum staff to describe its displays and public programs.

[2] Evaluation of the Australia Gallery was carried out in three stages:
  1. Four 1.5–2 hour long, internal audits with museum staff who worked closely with gallery.
  2. Eight in-depth interviews with Melbourne-based visitors recruited per Museum Victoria's motivational segmentation model, and four workshops with Melbourne-based residents over 18 years of age.
  3. A series of 16, 1.5 hour, in-depth interviews with tourists (regional, interstate and international) visiting Melbourne Museum.

As is evidenced by Museum Victoria's commitment to displaying the Little Lon assemblage, curators have understood the historical significance and interpretive value of the Little Lon assemblage. Until 2009 however, it was never a curatorial priority and consequently received minimal collection management attention. An outcome of this indifference was that aside from the 400 artefacts on display, the assemblage of over 508,000 fragments was effectively invisible: to the public, curators and researchers. The magnitude of the problem was discovered in 2007 when selecting material for display in Melbourne Story, for example: artefacts from seasons 2 and 3[3] were not registered; the electronic catalogue was populated with tens of thousands of records with the object name 'unidentified'; and location information was too generic (i.e. Store F) to be useful. It became clear that in order to make the assemblage physically (and intellectually) accessible an assessment of its management was required.

To this end, in 2009 Museum Victoria embarked on an Australian Research Council Linkage project with La Trobe University: *A Historical Archaeology of the Commonwealth Block 1850–1950* (LP0989224). The project had both research and museological objectives. The research focused on what the consumption of consumer goods can tell us about production, trade, ethnicity, class and gender, and the nature of the modern city as a global phenomenon. The two stated museological objectives were: to articulate a sustainable framework for the management of large archaeological assemblages, and to develop a relational database to which archaeological and historical documentation from all seasons of excavation could be uploaded. To realise these objectives, staff from the museum and La Trobe University undertook a comprehensive rehabilitation of the Commonwealth Block assemblage.

As the team discovered while researching ways to manage such a large assemblage, the situation at Museum Victoria is not unique. Archaeological repositories across the Western world are dealing with a 'curation crisis' (Childs 1995): they are groaning under the weight of poorly housed, insufficiently documented, and in many cases unregistered assemblages. As excavations continue apace, generating more artefact assemblages and compounding an already unsustainable situation, repository staff have started to influence procedures by engaging in the process of fieldwork design; legislation, permitting and consent approvals; archaeological reporting, and training.

This chapter examines how the global 'curation crisis' came to pass. It reviews concurrent developments in museum collection management and archaeological practice from the early 1970s – the period when museums began to be disenfranchised from the archaeological process (Owen 2004: 180) – and recent efforts by museums and heritage agencies to address the problems. The use of databases to manage information and improve access to assemblages is presented as an essential measure in the process of eliminating the crisis. Museum Victoria's experiences provide a lens through which these broader issues are explored.

Archaeology Collections at Museum Victoria

Archaeology assemblages constitute well over half of Museum Victoria's cultural collections. The Indigenous Archaeology Collection contains more than 100,000 objects; it includes small sub-collections from Old and New World sites, with the major component comprising artefacts sourced from south-eastern Australia. The Historical Archaeology collections total close to three quarters of a million artefacts. The finds are predominantly from inner-city Melbourne, and all were excavated after 1984. The largest assemblage in the museum's care is the Commonwealth Block; it comprises approximately 508,000 fragments, making it the largest 19th-century urban assemblage in the world. The history of acquisition and management of both the Indigenous and Historical Archaeology collections at Museum Victoria illustrates a typical tale for repositories around the world.

The Indigenous Archaeology Collection was acquired mostly from private donors over a period of 100 years. Following the passage of the Victorian *Archaeological and Aboriginal Relics Preservation Act 1972,* the museum became the legislated repository for archaeological relics in Victoria, which resulted in the acquisition of professionally excavated archaeological assemblages. Changes to legislation and the introduction of the Victorian *Aboriginal Heritage Act 2006* (updated in 2016) mean that the museum is no longer the mandated repository, though finds of significant archaeological assemblages can still be deposited with the museum.

Years of benign neglect saw the Indigenous Archaeology Collection – once a significant source of exhibition material, and the subject of much research and publication – become effectively inaccessible to community members, researchers and curatorial staff. In 2011, the museum commissioned a review of the Australian component of the Indigenous Archaeology Collection to 'establish its ... cultural, historical and scientific value and establish requirements for its long-term management' (Museum Victoria 2011).

This external review coincided with two museum-initiated collection projects: a review of

---

[3] Black Eagles & Oddfellow Hotels, 1990 and 17 Casselden Place, 1995.

Figure 8.1: The Historical Archaeology collections at Museum Victoria before commencement of the ARC-funded Commonwealth Block rehabilitation project (Source: Museum Victoria).

the Humanities Department collection plans and a collection risk assessment of the Indigenous Archaeology collections. The outcome of these projects is a better understanding of the museum's holdings in terms of artefacts and associated documentation. The findings have led to the creation of a new page (tab) for data-entry in EMu (the museum's collection management system), and a proposed system for rehousing the collections. A new storage area was created in one of the museum's off-site storage facilities to enable consolidation of the collection: yet to date the lithic material has been moved to this area but not yet rehoused or registered.

Additional resources – in terms of both personnel and funding – have not been provided to implement the review's findings and as a consequence work on relocating, rehousing and registering the bulk of the material has not yet commenced. The one exception is the museum's collection of over 800 Cyclons (personalised conical-shaped stone objects) identified in the review as highly significant, rare artefacts requiring priority attention. The museum employed an Indigenous collection manager to manage the project. He consulted with traditional custodian groups 'to determine cultural protocols for storage, handling and ongoing management'; repatriation options were also a part of those discussions (Allen 2016). As a result of this focused attention the museum's collection of Cyclons is now appropriately housed, documented and accessible.

The museum's historical archaeology collections are beset with the same access issues as its Indigenous archaeology material. In 1995, Museum Victoria became the mandated repository for historical archaeology excavated from Crown owned land in the wake of the passing of the Victorian *Heritage Act*. While amendments to the act (2004, 2016) relieve the museum of its obligation to act as a repository for all Crown-owned artefacts, the museum has remained the key 'option for lodgement of significant archaeological assemblages' (McCubbin 2011: 63).

Three Crown-owned assemblages were deposited at the museum, following the passage of the act: 300 Queen Street, excavated in 1984; the Australian Defence Industries (ADI), excavated in the mid-1990s; and seasons 1, 2 and 3 of the Commonwealth Bock, excavated between 1988 and 1995. In 2005, season 5 of the Commonwealth Block (excavated in 2002–2003) was deposited at the museum.[4] Two further assemblages have since been accessioned into the museum's collection: the Royal Exhibition Building Western Forecourt Collection in 2010 and season 1 of excavations at the former Carlton United Brewery site in 2013.

Prior to the commencement of the ARC Linkage project in 2009, data for seasons 1, 2 and 5 of

---

[4] Season 4, a test investigation, was carried out in 2001. The 4,646 artefacts were deposited with Heritage Victoria.

Figure 8.2: The Commonwealth Block assemblage at Museum Victoria after four years of labour-intensive rehabilitation (Source: Museum Victoria).

the Commonwealth Block assemblage had been uploaded into EMu. No audit of the data was conducted at the time of upload, so there were many errors and anomalies. The inventory material from the Little Lon season (1), had been washed, rehoused and physically labelled, as had all the material from the Casselden Place season (5). None of the artefacts from the Black Eagle and Oddfellows season (2) or 17 Casselden Place (3) were registered and the finds were still housed in the bags and boxes allocated onsite. The same was true for the 300 Queen Street and ADI assemblages: neither were registered in EMu, and both collections were still housed in their original packaging.

Over a period of four years, Museum Victoria and La Trobe University staff – with a team of 30 volunteers – rehabilitated the Commonwealth Block assemblage. All artefacts were registered, washed, re-bagged, labelled (with the registration number, season and site details, and object name), and rehoused in custom-made boxes; special finds were also photographed. Every bag and box was barcoded to allow for location tracking. The storage footprint of the Commonwealth Block assemblage was reduced by more than half as a result of the re-housing processes implemented.[5]

The model developed to rehabilitate the Commonwealth Block assemblage was later applied to the 300 Queen Street assemblage as part of the ARC funded *Suburban Archaeology* project: it too is now physically and intellectually accessible. The ADI assemblage is still invisible: no further resources have been committed to its rehabilitation.

Artefact analysis for the Commonwealth Block and 300 Queen Street assemblages was recorded in the *Exploring the Archaeology of the Modern City* (EAMC) database. EAMC is a relational database that enables comparative analysis of artefact data across sites by 'integrating artefacts, contexts and type series' (Crook and Murray 2006: 5). When the rehabilitation project commenced in 2009, EAMC hosted data from four Sydney sites: Cumberland and Gloucester Streets, First Government House, Lilyvale, and Paddy's Market. Adding data from the four seasons of the Commonwealth Block assemblage and 300 Queen Street to EAMC has offered scope for national inter-site analysis.

It was agreed at the commencement of the rehabilitation project that data in the EAMC database would be migrated to EMu upon completion. To better facilitate this process, the historical archaeology tabs in EMu were redesigned to allow for more detailed information to be recorded. Fields already in EMu, like site name and context, object name, type series, activity and function were kept, while new fields including pattern, portion, profile, section, percentage complete, weight, minimum number of individuals (mni), were added across two tabs. A third tab for faunal material was also created.[6] Museum Victoria has shared these tabs with Heritage Victoria, so that data for Victorian historical and maritime archaeology can be consistently recorded within the museum.

The transfer of data from EAMC to EMu was not straightforward. Not only are recording protocols subtly different for the two databases, a number of field names do not align. When dealing with small datasets like 300 Queen Street (840 artefacts), tweaking the data was manageable. However the transfer of the Commonwealth Block's over 90,000 records continues to cause problems for the museum's EMu team. These issues are not insurmountable, and can be resolved

---

[5] The processes developed to manage the project, and recommendations for receipting future accessions, are summarised in the paper 'Managing the Commonwealth Block Assemblage: An Australian Case Study' (Smith and Hayes 2010).

[6] The faunal tab fields are: Species Name; Common Name; Sex; Age; Butchering Unit; Skeletal Portion; CM Location; Cut Marks; Fore/Hind/Meta; Long Bone Portion; Meat Value; Sawn/Chop/CM; Measurements.

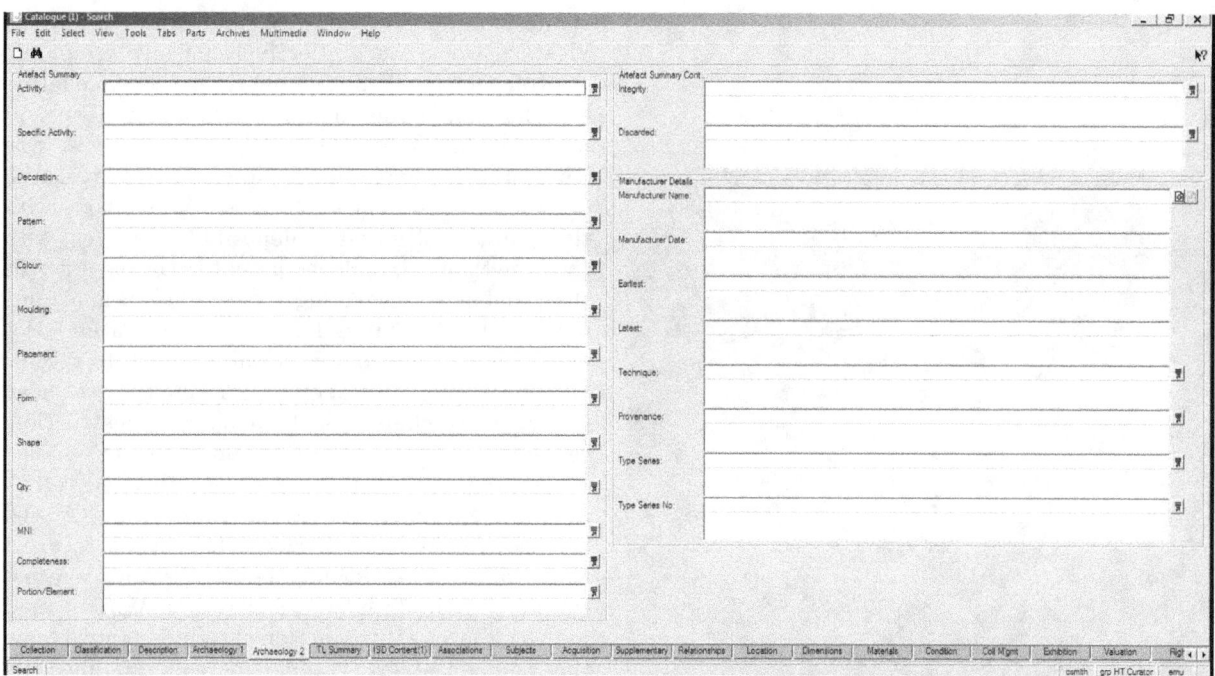

Figure 8.3: The second of three EMu Historical Archaeology tabs (Source: Museum Victoria).

with additional resources and time. Discussions have already commenced between the museum's Collection Information Systems (CIS) team and EAMC's developers to address ways to prevent similar problems occurring with future data transfers, and to consider ways to make the data in EMu more publicly accessible.

The data migration issues have brought to light the need for the museum to dictate a minimum dataset – drawn from EMu fields – for future acquisitions. To this end, when the museum engaged in an archaeological investigation of the Royal Exhibition Building[7] Western Forecourt (REB WFC), its staff worked closely with the artefact cataloguer to refine recording fields. Data was collated in an excel spreadsheet, then transferred to EMu where a registrar (employed from funds allocated to the management of the assemblage) cleaned up the data, labelled and barcoded all artefacts, photographed every group, and housed the artefacts following the protocols established from the rehabilitation project: i.e. by context then material type. Upon completion of the registration process, all data was uploaded to the museum's online collections database for public access.[8]

The success of the REB WFC project encouraged the museum to further refine the technique for the first season of excavation at the former Carlton United Brewery (CUB) site. Again working closely with the artefact cataloguer (who happily was the same specialist who worked on the REB WFC dig), a process for in-field artefact processing live into EMu was developed. Excavated finds were catalogued, registered, barcoded, and housed in museum-standard packaging on site. Museum CIS staff spent time on site helping the artefact specialists with the process. Upon completion of the excavation, the boxes were deposited at the museum and scanned to their new locations, thereby requiring no additional collection management resources.

The process had its flaws; specifically, the physical act of registering, barcoding and recording live into EMu was incredibly labour-intensive, but all parties acknowledged that the outcome – a physically and virtually accessible assemblage requiring no further collection management resourcing – outweighed the problems.

As soon as applications were made for the sixth (and final) season of excavation in the Commonwealth Block,[9] museum staff initiated discussions with the

---

[7] The Royal Exhibition Building (REB), built in 1879 to host Melbourne's first International Exhibition (1 Aug 1880 – 31 May 1881) is administered by Museum Victoria. It sits within Carlton Gardens, a landscape remodelled in 1880 for the Melbourne International Exhibition. The REB and Carlton Gardens were World Heritage Listed in July 2004. In 2009 the museum embarked on a three-phase project in which the 1950s carpark in the western forecourt was removed, an underground water tank was installed and the 1880 circular carriageway was reinstated (https://museumvictoria.com.au/reb/history/world-heritage-world-futures/). As custodians of the REB, the museum was the client and therefore in a position to actively engage in all aspects of the archaeological process. The REB WFC archaeology project is summarised in the paper 'Reconstructing Landscape – Archaeological Investigations of the Royal Exhibition Buildings Western Forecourt' (Major, Smith and Mackay 2017).

[8] http://collections.museumvictoria.com.au/articles/3541

[9] 271 Spring Street.

Figure 8.4: Museum staff member registering CUB finds onsite, direct into EMu (Source: Charlotte Smith, Museum Victoria).

is not unique. For decades, museums across the Western world were effectively passive recipients of archaeological finds, offering accommodation but not engaging in any further analysis or management. While archaeological fieldwork was led by university teams and determined by research questions, museums were largely able to cope with the quantity of material deposited. However, with the growth of urban development in the early 1970s the number of assemblages deposited in museums increased dramatically. The motivation for excavation began to shift from research to rescue; site selection, increasingly informed by a need to protect archaeological sites from destruction, resulted in a kneejerk approach to collect everything. After two decades of unbridled rescue archaeology, governments in the UK, USA and Australia introduced heritage legislation to exert some control over development to mitigate against the loss of the archaeological record. While sound in principle, the introduction of tighter controls saw the number of excavations increase significantly and so too the amount of predominantly historical archaeological material of 'marginal academic interest' (Swain 2007: 129) requiring storage. In Victoria alone the number of excavations tripled after the introduction of the *Heritage Act* in 1995 (Keene 2005: 54).

The introduction of heritage legislation in Australia compounded an already evident imbalance in the archaeological process, with its focus on research design, methodology, fieldwork and site interpretation. Recovered artefacts receive scant attention after initial cataloguing, and little provision is made for their long-term future (Crook 2002; Sonderman 2004). Victoria is the only state with designated archaeological repositories: across the rest of Australia, many assemblages still languish in basements, garages and sheds. As interpretation and research outputs are not required by legislation, consulting archaeologists have no basis from which to demand that developers pay for such work, and as Crook et al. point out, rescue archaeology is a competitive market and 'those who offer more than basic statutory compliance will not win the tender' (Crook 2002: 28).

The perilous fate of archaeological archives does not lie solely with the archaeology profession. Museums were slow to develop collection management procedures themselves, thereby compounding the problem.

Collections management is a relatively new discipline within the museum sector, its adoption and promotion by professional bodies – e.g. the American Alliance of Museums, Museums Association (UK) and Museums Australia – dating to the late 1970s/early 1980s. Collections management can be defined as 'the sum of all the activities which result in the preservation of the collection, the physical and intellectual control of the collection and the

consulting archaeologists and artefact cataloguer to articulate, and cost, collection management requirements. In-field artefact cataloguing was once again adopted. The CIS team updated its import spreadsheet to include barcode inventory control, so that once finds were documented in the spreadsheet they could be transferred to Moreland. Ideally, finds should have been scanned to museum-standard boxes, but delays in ordering the necessary housing materials meant all finds were stored and transferred in large, plastic tubs. The deposition fee includes money to contract a registrar to data enhance the records for publication on the museum's website so rehousing and scanning the artefacts to boxes will happen in the coming months.

Work space shortages, delayed responses by museum staff to pressing onsite issues, and hold-ups with the ordering of cataloguing supplies and housing materials hampered the in-field recording process. However, the creation of a dataset that can be imported directly into EMu and the live barcoding of all artefacts, once again outweighs the frustrations experienced by those onsite.

STOREHOUSES OF ARCHAEOLOGY

Museum Victoria's experience as a repository for the deposition of archaeological assemblages exploitation of the collection' (Game 1988: 19): i.e. acquisition, registration, storage, conservation, data management, inventory tracking, exhibition, loans and deaccession.

From the outset collection managers argued for standardised, institution-wide policies and procedures to enable an integrated management of collections. It was not until the establishment of collection management departments in the mid-1990s that more structured approaches to collections care were developed. The intervening years were typified by unsystematic procedures, resulting in poorly cared for collections, acquisition backlogs and the loss of associated documentation. In an attempt to address the situation, bodies like the Museums and Galleries Commission in the UK developed discipline-specific, standards of care guidelines in the 1990s (Knell 1994: 3). Though not mandatory, they went some way to ensuring more considered, institution-wide responses to collections care.

Concurrent with the recognition of collections management as a museum discipline was the development of personal computers, and it was recognised by many early collection managers that computer technology offered 'a viable solution to the kinds of collection management problems that museums have – inventory and information control over large bodies of objects and data' (Sarasan 1981: 196). Adoption of digital collection management systems however was slow and *ad hoc* across the sector: even within institutions it was not uncommon for 'different information standards, different hardware and different software' to be operating (Game 1988: 19).

Museum Victoria's approach to collections management was the same as that experienced across the museum sector. By the mid-1990s Museum Victoria's collections were spread across a number of sites. A new facility was opened in 1995 to consolidate off-site storage, while new collection stores for the museum's science and technology collections were created at the recently opened Scienceworks, while collection stores for social history, Indigenous cultures and natural history collections were integral to the design of Melbourne Museum, which opened to the public in 2001. While Museum Victoria recognised the need for better collection storage at this time, procedures for the management of collections were still inconsistent. As a result, when the first tranche of historical archaeology was deposited at the museum's new off-site facility c. 1995, a number of basic collection management tasks were not completed: e.g. rehousing into appropriate conservation-grade storage containers, applying registration numbers to artefacts, requesting associated documentation, providing an appropriate deposition receipt.

Catalogue data compiled by artefact specialists for the first three Commonwealth Block digs (Little Lon, Black Eagle and Oddfellows Hotels, and 17 Casselden Place) was uploaded to Texpress, a database developed in the 1980s by Museum Victoria in collaboration with the University of Melbourne and the Australian Museum. However, no audit to check the veracity of the data was undertaken, so when this content was transferred to EMu (the successor to Texpress) in 2005, problems in the original data were compounded.

In 2001 Museum Victoria established a Strategic Collections Management (SCM) department. Its remit was to standardise all areas of collections management across several areas including curatorial, conservation, exhibition collections management, collection information systems (e.g. EMu), and digital asset management. Since its inception SCM has overseen the development of collection plans, acquisition policies, disaster management plans, de-accession templates, etc.

The most recent initiative has been the introduction of a Collection Risk Assessment and Management (CRAM) framework to all areas of the collection. CRAM is a management model that is 'strategic, preventative, scalable, and systematic ... [that] encompasses short and long-term frames ... and ultimately guides priority settings' (McCubbin 2011: 72). The CRAM process involves multi-disciplinary teams – in the case of historical archaeology staff from curatorial, conservation, collection management, and facilities management – who assess how ten 'agents of risk'[10] may affect the permanency of a particular collection. Thanks to the rehabilitation work carried out as part of the ARC project, data for the CRAM assessment of the historical archaeology collection was comprehensive. The findings confirmed that the approaches adopted by the ARC team in terms of physical artefact management were appropriate. They also further informed the museum's minimum requirements for future depositions.

Why Bother?

From within the museum community there is a cry of 'Why bother'? Why do we keep these unwieldy assemblages that occupy so much storage space, and that the museum has had little say in collecting?

The answer is always 'research potential'. It is true for museums that the potential to uncover stories that may inform exhibitions and public programs is a legitimate reason for retaining assemblages. At Museum Victoria, research conducted on the Commonwealth Block Little Lon assemblage by museum staff and La Trobe University honours and PhD students has informed two long-term

---

[10] The ten agents of risk are: dissociation, criminals, contaminants, fire, light, pest, physical forces, relative humidity, temperature and water.

exhibitions and one foyer display.[11] These displays have in turn informed the museum's education program 'A Load of Old Rubbish' for years 7–9, which encourages students to consider the techniques and sources of evidence historians and archaeologists employ to learn about life in the past.

Yet anecdotal evidence shows that once lodged, assemblages are quickly forgotten by the archaeologists who created them; they rarely return to conduct further analysis (Swain 2007: 295). In the midst of a 'curation crisis' this apparent disinterest in the artefacts has encouraged museums to demand change.

In Victoria, fruitful cooperation between museum professionals, consultant and academic archaeologists, and Heritage Victoria staff has led to the refinement of artefact management procedures first developed in 2001 (updated in 2004). In 2014 Heritage Victoria released *Guidelines for Investigating Historical Archaeological Artefacts and Sites* (updated 2015): artefact management procedures have been further improved and, more importantly for the future of assemblages, 'the guidelines ... establish new requirements for the development of Research Designs and Statements of Significance for *both* assemblages and sites' (Heritage Victoria 2015: 6; author's italics). While the guidelines don't address the long-term fate of assemblages – or their use post-deposition – the emphasis on developing a rationale for artefact retention ensures more considered/refined collecting.

The guidelines also insist that the artefact catalogue use 'standard fields and terminologies' (drawn from the EMu archaeology tabs) to ensure consistent and searchable data. Building a dataset of comparable data will allow researchers to undertake comparative analysis across sites, and provide accurate information for those tasked with granting approvals, particularly site selection, research design, and artefact retention (sampling and discard).

A MOOD FOR CHANGE

The pace of development-led excavations is not likely to slow, so we – archaeologists, collection managers and heritage planners – must continue to respond to the challenges posed by this paradigm. How to prepare artefacts for deposition is well documented, and now museums are more engaged in the conversation more considered artefact retention policies that challenge 'the traditional approach of "quantity before quality"' (Owen 2004: 183) are being written. But as 'the majority of catalogue data are [still] stored in small, standalone spreadsheets or custom-built databases' (ADP 2010), the next step for museums is to dictate catalogue fields that correspond to their collection management systems, so that data across sites is standardised. The infrastructure is already in place. All museums use electronic Collection Management Systems (CMS) for inventory management, information (data) capture and object identification, and CMS like EMu are designed so that data can be interrogated several ways.

Concurrently, museums should rehabilitate the data for collections already in their care. Once this data clean-up has happened, museums are better placed to audit the artefacts in their care. This data can then be shared in a centralised system, like the Archaeology Data Service (ADS) in Britain. Established in 1996 by a consortium of universities and the Council for British Archaeology, the ADS works with archaeologists and planners 'to negotiate deposition of project data': e.g. 'text reports, databases ..., images ..., digitised maps and plans, numerical datasets related to topographic and sub-surface surveys and other locational data, as well as reconstruction drawings' (ADS 2016). The ADS informs future collection requirements through the publication of standards and guidelines, and assists in the sharing of unpublished fieldwork data. It is currently building 'an integrated on-line catalogue to its collections, and a gateway to other collections' (ADS 2016), which users/researchers will be able to access virtually.

Historical archaeologists in Australia have been campaigning for the development of a similar model to the ADS for more than a decade. Between 2001 and 2004, a group led by academics at La Trobe University developed the Exploring the Archaeology of the Modern City (EAMC) and People + Place databases. These databases offered a central electronic repository of hundreds-of-thousands of artefact records 'from multiple sites and a companion dataset of historical occupancy data' for the thousands of people who occupied those sites. In 2010, the same group received funding from the Australian National Data Service (ANDS) to 'redevelop the EAMC databases into an online platform and storage house for searching, entering and managing historical archaeological data' (ADP 2010). The result was the Australian Historical Archaeology Database (AHAD), a 'national online database for historical archaeological catalogue data and associated stratigraphic and historical records' (ADP 2010).

In 2013, the AHAD was subsumed into the FAIMS repository, a creation of the Field Acquired Information Management System (FAIMS) project. FAIMS is an Australian consortium of 41

---

[11] To coincide with a symposium on managing archaeological assemblages hosted by Museum Victoria, curators installed a 'table-top' display in the foyer of Melbourne Museum. The display, titled 'An Archaeological Time Capsule', contained all finds excavated from a cesspit in Irish labourer John Maloney's backyard. Initially installed for six months, it was so popular with visitors it stayed on display for one year, May 2010 – May 2011.

organisations including universities, archaeological consultancies and heritage agencies. The FAIMS repository was created 'to store data sets, documents, images, and sensory data produced by archaeological research in Australia or collected by Australian archaeologists working abroad' (FAIMS 2016).

From the outset the project partners' aims for the FAIMS repository were high: to 'enhance collaboration, reinterpretation and comparative study by facilitating the production and dissemination of compatible, high-quality archaeological datasets' (Intersect 2014). However, upload of datasets to the repository has been slow; in large part because the preparation of data for upload requires a considerable investment of time and money, and as research outputs are not required by current legislation funds for such work are hard to argue for at the research design phase.

At the time of writing the FAIMS repository is being migrated to The Digital Archaeological Record (tDAR), hosted by the Center for Digital Antiquity at Arizona State University. Australian archaeologists will still be able to upload datasets to the 'FAIMS Collection'. The expansion of tDAR since its inception in 2006 demonstrates that there is a recognition amongst researchers of the value of storing archival data that enables connections between sites nationally and transnationally. tDAR has already collaborated with the ADS in the 'Transatlantic Archaeology Gateway' project, enabling access to resources across two continents (ADS 2016). The inclusion of the FAIMS Repository in tDAR broadens the scope of resources for all researchers.

With the inclusion of the Commonwealth Block data in tDAR, researchers around the world will have access to information from the largest extant 19th-century urban assemblage in the world. This body of data will facilitate the 'archaeological contribution to writing the history of the modern world, contextualising new histories of migration, consumption and ... the city, in ways that support the broader goals of transnational histories' (Murray and Smith 2008). We can hope that as more historical research is undertaken through analysis of assemblages and sites, the archaeology profession will increasingly realise the value of creating standardised, consistent datasets, and uploading these to an international repository of comparative data.

From a collections management perspective, the creation of consistent, standardised and accessible catalogue data gives rise to the question: do we need to keep all excavated material in our collections? Heritage planners are now encouraging (insisting in Victoria) that an application for consent to excavate contain a reasoned artefact retention policy, with a rationale for retention, discarding and sampling. Furthermore, significance assessments prepared for the final report rank assemblages as high, medium and low. Heritage Victoria makes allowances for low-significance finds to be reburied on site, though a detailed catalogue is still required to ensure a record of finds exists.

For assemblages already in museum collections, once a comprehensive catalogue has been prepared, similar criteria should apply. Special finds and taxonomic material should be retained, but there must be scope to sample the rest of the assemblage and discard a percentage. I can hear the cry of panic from some in the archaeology profession at this suggestion. But the reality is: we cannot save every piece of material evidence of past generations in museums. As Tim Murray has observed, 'converting archaeological data into cultural capital ... has greater value than many boxes of artefacts gathering dust in anonymous store houses' (Murray 2011: 86). There is no denying that access to physical artefacts is limited, whereas access to data can be shared virtually with millions across the globe.

Conclusion

The approach Museum Victoria has taken to enhance access to its historical archaeology collections is a case study of best practice. In the process of rehabilitating the Commonwealth Block assemblage, museum staff have developed a model for storing, labelling, and registering assemblages that can be applied to already accessioned assemblages and future acquisitions. This approach allows for unimpeded physical access to the collections, and essential inventory tracking.

Museum staff have also learnt the value of direct engagement with heritage planners and consulting archaeologists at the commencement of new projects. Costing for the ongoing management of assemblages, involvement in the design of clearly articulated artefact retention policies, establishing a set of defined cataloguing fields, and continuing trials of onsite registration and cataloguing live into EMu will eliminate many current physical access issues.

Significant in terms of reach and research potential has been the museum's commitment to working with archaeology specialists to establish protocols for recording data in EMu and EAMC. Acknowledging that there are still communication issues between the two databases to resolve, the principle of enabling greater access to data and collections will continue to motivate museum staff to solve them. The next step is to find ways for EMu to be shared on a global platform, so that basic (though comprehensive) catalogue information can complement more in-depth analysis like that afforded the Commonwealth Block assemblage. Not all collections warrant the level of detailed study afforded the Commonwealth Block, however access to the complete archaeological record ensures robust analysis.

Enabling access to standardised catalogue data could prove to be the most significant collections management tool in the long term. A searchable, national (or international) repository of archaeological datasets will facilitate better understanding of sites and artefacts, highlighting areas well represented in the archaeological record and identifying those that are absent. This knowledge will allow heritage planners to make informed decisions regarding site selection, research design, and – significantly for museums – artefact retention. The archaeological record will continue to grow, but in a more considered way, so that collections deposited in museums will be smaller in scale and of higher quality.

REFERENCES

Allen, L. 2016. Re: Indigenous Archaeology Collection – post 2013 update. Personal email correspondence.

Archaeology Database Project (ADP), c. 2010. *Archaeology Database Project: Creating an Online Artefact Database for Historical Archaeology*, https://archaeologydatabase.wordpress.com/ahad-documentation/about-ahad/.

Archaeology Data Service (ADS), 2016. *Transatlantic Archaeology Gateway*, http://archaeologydataservice.ac.uk/TAG/intro.jsf.

Brown, D. 2007. *Archaeological Archives: A Guide to Best Practice in Creation, Compilation, Transfer and Curation*. Archaeological Archives Forum, UK.

Childs, S.T. 1995. The Curation Crisis. *Common Ground* 7(4): https://www.nps.gov/Archeology/cg/fd_vol7_num4/crisis.htm.

Childs, S.T. 2011. Archaeological Collections Management in the United States: Developing a Path to Sustainability. In Smith, C.H.F. and T. Murray (eds.), *Caring for Our Collections: Papers from the Symposium 'Developing Sustainable, Strategic Collection Management Approaches for Archaeological Assemblages'*, pp. 19–36, Melbourne: Museum Victoria.

Crook, P., S. Lawrence and M. Gibbs, 2002. The Role of Artefact Catalogues in Australian Historical Archaeology: A Framework for Discussion. *Australian Historical Archaeology* 20: 26–38.

Crook, P. and T. Murray, 2006. *Guide to the EAMC Archaeology Database*. Sydney: Historic Houses Trust of NSW.

Edwards, R. 2013. *Archaeological Archives and Museums*. Society of Museum Archaeologists, England.

FAIMS 2016 *The FAIMS Repository*, https://www.fedarch.org/faims-repository/.

Game, J. 1988. Overview of Collections Management Practice in Australia, New Zealand and Papua New Guinea. In Roberts, D. A. (ed.), *Collections Management for Museums: Proceedings of an International Conference Held in Cambridge, England, 26–29 September 1987. The First Annual Conference of The Museum Documentation Association*, pp. 18–31, Cambridge: The Museum Documentation Association.

Heritage Victoria, 2004. *Archaeological Artefacts Management Guidelines*, Version 2, https://www.academia.edu/1747447/Heritage_Victoria._2004._Archaeological_Artefacts_Management_Guidelines_Version_2.

Heritage Victoria, 2015. *Guidelines for Investigating Historical Archaeological Artefacts and Sites*, Version 2A, July, http://www.dtpli.vic.gov.au/heritage/historical-archaeology-and-heritage-inventory/archaeology-and-heritage-inventory-forms-and-guidelines.

Intersect, 2014. *Federated Archaeological Information Management System*, http://www.intersect.org.au/FAIMS.

Keene, S. 2005. *Fragments of the World: Uses of Museum Collections*. Oxford: Elsevier Butterworth-Heinemann.

Knell, S. (ed.) 1994. *Care of Collections*. London: Routledge.

Knell, S. (ed.) 2004. *Museums and the Future of Collecting*, 2nd edition. Surrey: Ashgate.

Major, J., C. Smith and R. Mackay, 2017. Reconstructing Landscape: Archaeological Investigations of the Royal Exhibition Buildings Western Forecourt, Melbourne. *International Journal of Historical Archaeology*, DOI 10.1007/s10761-017-0414-5.

McCubbin, M. 2011. Applying a Collection Care Framework to Archaeological Collections. In Smith, C.H.F. and T. Murray (eds.), *Caring for Our Collections: Papers from the Symposium 'Developing Sustainable, Strategic Collection Management Approaches for Archaeological Assemblages'*, pp. 67–75, Melbourne: Museum Victoria.

Merriman, N. and H. Swain, 1999. Archaeology Archives: Serving the Public Interest? *European Journal of Archaeology*, 2(2): 249–267.

Murray, T. and C.H.F. Smith, 2008. A Historical Archaeology of the Commonwealth Block 1850–1950, ARC Application, Section E2, unpublished document.

Murray, T. 2011. Research Using Museum Collections Need Not be a Vale of Tears, Though It Often Is. In Smith, C.H.F. and T. Murray (eds.), *Caring for Our Collections: Papers from the Symposium 'Developing Sustainable, Strategic Collection Management Approaches for Archaeological Assemblages'*, pp. 79–88, Melbourne: Museum Victoria.

Museum Victoria, 2011. Bunjilaka Project Australian Indigenous Archaeology Collection Review. Unpublished Museum Victoria RFT, Melbourne.

Owen, J. 2004. Who is Steering the Ship? Museums and Archaeological Fieldwork. In Knell, S. (ed.), *Museums and the Future of Collecting*, pp. 179–184, Surrey: Ashgate.

Sarasan, L. 1981. Why Museum Computer Projects Fail. Reproduced in Fahy, A. (ed.) 1995 *Collections Management*, pp. 187–197, London: Routledge.

Sonderman, R. 2004. Before You Start That Project, Do You Know What to Do with the Collection? In Childs, S.T. (ed.), *Our Collective Responsibility: The Ethics and Practice of Archaeological Collections Stewardship*, pp. 107–120, Washington DC: Society for Museum Archaeology.

Sullivan, L. 1992. Managing Archaeological Resources from the Museum Perspective. Technical Brief no. 13, April, National Park Service.

Swain, H. 2007. *An Introduction to Museum Archaeology*. Cambridge: Cambridge University Press.

Smith, C.H.F. and S. Hayes, 2010. Managing the Commonwealth Block Assemblage: An Australian Case Study. *Collections: A Journal for Museum and Archive Professionals* 6(3): 171–188.

Smith, C.H.F. and D. Tout-Smith, 2010. Recreating Place: Little Lon. *Museum Management and Curatorship* 25(1): 37–51.

9
Diversity and Change in Little Lon: Ongoing Historical and Archaeological Research

Sarah Hayes and Barbara Minchinton

Research on Little Lon over the past decades has deepened our appreciation of the kaleidoscopic nature of the area and this chapter adds a further level of detail to that work. At the same time the discovery during this phase of research of a set of archival records that precisely dated the closure of many of the cesspits has upturned previous understandings about the nature of the archaeological evidence and led to questions about the patterns of residence in the area across the last third of the 19th century. By studying the people and the archaeological evidence from Little Lon together in detail – comparing and contrasting their life stories and material culture – research has revealed even more of the fluidity and diversity of this community in that period, but also suggests that it might have undergone a substantial change in the years following the cesspit closures. Certainly there were brothels, crime, cramped living conditions and poor waste disposal both before and after the early 1870s, and in both eras there were home owners, both male and female, with businesses, children and carefully chosen possessions. But the new evidence suggests that the balance between sex workers and others may have shifted in the decades after 1870, increasing the number of brothels and decreasing the number of poor families in the area. In any case research has shown that the traditional categories were unstable – 'bad houses' could also contain children, and criminals might be the sons of respectable bootmakers. Challenging the slum stereotype, then, is producing further questions about Little Lon as a neighbourhood: How did it change over time? To what extent was it a unified community? How many people were moving on and up the social ladder? How did people negotiate changes in their status? This chapter begins by explaining the new understandings about Little Lon and the questions they raise for future research, and then moves beyond labels such as 'prostitute', 'criminal' and 'respectable labourer' to look at individual lives. Recent research has been focused on comparative studies of individuals, their houses and their rubbish within the block and forms a requisite precursor to comparative studies at broader scales (see Murray 2006: 302). The history and archaeology discussed in this chapter draws on research conducted by the authors on Little Lon since 2009 under the *Commonwealth Block* (ARC LP0989224) and *Suburban Archaeology* (ARC DP1093001) projects, research which is still under way at the time of writing.

NEW UNDERSTANDINGS

Dating Cesspit Closures – the Process

The majority of the deposits that were identified as being of interest for this phase of research were located in old cesspits. In order to pinpoint when these cesspits were closed, the transition process from cesspits to nightpans in Little Lon was tracked through *The Argus* and the Melbourne City Council (MCC) records at the Public Record Office Victoria (PROV) (Hayes and Minchinton 2016). *An Act to Amend the Laws Relating to or Affecting Public Health* 1867 had empowered the MCC's Health Committee (in its role as a Local Board of Health) to order the 'remedying' or closure of leaking cesspits, and although it took some time for the MCC to develop an effective process for administering the act, a set of records was located at PROV giving exact closure dates for cesspits closed by Council notice following a report from the Inspector of Nuisances (PROV VA 511 VPRS 3103). Correlating these records with the MCC Rate Books (PROV VA 511 VPRS 5708 P9) can pinpoint the closure of a cesspit to within a week (Council notices required that a problem be remedied within seven or 30 days). Not all cesspits were closed by council notice – some were closed voluntarily once earth-closets became available in the mid-1860s, and many more were closed when municipal nightpan collection was made available in 1870 – but the combination of archival records with archaeological evidence can often establish a date of closure. Useful information was obtained from this source for all of the cesspits identified for this project (see Hayes and Minchinton 2016: 15, 17).

The Inspector of Nuisances' lists proved invaluable for accurately dating cesspit closures on the sites in this study, but they only recorded 'Name' (usually the owner, sometimes the tenant) and 'Situation of premises' of the cesspit being closed (usually the street address, but sometimes no more than a laneway), so that verified lists of owners and tenants in that period were critical to any attempt to link artefacts with their owners.

Establishing Lists of Owners and Tenants – the Process

Previous projects had compiled substantial data on owners and tenants (McCarthy 1989: 53–453; Murray 2004: 37), but there were many gaps and a few puzzling discrepancies relating to occupants. Since the completion of those earlier projects, however, the MCC Rate Books (PROV VA 511 VPRS 5708 P9 1861–1863 and 1866–1975) had been digitised and made available online, making it possible to interrogate this source more thoroughly. The use of this data together with intensive consultation with other historical sources concentrating on the time of cesspits closures (for example newspapers, land transfer records and prisoner registers) showed that there was a high incidence of unrecorded tenant turnover on several of the sites being studied, and there were also many known residents who did not appear in the traditional sources for 'occupier' data. This research has been reported in *Australasian Historical Archaeology* (Minchinton 2017a). As a result the basis for interpretation of the artefacts recovered from the cesspits – while still holding out the promise of clear correlation with some owners – has changed.

The Outcome

The picture that emerged from this study of 22 sites in Little Lon was clearly similar to that reported by Murray and Crook (2005: 95) for The Rocks area in Sydney, where there was 'a high level of house-to-house mobility' of tenants and 'longer-term loyalty to the local area'. It was not unusual – especially in the inner lanes – for tenants in Little Lon to move house within, for example, the same row of cottages, or to move elsewhere in Little Lon or rent an extra cottage for a period, perhaps in response to changing family size or increased income. The research also confirmed previous findings relating to owners living alongside tenants (Mayne 2006: 320). But two other factors were found to be important in relation to the question of interpreting artefacts retrieved from cesspits. First, that numerous cesspits served more than one house, and it cannot always be determined which houses were served by and/or contributed rubbish to the cesspit at the time of closure (information on cesspits serving multiple houses can be found in PROV VA 511 VPRS 3103). Second, the presence of numerous unrecorded sex workers and lodgers in the area means that artefacts retrieved from cesspits cannot necessarily be attributed to particular families or individuals on the basis of traditional records of occupation (rate books and directories). Two room cottages in Little Lon often had three or four sex workers living in them – none of whose names were listed in the standard sources – and petitions from residents against the brothels show that 'respectable' houses often held a similar number of lodgers, who, again, were not listed as occupants in traditional records (Minchinton 2017a). This could help to explain what Murray and Mayne (2003: 98–99) described in relation to Casselden Place as a 'remarkably low level of variability in assemblage structure and composition' between houses with apparently different kinds of occupancy, which they characterised as 'long-term' and 'short-term'. Perhaps, in fact, they had the same kind of 'shared house' occupancy over a long period, despite what the written records appeared to show.

Other Developments

Despite these reservations, 'timelines' were developed for 144 families of owners and known tenants for the 22 sites, including 75 full family trees showing where they had come from and the occupations their children followed. Owners, of course, were generally easier to track than tenants because of their footprint in the land title records, but many tenants – especially those who led colourful lives (thieves and sex workers, for example) – could also be traced in detail. This phase of the research produced a number of new findings.

One surprising element of the ownership lists was the high incidence of women. Most were widows, some with outright ownership and others with a life interest only, but many were married women (such as Mrs Bond, Anne Monks and Honora Judd) who were investing their own earnings in land, and using a variety of strategies to circumvent the common law prohibition on married women owning property. This research has been reported in *History Australia* (Minchinton 2017b), but its implications for interpretation of the archaeological material have yet to be examined.

Another element of the research which has yet to be fully explored is the apparent shift in the pattern of tenancy across the later decades of the 19th century. It has been noted elsewhere (Lawrence and Davies 2017: 4–5) that the firm dating of the cesspit closures to the early 1870s is earlier and occurred over a shorter period of time than previously thought, but the significance of that change has yet to be established. Preliminary research indicates that the number of sex workers in the area increased dramatically through the 1870s and 1880s, and that they paid higher rents than other tenants. Their presence appears to have reduced the number of 'respectable' tenants in the area, and rendered landlords increasingly unwilling to maintain housing stock for either the back lane sex workers or the very poor labouring people who remained. It is possible therefore that the contents of the cesspits closed in the 1870s belonged to people with a higher standard of living than those who lived there in the following decades up to 1907 at least, when the laws around prostitution changed. This supposition will be tested in our ongoing research.

Artefact Research

Over 2000 boxes of artefacts from the various excavation seasons at Little Lon are housed at Museum Victoria. In the sheer size of the assemblage lies both its value and its greatest challenge. To physically handle and catalogue all the artefacts presented a time consuming and overwhelming task for the Commonwealth Block project. While catalogues existed for all artefacts from Little Lon, there were inevitable differences between how data was recorded by different cataloguers and varying levels of detail largely due to the constraints of time and funding (see Smith and Hayes 2010; Hayes 2011). The first step for this project was to amalgamate artefact records from all five seasons of excavation into one database. Data for each of the excavations was transferred into the Exploring the Archaeology of the Modern City (EAMC) database. Artefact records for the Little Lon, Black Eagle and Oddfellows Hotels, and Casselden Place excavations were taken from Museum Victoria's EMu database to ensure that any changes made to the records by the museum were reflected in EAMC. The 17 Casselden Place data was transferred into EAMC from the original Excel catalogue as this had never been entered into the museum's database in spite of the artefacts being held at Museum Victoria. The phase 3 testing artefacts held at Heritage Victoria were added to EAMC from Heritage Victoria's database. It quickly became apparent that the records now in EAMC did not, in some cases, accurately reflect the artefact bags in boxes on shelves. A number of causes were identified (see Smith and Hayes 2010; Hayes 2011), but the most significant were changes to records and locations of artefacts for display at the museum or for further research by archaeologists that were then not recorded in the EMu database.

The cataloguing for the Commonwealth Block project commenced in 2009 and was continued as part of the Suburban Archaeology project; it is ongoing. Collectively this work aims to:

1) rehabilitate the assemblage by conducting a box audit to ensure all artefacts were located and accurately matched to a corresponding record
2) apply Museum Victoria's inventory tracking system – Museum Victoria Wireless Input System for EMu (MvWISE) – to the entire collection
3) consolidate site records and enter context data from the fieldwork into the EAMC database
4) conduct detailed cataloguing on a selection of deposits.

The cataloguing of selected deposits applies consistent terminology and type series across the seasons, and adds tools for analysis to the records including matching sets analysis, calculation of minimum numbers of individuals (MNIs) and recording of flaws which improve the overall research value of the assemblage (see Hayes 2011 for further details). Recording this additional information can be prohibitively time intensive in initial cataloguing phases especially in the case of such large assemblages. MNIs, type series and matching sets analysis had not been systematically or extensively included in the earlier catalogues. The exceptions were MNIs recorded for the glass and stoneware containers from Casselden Place (Godden Mackay Logan, Austral Archaeology and La Trobe University 2004: 229–288) and type series created for the Casselden Place 2002–2003 and *Vanished Communities* (Murray and Mayne 2002) catalogues. This type series grouped records with identical patterns and shape with types illustrated in pencil in a master document. Matching sets and flaws were not recorded in the catalogues for any of the assemblages. The importance of this additional layer of detail has long been advocated (e.g. Birmingham 1990: 19; Crook, Lawrence and Gibbs 2002) and forms an important part of the current project. All cataloguing has been done in the EAMC database and has been uploaded to the museum's EMu database at various stages throughout the project. The terminology and systems of cataloguing, including the format of the type series, that are integrated into the EAMC database have been utilised for this project (see Crook and Murray 2006).

Due to the size of the assemblages and the labour intensive work needed to rehabilitate the collection, it was decided to prioritise for cataloguing a selection of households that best represented different occupation types across the site. Both the Little Lon and Casselden Place reports provided shortlists of households of primary interest (McCarthy 1989: 107; Godden Mackay Logan, Austral Archaeology, and La Trobe University 2004: 17–28). These shortlists were used as a starting point, but as the research objectives of the Commonwealth Block project differed from those of earlier phases, all excavated areas from all five excavation seasons at Little Lon and Casselden Place were reviewed and considered for the shortlist for this current project, taking into consideration both the historical record and the presence of stratified deposits.

In order to identify households of interest a review of context sheets, trench reports, historical reports and excavation photographs was undertaken (see Hayes 2011). The first step in creating the shortlist required the identification of stratified, intact deposits such as cesspits, refuse pits and underfloor deposits. Artefacts recovered within the houses on the Commonwealth Block, including subfloor deposits, were largely from mixed deposits of 19th- and 20th-century artefacts (Mayne and Murray 2001: 98) and would be much harder to associate with specific phases of occupation. For each stratified deposit, location, type, associated structure, summary of history and dates were recorded. All of this was based solely on the excavation record without the benefit of seeing the site and it is possible that important deposits not highlighted in the reports have been overlooked. While cesspits and rubbish pits were comparatively easy to identify by the context sheets and reports, other potential deposits of interest were harder to distinguish.

Once deposits of significance and integrity were identified, factors such as location of the lot (i.e. Site A, Site B and Site C), type of deposit (i.e. different types of cesspits – barrel, bluestone, brick lined etc.) and historical information on the type of occupation (i.e. families, singles, tenanted with frequent changeovers, owner occupied, business, brothel etc.) were considered. The final shortlist for the first phase of cataloguing was spread across 12 households and included a total of 14 cesspits, five rubbish pits and a deposit of clay pipes, which when combined provided a comprehensive picture of the different types of occupation across Little Lon. When additional funding was made available through the Suburban Archaeology project a second phase of cataloguing was initiated and a second shortlist was compiled (see Woff this volume).

In accordance with the integrated, recursive model of historical archaeology (Mayne, Murray and Lawrence 2000: 143; Murray, Karskens and Mayne 2004), the shortlists were developed based on archaeological and historical evidence in tandem, and similarly the cataloguing work was undertaken in conjunction with additional historical research. The initial question taken to the archives was: when was each of the shortlisted cesspits closed and filled with artefacts? Once that was established (Hayes and Minchinton 2016), timelines of occupants were developed in order to establish which individuals, families or groups of occupants might have been related to the cesspit closures and fills. Historical timelines and personal histories were then constructed for all of the traceable individuals who either lived in or owned the studied properties at Little Lon.

Historical Research

For working-class individuals, immigration to Melbourne brought with it the hope of bettering one's position in life, and perhaps even moving into the middle class. But this phase of research has shown that aspirations and levels of success were by no means uniform for the residents of Little Lon. The emphasis of the recent work has been on studying a cross section of the neighbourhood (small inner-lane residences, larger outer-lane properties, owner occupied, tenanted, families, individuals, businesses, brothels etc.) through extensive additional historical research and in-depth re-cataloguing of a selection of house lots. The approach has been intrinsically multidisciplinary, following both historical and artefact narratives and their cross sections. Deposits have been carefully correlated with occupants where possible, or used to tease out the nature of occupation (type of tenancy, including prostitution). The diversity and varying aspirations of the residents has been brought to the fore, but with the dating of the cesspit closures to the early 1870s it is now clear that the owners of the artefacts found in them may not be representative of the kind of people living in Little Lon by the end of the century.

The House Lots

As previously noted, the 22 sites in this study were chosen on the basis of providing evidence relating to a variety of factors: main street and inner-lane frontages, long-term and short-term tenancies, homes and businesses. The historical research on these sites has produced substantial additional detail confirming conclusions from previous studies about occupational use (Mayne 2006; Leckey 2004), beginning with the broad scale transition from providing basic housing and business premises in the 1840s and 1850s to increasing numbers of 'houses of ill-fame' throughout the century, both in the poorer inner-lane cottages and in the larger main street properties. The mixture of industrial, retail, trade and residential premises was also present in the 22 sites, with the activities on most sites changing throughout the second half of the 19th century. The coal merchant's yard on lot 43 in the 1850s, for example, became a 'coal and timber yard' in the 1870s, a 'box factory' in the 1880s and a Chinese cabinetry works in the 1890s, while lot 33A changed from a bowling saloon to a synagogue to a drill hall before being used for furniture-making, then blacksmithing and the production of earth closets until it was rebuilt for use as a butcher shop in 1872. Most of the buildings – both main street and inner-lane frontages – appear to have been used as both businesses and residences at various (and often the same) times, with periods of vacancy not uncommon.

Confirmation of previous research was also found in relation to the dilapidation of inner-lane cottages, with those built of timber gradually deteriorating to the point where they either fell down or became uninhabitable. Some were replaced with brick cottages, and others were rebuilt at various times, but the increasingly erratic tenancy of many reflects the gradual erosion of the housing stock considered undesirable as dwellings and not useful for industry.

Peter Tucker, for example, owned four houses in Leichardt and Little Leichardt Streets, and when he died in 1896 it was noted that the four-roomed brick house was 'let to a weekly tenant', but the '3 small cottages composed of brick each containing two rooms' were 'seldom let' (PROV VA 2620 VPRS 28 P2 Unit 452). Unfortunately annual point-of-time records such as the Post Office Directories and MCC Rate Books could not distinguish between permanent and weekly tenants, although newspaper reports were sometimes able to provide incidental evidence. Late in 1865, for example, 19 half-chests of tea were stolen from a warehouse in Flinders street west; some of the stolen goods were subsequently found in one of the Leichardt Street houses, which had been rented on a weekly basis by the tenant of an adjoining house which was part of this study (*The Argus*, 19 December 1865, 1S).

Discussion: Diversity and Change in Little Lon

Little Lon's reputation as a haven for ruffians and houses of ill-fame has been noted and explored by many researchers (McConville 1980; Davison, Dunstan and McConville 1985; McCarthy 1989; Graeme Butler & Associates 2010). The current project has found ample evidence to support this reputation, but also to confirm the findings of recent historical archaeology projects which indicate honest families and workers could be found there as well as sex workers and rogues (Mayne 2006; Mayne and Murray 2001; Mayne, Murray and Lawrence 2000; Murray 2004). In their review of the archaeology of Melbourne, however, Lawrence and Davies (2017: 4–5) argued that the chronology developed by our paper on cesspits (Hayes and Minchinton 2016) has altered previous understandings of the Little Lon site, such that the vast majority of its stratified artefact evidence dates to the 20 years immediately after the gold rush. If the majority of artefacts predate the period in which Little Lon developed its reputation as a slum (Lawrence and Davies 2017: 5) it could explain why artefacts recovered from some cesspits showed a higher than anticipated level of respectability (McCarthy 1989: Vol 1, 6–7; Karskens and Lawrence 2003). It also leaves open the question of what effect the influx of sex workers in the 1870s and 1880s had on the overall economic status and community of Little Lon.

The family histories compiled for this project provide a beginning point for exploring this question. They show the trajectory of individual lives from occupations in their country of origin, circumstance of their immigration, employment and level of success in the colony, family situation, criminal activities etc., but people without property or prison records or court appearances reported in the newspapers were far harder to track with certainty in the records. Without a historical narrative supporting their existence, they had little influence on its reputation compared with the 'disorderly' women and criminals (see Mayne 1993). Another twist on this skewing of influence can be found when tracing people of different ethnic origins. The clear influx of people of Chinese, Indian and other nationalities in the 1890s, for example, proved almost impossible to trace in detail because they were often listed without names (the Melbourne City Council Rate Books, for example, often noted simply 'occupied by Chinese').

Nevertheless, beginning with the cross-section of house lots selected for this study and delving into the personal histories of owners and tenants, it is clear that the people who lived and worked in Little Lon in the 19th century came from diverse backgrounds and gave rise to generations with varying levels of material success. Alan Mayne's observation of a 'trend from initial owner-occupation to landlordism over an individual's lifetime' held true in our research (Mayne 2006: 324), with the added curiosity of labourers who accumulated property portfolios without any accompanying increase in middle-class material goods. Timothy Cleary and George Howes, for example, began as labourers but left estates including at least five pieces of real estate each in the Little Lon area, but very few goods and chattels (PROV VA 2620 VPRS 28 P0 Unit 143 and P2 Unit 101). Combining the personal histories with our detailed waste management history provides a nuanced understanding of the types of occupation in the area, especially prior to the cesspit closures, and suggests a basis for the differentiation of deposits in the future (Hayes and Minchinton 2016).

From the 22 selected sites, a number of themes emerged, three of which will be discussed below: the different material culture signatures of short-term and long-term residents, the diversity in the life stories of women involved with sex work, and the predominantly gradual nature of movement into the middle class.

Short-Term Versus Long-Term Residents

The selection of house lots for this phase of research was driven by the question of whether distinctions might be drawn between short-term and long-term tenants in terms of their aspirations as reflected in their material possessions. However, as noted above, this phase of historical research has disrupted the concept of the 'household' in relation to the archaeology of these sites. Careful consideration is required to determine 'short-term' versus 'long-term' tenancies in Little Lon, because the prevalent use of aliases, the constant moving of tenants, the inconsistent spelling of many (illiterate) people's names, and the high incidence of unnamed people residing as lodgers and sex workers make it hazardous to specify the tenants of any given property (Minchinton 2017a). This is true for both the inner-lane cottages and the buildings with main street frontages, so that in Little Lon linking artefacts with individuals requires very careful assessment and fortuitous circumstances. Nevertheless the recursive integration of archival research with archaeological evidence revealed patterns of short-term and long-term occupation on several sites prior to the closure of the cesspits. For example, the cesspit deposits on lots 74B (Casselden Place), 25C (Leichardt Street), and 36A (Little Leichardt Street) could be confidently associated with short-term tenants because the names of occupiers changed frequently in and across the records. The cesspit on lot 36A, however, was shared with a long-term owner-resident on lot 36B, and the pit on 25C was shared between four houses on lots 25A/B/C/D with some long-term residents, leaving lot 74B as the best single-house example of short-term tenancy.

We anticipated that short-term tenants would invest little in domestic possessions as they would need to discard or pack anything they purchased to take with them. Lot 74B on Casselden Place was occupied by a series of tenants for two to three years including John Fermerly, C McDonald and Michael Cummings (butcher) around the time when Cesspit C on this lot was closed in 1871 (Hayes and Minchinton 2016: 15). As expected, it contained few artefacts compared to other Little Lon cesspits: a MNI of 77 (not including faunal and building materials). Despite the low numbers, some modest investment in home and self is evident with three ceramic figurines, a flower pot, two simple hygiene vessels, a medicine bottle, two ointment jars, a slate pencil (suggesting literacy) and two clay pipes in the assemblage. 'Food and Tea Service' vessels were the largest single group in the assemblage (39%) and largely comprised cheap wares, predominantly whiteware and transfer-prints. The only hint of a matching set was two Willow pattern plates and a platter that could have functioned as a complementary set, but in this high turnover tenancy scenario each vessel could equally have belonged to a different owner. The very simple hygiene vessels suggest that money was not invested on decorative items for private use (see Praetzellis and Praetzellis 1992: 91). The most expensive ceramics, perhaps saved for guests, were a porcelain tea cup and saucer with multi-colour enamelled decoration (see Brooks 2005: 38) and, arguably, two platters. The cesspit assemblage from lot 74B is certainly modest – the necessities with just a handful of nicer items, selectively chosen – but in this period of burgeoning consumer culture it shows that at least some short-term tenants were investing in ornaments and flower pots.

Our research indicates that there were many common circumstances leading to short-term tenancies in Little Lon but the predominant ones were poverty and/or prostitution. The tenants of lot 74B after 1871 included known sex workers, but the timing prohibits any evidence of that occupation appearing in the cesspits. The cesspit from lot 74B showed signs of some investment in domestic wares, but the items retrieved, for example, from lot 27 – occupied by poor sex workers – showed that money was largely spent on cheaper alcohol (further discussion below).

Alongside the transient population of Little Lon our research indicates that there were also many long-term residents, especially labourers, but they tended to move from one property to another, while owner-occupants were more likely to be living and raising families in the same property over a long period. Only five of the cesspits we examined proved to have long-term residents who were its sole users at the time of its closure, and they were all owner-occupied by three owners (two owners had two each). Two owners had been identified and discussed in earlier phases. The third (on lot 57B, owned and occupied by Thomas and Mary Player) was catalogued as part of phase 2 (Woff this volume), while this chapter was in preparation, and is yet to be analysed. The Moloney family at lot 69A/B on Casselden Place lived across the road from the short-term tenancy discussed above, and have been discussed in previous research (Mayne, Murray and Lawrence 2000: 141; Mayne and Murray 2001: 101). The photograph of the Moloney assemblage in Figure 9.1, however, provides an immediate and sufficient contrast with the description of the minimal contents of the cesspit at lot 74B given above. A more detailed interpretation of this collection in terms of respectability is also in preparation by Hayes. Briefly, situating the Moloneys against other residents of Little Lon, it becomes clear that this family valued possessions in a different way to their neighbours and engaged with respectability as best they could from within their means.

John and his siblings were all illiterate, and no children lived at lot 69A/B, yet two slate pencils, a doll's tea set and marble were recovered from the cesspit. Together they suggest that John Moloney's brother Thomas's children (who lived across the lane) visited their uncles and aunts at lot 69A/B, providing a clear contrast with Henry Cornwell's version of parenting (see below).

The cesspits at lot 74B and lot 69A/B show that before 1870 at least, both transient and more settled residents in Little Lon were buying into the world of goods, but as the above examples indicate short-term occupants were less likely to be investing significant amounts of money in quality goods.

Prostitution: Deviance, Choice or Necessity?

Prostitution was not illegal in Victoria until soliciting was prohibited in 1891, but it was controlled through the use of legislation relating to vagrancy. Previous research on Little Lon has emphasised the prevalence of prostitution in the area without investigating how central or integrated it was

Figure 9.1: The contents of the Moloneys' cesspit on display at Museum Victoria as part of the Commonwealth Block project (Source: Sarah Hayes).

in the economy of the neighbourhood or how the industry changed over time (Davison, Dunstan and McConville 1985; McCarthy 1989; McConville 1980). The women were described as 'outcasts' and it was thought that it was the neighbourhood's relatively low rents that attracted the sex workers, but our research indicates that sex workers were paying higher rents than others in Little Lon, and that as a group they were an accepted part of the Little Lon community. Many of the longer-term occupants were either involved with prostitution or benefiting from it through rents, employment or the sale of goods (groceries, beverages etc.). Two property-owning madams appeared in this research, owning three of the 22 properties at various times, and at least one other site was being used as a brothel in the period under study. Lots 26 and 27 Leichardt Street conveniently encompass both of the brothel owners and one of the sex workers whose personal histories could be reconstructed to a meaningful degree. Lot 26 had been occupied from about 1861 by a family with long and multiple criminal histories not including prostitution, but from 1871 onwards under the ownership of Madame Diana de Beaumont both sites were being run as a rough back-street brothel. Madame de Beaumont was prosecuted in 1873, and although she was found not guilty she was forced to leave the area; she sold lots 26 and 27 to Mrs Bond, who continued the brothel with Mary Williams and her husband as tenants. Names were a moveable feast for all three of these women, but there the similarities end. By drawing out some of the nuances of the individual lives carried on in Little Lon's 'dens of infamy' we can understand more about Little Lon as a community.

Diana de Beaumont came from Sydney in the 1860s; in 1871 she was running a fruit shop as a cover for a brothel in Russell street, Melbourne (*The Argus*, 9 February 1871: 4), as well as the two properties in Leichardt street which form part of this study (lots 26 and 27). It was a lucrative business until December 1872 when she was accused of procuring young girls for her establishment in Russell Street. Running a house of ill-fame was one thing, but decoying and ruining innocent girls was something else. She was discharged on the condition that she took her business elsewhere within a week (*The Argus*, 17 December 1872: 7). In the newspaper reports of the time Madame de Beaumont's style and reputation were enough to condemn her, unlike the woman who very quickly bought her Leichardt street cottages: Mrs Bond.

Mrs Bond was an Irish widow who first came to public notice in 1862 when she was reported as running a 'disreputable house' in Stephen (Exhibition) Street. Her (at that time) de facto husband, William Bond, had been attacked by her son from her previous marriage, and her evidence at the trial revealed that her husband barely worked, and 'she could not see her children starve, and had at first taken in washing, and then had to keep a brothel to support the family' (*The Argus*, 30 April 1862: 5). Mrs Bond was raising three children in this manner until her drunken, violent husband died of tuberculosis in 1863. Then she began accumulating assets; she first bought a two-roomed cottage off Lonsdale Street, and when Diana de Beaumont had to leave she also bought her two properties in Leichardt Street. Within a few years she had purchased three more houses in Lonsdale Street; two were rented to sex workers, but she turned the third one into a grocer's shop. The historical records represent it clearly as a genuine shop, but a close inspection of a rubbish pit on the lot (Pit N) supported McCarthy's conjecture that the site was used as a brothel (McCarthy 1989: 129). The pit was distinctive with regard to artefact types and distributions: it contained a large number of champagne, imported spirits and absinthe bottles (Figure 9.2), and over 300 oyster shells (McCarthy 1989: 126). Further, the variety and depth of the bottle identification resources now available allowed 10 bottles recovered from the tip to be identified as absinthe bottles by our research. The absinthe bottles (representing 28% of all beverage storage bottles from the pit) were particularly noteworthy, given their absence across the rest of Little Lon. The only other deposit which yielded absinthe bottles was the cesspit on the same lot. Absinthe, or 'the green fairy', was an alcoholic drink with a reputation for being hallucinogenic; it was available from the 18th century but reached new heights of popularity in bohemian Paris in the late 19th century, coinciding with the timing of Mrs Bond's occupancy of lot 30. While Mrs Bond was never prosecuted for running a 'bad house', her grocer's shop was likely to have been a cover for a better class brothel than lots 26 and 27. Not that she missed the opportunity to make money from the grocery business: her probate inventory includes 'Stock in trade of a grocer Draper &c' valued at £75 (PROV VA 2620 VPRS 28 P2 Unit 80). This was a significant amount of stock, and some of it probably wound up in rubbish pit N after her death in 1877. It seems most likely that the majority of the contents of that pit came from Mrs Bond's brothel and grocery as well as from the clear-out of George Jameson's pawnshop in about 1870.

While a brothel serving absinthe would have been catering for relatively expensive tastes, one of Mrs Bond's tenants in Leichardt Street was, by contrast, catering for poorer clientele. Mary Williams came from Ireland via a brief marriage in Adelaide, but in 1870 when she was still in her 20s she left South Australia with George Williams; they ended up in residence at one of Madame de Beaumont's houses (lot 26). George was an English carpenter but within months of arriving in Melbourne he was in prison for theft – the first of at least four stretches (PROV VA 1464 VPRS 515 P1 Vols 15 and 29). Mary ran the brothel at lot 26 while he was away, and had at least two babies in Little Lon; both died in infancy. She was described by a police sergeant in 1872 as a 'drunkard' who ran one of the most disorderly houses in Leichardt Street and had been fined numerous times at the City Court for bad language (PROV VA 724 VPRS 937 P0 Unit 292). Mary and George Williams ran a number of brothels in the Little Lon area both before and after their sojourn at lot 26, and Mary's history as a madam can be found in the newspapers (e.g. *The Argus*, 1 November 1871: 4 and 18 February 1879: 6).

Clear distinctions are observable between the brothels. Mrs Bond's absinthe drinking, oyster shucking brothel was a brick shop with five additional rooms (at least eight rooms in total), with a prominent Lonsdale Street frontage, but the brothel at lots 26 and 27 comprised two very basic detached two-room brick and wood cottages down a side street. A woman supporting herself or her children through prostitution in her bedroom at home would probably leave the same material cultural signature as a domestic occupant – there would be no lavish accoutrements and her profession would not be visible in the archaeological record. The cesspit contents on lot 26 were not associated with the brothel phases, but next door at the three-room

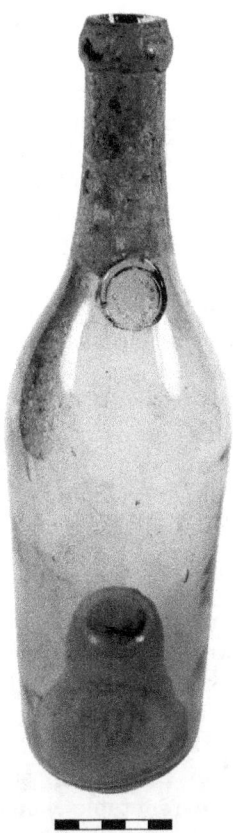

Figure 9.2: Absinthe bottle from Mrs Bond's rubbish pit (Source: Bronwyn Woff).

brick building on lot 27 the cesspit fill was probably created, at least in part, by the sex workers living there from 1872. The deposit lacked the luxury imports of champagne and absinthe present in Mrs Bond's rubbish pit, but there was still a strong representation of beverage bottles (33%) including 90 beer/wine bottles, two gin/schnapps bottles and one cognac bottle. There were also 165 oyster shell fragments, two perfume bottles and an ointment pot. The sex workers living in the cottage brothel were likely earning less and attracting less well-to-do clients than their expensive counterparts.

Madame Diana de Beaumont, Mrs Bond and Mrs Williams were all involved in the same business, running brothels in the same area in the same era, but Madame Diana was 'an elderly French woman' (*The Leader*, 21 October 1871: 13) – her first advertisements in Sydney were in both French and English (e.g. *Sydney Morning Herald*, 7 July 1862: 1) – with a love of diamonds (*The Argus*, 18 September 1871: 4), whereas Mrs Bond began as a poor Irish woman and poured her earnings into property. Mary Williams was probably the epitome of what reformers of the era would have called 'low-life' and judged harshly for both her poverty and her morals, but Mrs Bond raised three sons and when she died her property portfolio would have been the envy of many (PROV VA 2620 VPRS 28 P2 Unit 80). Comparing the life stories of these three contemporaries in Little Lon gives considerable depth to the generic label 'prostitute'.

Moving to the Middle Class

This phase of research sought to identify people who could be characterised as stepping on the ladder up to the middle classes, but only three examples of a dedicated single-family cesspit of this kind were found. One has yet to be analysed (lot 57B), and the other two belonged to Henry Cornwell, who operated a butcher shop in Little Lon for three decades (Godden Mackay Logan, Austral Archaeology and La Trobe University 2004: 19; PROV VA 862 VPRS 460). This finding will be discussed in future research. The Cornwells, like the Moloneys, have been discussed in previous research (Godden Mackay Logan 2004: 55–57; Mayne 2006: 326) but not in the context of how they displayed 'respectability' and the role this played in their social mobility, which is a central aspect of our research. Henry and his wife Isabella initially lived in a three-room home which also housed their shop. By 1873, they were occupying this tiny space with six children and a baby. It was at this point that they moved next door to a house with seven rooms. When Isabella died in 1889, Henry (in his 60s), sold up their properties in Little Lon and moved to Northcote. The Cornwells occupied lot 33B long enough to have two cesspits closures associated with them (Hayes and Minchinton 2016: 22). The bluestone cesspit (2.722), closed between 1861 and 1867, was used to discard rubbish before a new leak-proof barrel cesspit (2.631) was installed inside it over the layer of artefacts, and subsequently closed in October 1871. The lower deposit comprised a MNI of only 17 (excluding faunal and building materials) including six mostly unremarkable tea wares. The barrel cesspit contained 157 individual items (not including faunal and building materials) 38.4% of which were food and tea service related. This seems to be where the Cornwells invested most of their expenditure in material goods, and their choices are significant in the context of their move into the middle class. The Cornwells discarded five matching sets including a complementary Willow (15 vessels), two complementary and two matching tea sets three of which comprised both teacups/saucers and plates. The emphasis in matching sets for serving tea suggest that the Cornwells were more concerned with keeping up appearance while serving tea to guests than dining (see Wall 1992: 79), which was probably a private family affair. The Cornwells also had a range of patterns beyond the most commonly available including Wild Rose, Corinthian and Tyrol. Transfer-prints dominated with only a handful of relatively more expensive hand-painted vessels. Beyond the tea and tableware there are only small hints at investment in the home. They discarded a Staffordshire figure and a flower pot in the cesspit, suggesting that they had some interest in decorating their house. They also chose a hand-painted and flown chamber pot rather than the standard undecorated versions. At the same time, not a single toy or childhood related item was found in spite of the fact that seven children lived at lot 33B. The comparison with the Moloneys is stark, and will be discussed in a future publication.

When comparing the assemblages discussed here, it can be argued that respectability in the choice of material goods was more important to those who settled in Little Lon for the longer term like the Moloneys and Cornwells. Yet, what kept these families in Little Lon differed, as did their brands of respectability. For the Moloneys, their brand of respectability sits with Karskens' (1997: 230–232) argument of situating themselves with a sense of belonging within the working-class, as hard working, respectable people doing their best for their children. In contrast, the Cornwells focused their expenditure on tea and there is an implied emphasis on display, appearances and middle-class values that goes with this (see Wall 1992: 92). In this regard they were also engaging with respectability as a strategy, using possessions to communicate their status to those who dined or took tea at their home (Hayes 2017: 7).

Henry's move to the suburbs occurred late in life once his children were grown (Figure 9.3). It was a gradual hard slog up the ladder, and research on the selected house lots has shown that it was not a common path in Little Lon, though there were certainly others who made the journey. Honora

Figure 9.3: Henry Cornwell's houses in Westgarth Street Northcote, 'Aliceville', 'Edithville' and 'Belleville' (Source: Barbara Minchinton).

Judd, for example, and her husband, after living in Little Lon for most of their married lives (lot 55A), died in a double-storey terrace on Beaconsfield Parade overlooking Port Philip Bay (PROV VA 2620 VPRS 28 P0 Unit 775 Honora Judd). They left their children with a substantial legacy of properties and middle-class accoutrements such as a piano and a sewing machine (PROV VPRS 7591 P2 Unit 248 Honora Judd). It was not only the Judds' and the Cornwells' children who were able to establish their own businesses and enter the world of Family Notices in *The Argus* and wives labelled 'home duties' in the electoral rolls, either; some of the labourers' children and even more of their grandchildren were there as well. At the same time there were many who never found the ladder much less made the climb.

The Moloneys, Cornwells, Judds and other families who appeared in this phase of the research provide examples along the spectrum of Little Lon 'success', but few of the residents of Little Lon moved quickly or directly into the middle class, and those who did were often indebted to the business of prostitution for their achievement. Mrs Judd was not a madam or a sex worker herself, but she accumulated property through profits obtained by renting houses to those who were. According to one police inspector, property owners preferred renting to sex workers because 'they obtain three times the amount of rent with only half the trouble of collecting' (PROV VA 724 VPRS 937 P0 310). Henry Cornwell, despite his vociferous condemnation of the brothels surrounding his butcher shop, no doubt sold his meat to them (e.g. PROV VA 724 VPRS 937 P0 Unit 314). The situation was complex, and the economic history of Little Lon in relation to prostitution is the subject of another study by Minchinton.

So far we have found no evidence that a significant number of the tenants of Little Lon were striking it rich on the goldfields or making rapid moves into the middle class in the 19th century, in fact gaining direct entry to the middle class was a rare achievement for residents of Little Lon. Nevertheless they were purchasing and discarding consumer goods in revealing ways. Our research has shown that while there are some indications of upward social movement in the following generations, children who grew up in Little Lon often moved out to Carlton or Fitzroy when they started their own families, and they were not necessarily moving 'up' – conditions in the nearer suburbs could be every bit as difficult as those in Little Lon (McConville 1985). Social movement of this kind has not been studied in any depth as yet, but will be researched further for the Gold Rush Lives project.

Conclusion

The research undertaken for this project unearthed a number of thieves and madams amongst the occupants of the 22 selected sites, but the number relating to the cesspit closures was much smaller than Little Lon's reputation would have predicted, and while some were scattered amongst respectable business people and poor but decent workers, others defied differentiation. At the same time, by beginning with a list of owners' and tenants' names rather than with a grand narrative of 'red-light district' or 'slum', the researcher is able to build up a picture of the person and their family by learning about their parents, their marriage(s) and their children, for example, before the evidence of court reports and multiple dead babies culminates in a search through prison records where charges of 'vagrancy' or 'theft' might appear. For the researcher, therefore, the names become characters with nuanced identities before they are defined by derogatory labels, and the differences in their individual life stories can be striking. While social history might apply pejorative descriptors such as 'prostitute' and 'criminal', the timelines constructed for the individual families make it clear that the trajectories of the lives described in such terms were by no means uniform or predictable.

As a result, this phase of research has changed the authors' views of Little Lon. It might have been a low-rent place for transients in the 1850s and 60s, but by the mid-1870s it appears that only tradesmen or poverty-stricken families would rent an inner-lane cottage alongside the sex workers. Yet the ties of home ownership, family connections or business convenience kept others in the area for the long-term. It was through these long-term residents – families like the Moloneys, Judds and Cornwells – that the cultural cache of respectability found its way in to Little Lon. Unsurprisingly, much of the 'moving up in the world' that was done in Little Lon in the 19th century came from the profits of prostitution, whether through running 'bad houses', owning property and renting it to sex workers, or running businesses that profited from them (grocery shops, hotels, furniture hire etc.). The main-street frontage businesses were more varied, and people like Henry Cornwell (who resided there, unlike many of the manufacturers) complained bitterly and often about the brothels. Yet some of those who complained about sex workers in public were renting houses to them in private: it was a district built on the back of prostitution, and the resulting social conditions defined the area. We now know that future research will need to explore what effect the influx of sex workers in the 1870s and 1880s had on the social fabric of the area without the assistance of cesspit archaeology. We can be confident that by the 1890s, hit by the depression and legislation prohibiting soliciting, the material deposited in Little Lon at the time of the cesspit closures was no longer representative of the people living in the area.

Having further unpacked the diversity within Little Lon in this phase of research, new questions can now be asked of the archaeology. How did the residents' choice of possessions differ from Victorians' of different class backgrounds and why? To what extent did immigration improve the lives of Little Lon's residents? How easy was it for immigrants to Victoria to improve their lot in the gold rush period? And what factors limited their advancement? These are the driving questions of the next phase of research for the authors (under the Suburban Archaeology and Gold Rush Lives projects). Other questions relate to the period after the cesspit closures: How did the increase in prostitution in the area affect Little Lon's economy? In what ways did the community change between the closure of the cesspits in the 1870s and the closure of the legal brothels in the early 20th century?

The long legacy of research on Little Lon, of which this chapter is a small part, is not set to come to its conclusion any time soon. Murray (2006: 302), in his introduction to the 2006 IJHA volume on Casselden Place, noted that the papers in the volume constituted 'a work in progress rather than the end point of research on the archaeology of the "Commonwealth Block"'. It's a statement which feels as true today as it did a decade ago. This phase of research has upturned previous understandings about the area by producing precise dating for many of the cesspit closures and teasing out the nature of 'occupancy'. While the full ramifications of that have yet to be explored, the picture of Little Lon created by earlier historical and historical archaeological research has already been considerably augmented by our detailed research on individuals and their material possessions. Combining archival research with the archaeological record has been collaborative, consistent and valuable throughout this phase, and there have been instances where the archaeology has led to the reinterpretation of the history (as in the case of Mrs Bond's grocery/brothel) and vice versa (including the association of cesspits with occupants). The resultant understanding of the diversity of Little Lon's residents, of what they chose to purchase and use, and of their life histories, gives a real and gritty sense of the hardships and joys of life at Little Lon. This detail provides the bedrock for further comparative studies within Melbourne, and between Melbourne and cities elsewhere (a major objective of the Commonwealth Block and Suburban Archaeology projects).

Acknowledgements

The research presented here draws on two Australian Research Council funded projects:
- A Historical Archaeology of the Commonwealth Block 1850–1950 (LP0989224) undertaken at La Trobe University and Museum Victoria. Chief investigators Tim Murray and Charlotte Smith.
- Suburban Archaeology: Approaching an Archaeology of the Middle Class in 19th-Century Melbourne (DP1093001) undertaken at La Trobe University, Deakin University and University of Melbourne. Chief investigators

Tim Murray, Susan Lawrence, Andrew Brown-May and Linda Young. Post-doctoral Fellow Sarah Hayes.

Two research assistants have carried out artefact cataloguing for the above projects: Paul Pepdjonovic who worked on the first phase, and Bronwyn Woff who undertook the second phase. A special thanks to the volunteers who have put in many hours to assist with this work.

Thank you to the Department of Archaeology and History at La Trobe University for the technical and intellectual support that facilitated these projects. Also, Museum Victoria kindly provided access to the collection and lab space for the project and were jointly involved in the rehabilitation of the collection.

The research discussed here will also form part of the Australian Research Council Discovery Early Career Researcher Award project An Archaeology of Quality of Life During Victoria's Gold Rush (DE150101203) undertaken at La Trobe University. Chief investigator Sarah Hayes.

Thank you to Tim Murray for the opportunity to work on the above projects and the invitation to contribute to this volume, and to Kristal Buckley for considered comments on early drafts.

REFERENCES

Archival Material

Public Record Office Victoria (PROV), Agency (VA), Public Record Series (VPRS):

PROV VA 724 Victoria Police (including Office of the Chief Commissioner of Police) VPRS 937 Inward Registered Correspondence P0 Unit 292 'Brothel nuisance in Leichardt street', 27 February 1872; Unit 304 Bundle 1 'Mr Cornwall writes on Prostitutes', 20 January 1881; Unit 310 'Prostitutes in Lonsdale Street', 20 November 1883; Unit 314 'Mr Cornwell v Const Wall', 23 February 1885.

PROV VA 511 Melbourne (Town 1842–1847; City 1847-ct) VPRS 3103 Melbourne City Council (MCC) Committee Reports.

PROV VA 511 Melbourne (Town 1842–1847; City 1847-ct) VPRS 5708 P9 MCC Rate Books 1861–1975.

PROV VA 2620 Registrar of Probates VPRS 28 Probate and Administration Files P0 Unit 143 Timothy Cleary; Unit 775 Honora Judd.

PROV VA 2620 Registrar of Probates VPRS 28 Probate and Administration Files P2 Unit 452 Peter Tucker, Statement of Assets and Liabilities, 4; Unit 101 George Howes; Unit 80 Alicia Gleeson, Inventory.

PROV VA 2620 Registrar of Probates VPRS 7591 Wills P2; Unit 248 Honora Judd; Unit 539 Henry Cornwell.

PROV VA 1464 Penal and Gaols Branch, Chief Secretary's Department VPRS 515 Central Register of Male Prisoners P1 Volume 15, page 17 Prisoner No 9722 and Volume 29 page 87 Prisoner No 17090, William Williams alias George Williams.

PROV VA 862 Office of the Registrar-General VPRS 460 Applications for Certificates of Title P0 Unit 2311, Henry Cornwell statutory declaration 6 January 1887.

Newspapers

The Argus (Melbourne)

Leader (Melbourne)

Sydney Morning Herald (Sydney)

Published

Birmingham, J. 1990. A Decade of Digging: Deconstructing Urban Archaeology. *Australian Historical Archaeology* 8: 13–22.

Brooks, A. 2005. *An Archaeological Guide to British Ceramics in Australia 1788–1901*. Sydney: Australasian Society for Historical Archaeology and the La Trobe University Archaeology Program.

Crook, P., S. Lawrence and M. Gibbs, 2002. The Role of Artefact Catalogues in Australian Historical Archaeology: A Framework for Discussion. *Australasian Historical Archaeology* 20: 26–38.

Crook, P. and T. Murray, 2006. *Guide to the EAMC Archaeology Database*. Archaeology of the Modern City 1788–1900 Series, Volume 10. Sydney: Historic Houses Trust of New South Wales.

Davison, G., D. Dunstan and C. McConville (eds.), 1985. *The Outcasts of Melbourne*. Sydney: Allen & Unwin.

Godden Mackay Logan, Austral Archaeology and La Trobe University, 2004. Casselden Place, 50 Lonsdale Street, Melbourne, Archaeological Excavations Research Archive Report, Volume 1: Introduction and Background. Report. Melbourne: ISPT and Heritage Victoria.

Graeme Butler & Associates, 2010. *Heritage Assessment of Buildings at 116–132 Little Lonsdale St, Melbourne: For the City of Melbourne*. http://www.melbourne.vic.gov.au/about-council/committees-meetings/meeting-archive/MeetingAgendaItemAttachments/491/8099/5.2%20att2.pdf

Hayes, S. 2017. A Golden Opportunity: Mayor Smith and Melbourne's Emergence as a Global

City. *International Journal of Historical Archaeology*, Online First.

Hayes, S. 2011. Amalgamation of Archaeological Assemblages: Experiences from the Commonwealth Block Project, Melbourne. *Australian Archaeology* 73: 13–24.

Hayes, S. and B. Minchinton, 2016. Melbourne's Waste Management History and Cesspit Formation Processes: Evidence from Little Lon. *Australian Archaeology* 82(1): 12–24.

Karskens, G. 1997. *The Rocks: Life in Early Sydney*. Carlton: Melbourne University Press.

Karskens, G. and S. Lawrence, 2003. The Archaeology of Cities: What is It We Want to Know? In T. Murray (ed.) *Exploring the Modern City: Recent Approaches to Urban History and Archaeology*, pp. 89–111. Melbourne: Historic Houses Trust of New South Wales and La Trobe University.

Lawrence, S. and P. Davies, 2017. Melbourne: The Archaeology of a World City. *International Journal of Historical Archaeology*, Online First.

Leckey, J. 2004. *'Low, Degraded Broots'? Industry and Entrepreneurialism in Melbourne's Little Lon, 1860–1950*. Melbourne: Australian Scholarly Publishing.

Mayne, A. 1993. *The Imagined Slum: Newspaper Representation in Three Cities, 1870–1914*. Leicester: Leicester University Press.

Mayne, A. 2006. Big Notes from a Little Street: Historical Research at Melbourne's Little Lon. *International Journal of Historical Archaeology* 10(4): 317–328.

Mayne, A. and T. Murray, 2001. Imaginary Landscapes: Reading Melbourne's Little Lon. In Mayne, A. and T. Murray (eds.) *The Archaeology of Urban Landscapes: Explorations in Slumland*, pp. 89–105. New Directions in Archaeology Series. Cambridge: University of Cambridge.

Mayne, A., T. Murray and S. Lawrence, 2000. Historical Sites: Melbourne's Little Lon. *Australian Historical Studies* 31(114): 131–151.

McCarthy, J. 1989. Archaeological Investigation: Commonwealth Offices and Telecom Corporate Building Sites, The Commonwealth Block, Melbourne, Victoria, Volume 1: Historical and Archaeological Report. Report. Melbourne: Department of Administrative Services and Telecom Australia by Austral Archaeology.

McConville, C. 1980. The Location of Melbourne's Prostitutes, 1870–1920. *Historical Studies* 19(74): 86–97.

McConville, C. 1985. From 'Criminal Class' to 'Underworld'. In Davison, G., D. Dunstan and C. McConville (eds.) *The Outcasts of Melbourne*. Sydney: Allen & Unwin.

Minchinton, B. 2017a. 'Prostitutes' and 'Lodgers' in Little Lon: Constructing a List of Occupiers in Nineteenth-Century Melbourne. *Australasian Historical Archaeology* 35: 64–70.

Minchinton, B. 2017b. Women as Landowners in Victoria: Questions from Little Lon. *History Australia* 14(1): 67–81.

Murray, T. 2004. Plain English Report. In Godden Mackay Logan, Austral Archaeology and La Trobe University, Casselden Place, 50 Lonsdale Street, Melbourne, Archaeological Excavations Research Archive Report, Volume 1: Introduction and Background, pp. 29–61. Report. Melbourne: ISPT and Heritage Victoria.

Murray, T. 2006. Introduction. *International Journal of Historical Archaeology* 10(4): 297–304.

Murray, T. and P. Crook, 2005. Exploring the Archaeology of the Modern City: Issues of Scale, Integration and Complexity. *International Journal of Historical Archaeology* 9(2): 89–109.

Murray, T., G. Karskens and A. Mayne, 2004. Explorations in Slumland: A Reprise. *Australasian Historical Archaeology* 22: 94–97.

Murray, T. and A. Mayne, 2002. *Vanished Communities: Investigating History at Little Lon, An ARC Funded CDROM*. Melbourne: La Trobe University and Swish Group.

Murray, T. and A. Mayne, 2003. (Re)Constructing a Lost Community: Little Lon, Melbourne, Australia. *Historical Archaeology* 37(1): 87–101.

Praetzellis, A. and M. Praetzellis, 1992. Faces and Facades: Victorian Ideology in Early Sacramento. In Yentsch, A.E. and M.C. Beaudry (eds.) *The Art and Mystery of Historical Archaeology: Essays in Honor of James Deetz*, pp. 75–99. Florida: CRC Press.

Smith, C.H.F. and S. Hayes, 2010. Managing the Commonwealth Block Archaeological Assemblage: An Australian Case Study. *Collections: A Journal for Museum and Archives Professionals* 6(3): 171–187.

Wall, D.D. 1992. Sacred Dinners and Secular Teas: Constructing Domesticity in Mid-19th-Century New York. *Historical Archaeology* 25: 69–81.

10
An Update on the Commonwealth Block Project: A Second Phase of Targeted Feature Cataloguing

Bronwyn Woff

The second and most recent phase of work on the Commonwealth Block collection, also known as the Little Lon collection, began in May 2015 and was completed March 2017. This paper reports on this phase of the project, its methodologies and outcomes, then discusses the use of the Exploring the Archaeology of the Modern City (EAMC) database and Museums Victoria's KE Electronic Museum (EMu) collections management system, and the challenges that the tandem use of these two databases creates.

THE COLLECTION

The Commonwealth Block artefact collection, as well as being the most completely analysed assemblage in Australia, is the largest urban 19th-century collection in the world. The artefact collection resides in the custody of Museums Victoria (MV), which previous to 2016 was known as Museum Victoria. Artefacts from the collection that are not on display are kept at an MV storage facility, forming part of the wider historical archaeology collection for the history and technology department (Smith and Hayes 2010). Due to the sheer volume of material collected during the various excavation seasons, some artefacts in the past have been bulk bagged, and some records contain only basic information. Bulk bagged records can contain hundreds of fragments which may represent hundreds of vessels. Other records contain only basic information, which began to be updated during the first phase of works on the collection which commenced in 2009 (Hayes 2011a).

THE PROJECT

A precursor to the Commonwealth Block project was the ARC Linkage project 'Exploring the Archaeology of the Modern City, 1788–1900', which began in 2001, and investigated archaeological assemblages from Sydney (Murray and Crook 2005: 94; Hayes 2011a: 14; Crook et al. 2003, 2005). The EAMC database was created during this project using Microsoft® Access®, and at first contained historical and archaeological data from multiple Sydney sites including First Government House, the Cumberland and Gloucester Streets site and the Hyde Park Barracks (Murray and Crook 2005: 93; Crook and Murray 2006: 5).

During the first phase of the Commonwealth Block project, which aimed to combine and enhance excavation and artefact records, the EAMC database was expanded to contain historical and archaeological data from the various Commonwealth Block sites. The various physical and digital records were combined, including field notes, artefact records, and historic records in order to provide the opportunity for new and more detailed analysis and interpretations, and for inter-site comparisons to be made (Smith and Hayes 2010; Hayes 2011a: 14). From this data Hayes compiled a list of significant features and contexts (Hayes 2011a: 17). Hayes and Pepdjonovic then worked on the artefact records to combine the various original databases, and to complete a full box audit and rehousing and reorganisation of the artefact collection (Hayes 2011a: 17–21).

The second phase of the project builds on these earlier processes and was carried out over two years. The project targeted artefacts from Little Lon pit and cesspit features that had been flagged as being of high significance by Hayes (2011a: 17) (see Figure 10.1). These features were excavated during the 1988 Little Lonsdale Street and 2002–2003 Casselden Place excavation seasons. It aimed to create more detailed information about these artefacts, by expanding basic records previously added to EAMC and creating new individual records for previously bulk bagged artefacts. Being part of the wider project, these tasks were guided by previous processes, and the overarching aim of ensuring that artefacts in the EAMC database were comparable with the previously entered assemblages from the various Sydney sites (Mayne and Murray 2001: 1–7; Murray 2006: 396; Murray and Crook 2005: 94).

METHODOLOGIES

The methodologies of the project followed the instructions of the *Guide to the EAMC Database*

Feature Name	Status
Cesspit N	Complete 2015
Cesspit O	Complete 2015
Refuse pit 27/04	Complete 2015
Pit 1.251	Complete 2015
Pit 2.290	Complete 2015
Pit F	Complete 2015
Cesspit 3.340	Complete 2015
Cesspit 3.341	Complete 2015
Cesspit 3.383	Complete 2015
Cesspit H	Complete 2016
Cesspit I	Complete 2016
Pit 3.035	Complete 2016
Pit 3.040	Complete 2016
Pit 3.041	Complete 2016
Pit 3.177	Complete 2016
Pit 3.197	Complete 2016
Pit 7.091/7.086	Complete 2016
Pit 1.401	Complete 2016
Pit 1.169	Complete 2016
Pit 1.210	Complete 2016
Pit 2.400	Complete 2016
Cesspit 2.402	Complete 2017
Pit 1.023	Complete 2017
Pit 1.165	Complete 2017
Pit 8.044/8.045	Complete 2017
Pit 3.566	Three associated artefacts – investigation needed
Pit 37/09	No associated artefacts – investigation needed
Deposit 2.453	No associated artefacts – investigation needed
Pit 3.336 (3.338, 3.611)	No associated artefacts – investigation needed

Figure 10.1: Status of all significant features.

(Crook and Murray 2006), and methodologies developed for *A Historical Archaeology of the Commonwealth Block 1850–1950: Artefact Processing Project Report* (Hayes 2011b) as well as suggestions from various current and past LTU staff.

Artefacts were catalogued using the EAMC database, supplemented by information in Museums Victoria's KE Electronic Museum (EMu) collections management system. The cataloguing side of the EAMC database includes standardised lists for artefact information, as well as free-fill text fields. The database contains context data, type series data, and images (Murray and Crook 2006). In the previous phase, the EAMC database was altered to work with the EMu collections management system (Hayes 2011a: 14). The EMu collection management system is a database and location system used by MV in order to record and track objects, whereby each object record is allocated a barcode and registration number, which is then aligned with a location barcode allowing the object to be located and tracked (Smith and Hayes 2010). Within EMu three archaeology tabs have been created, as well as other general tabs for information such as the object description, location and images. The Archaeology tabs were revised and updated by both Commonwealth Block project and MV staff during the first phase of the project (Hayes 2011a: 14). In accordance with the project's previous phase, the MV barcoding and location system was used during this phase as developed by the previous Commonwealth Block project team (Hayes 2011a: 14). Barcode ranges were received from the MV Collection Location Systems department, and were then allocated to new records in EAMC.

PROJECT OUTCOMES AND STATUS

Various tasks were completed throughout the course of the project, relating to both the cataloguing aims and to the collection as a whole. The aim of this phase of the project – namely the cataloguing of the 55 significant artefact bearing contexts – was completed, amounting to more than 7,700 new and updated records. This has created new and more detailed information about individual vessels from significant contexts and the collection more generally, making the recorded data more useful and accessible for future study and analysis.

Four features flagged as significant in the field records were found to have few or no associated artefact records in EAMC or EMu. These artefacts may have been misplaced over time, and the contexts will need to be investigated in order to determine their status, involving re-examination of field notes, field data and data in EAMC and EMu, and possibly a full audit of the more than 2,000 boxes in the collection. This was not completed during this phase of the project due to time constraints.

Three data merges from EAMC to EMu were completed throughout the project. Each record in EAMC contains information including the dates the record was created or modified, and which user carried out these tasks. Due to the size of the database, only data 'created by' and 'upgraded by' the user BW was merged with EMu in each merge in order to keep sets of data at manageable sizes, and so that the opportunity for errors was minimised.

Difficulties which arose during the project were discussed with MV staff where necessary and resolved where possible. Rectifying these issues as they arose was beneficial to the collection as a whole. Tasks completed during the project which were related to the wider collection, but not necessarily the project tasks specifically are as follows:

- Capturing type series images, which were later cropped and added to both EAMC and EMu
- Completing a small quality check audit, approximately 0.5% of the collection
- Returning of more than 280 boxes of bone loaned to LTU for research
- Discussing and remedying of access and conservation issues with MV staff
- Organising processes for future phases of data merges with MV staff
- Providing general assistance to MV staff regarding Little Lon artefact identification
- Providing a basic guide for MV staff regarding archaeology and the original Little Lon ID numbers.

The aim of the most recent phase – to create more detailed information about artefacts contained within the significant Little Lon contexts – has been largely completed. These records are now not only more physically and digitally accessible, but the updated data of the significant features is now more tailored to completing artefact analyses and comparisons between the various sites contained in the EAMC database, an important aim of the broader project (Murray 2006: 396; Smith and Hayes 2010; Hayes 2011). The enhanced catalogue data created during this project provides the possibility of new interpretations through the records which are now contained within EAMC and consistently recorded. This in turn will lead to a better understanding of the people living and working in the Little Lon area of Melbourne, as well as the inhabitants of other sites contained within the database.

Ongoing EAMC and EMu Relationship Issues

In the previous phase of the Commonwealth Block project several reoccurring issues were identified (Hayes 2011a). These generally stem from the fact that the two databases – EAMC and EMu – were created for different purposes, although each were modified to allow for better communication. The following section summarises the main issues, and proposes solutions.

Data Compatibility

As EAMC is used for archaeological recording and research of artefacts, whilst EMu is used for collection management and as a location system by the various departments of MV there are understandably differences between the data fields in EAMC and the fields available in EMu. Due to this difference, tabs with information specifically related to archaeology were created in EMu to facilitate the transfer and recording of data relating to archaeological artefacts by the Commonwealth Block team (Hayes 2011a: 14). The EMu database contains fewer fields for archaeological data than are available in EAMC, with any extra information recorded from EAMC being stored in the 'Notes' field of EMu. As the data fields are not completely compatible, an upgrade of either database could enable this disparity to be reduced, without altering the function of the data in each database.

In order to improve data compatibility, free text fields and differing uses of capitalisation and spacing in lookup lists in EAMC (for example: Tea Cup, tea cup, Teacup and teacup) should be further standardised to align with EMu system standards, and in particular legacy data from previous databases and phases of the project would benefit from being standardised. In a similar vein, the standardisation of field sizes between the two databases would also be beneficial, so that partial fields of data are not transferred. This would improve the merging process to the advantage of both institutions, and reduce the amount of manual editing the MV staff carries out to fit standardisation rules in EMu.

Archaeological versus Museum Recording Methods

Due to the differing functions and priorities of the two databases and systems, three main issues regarding artefact recording affect the Little Lon collection. These can be summarised as: the misunderstanding of the original Little Lon 1988 identification numbers; the use of part records; and a misunderstanding of the importance of provenance information to archaeological collections.

The ways that archaeologists and museum staff record information differ. As MV is the custodian of this collection, MV staff have, of course, had access to and have altered records in the past. This has especially been the case for displayed items, and unfortunately through this activity some archaeological information has been lost. This is an ongoing concern, and throughout this phase of the project the majority of queries made by MV staff were regarding the identification of Little Lon artefacts with ID numbers in the original format, which involves a series of numbers separated by forward slashes.

In MV collections, objects are organised based on their description. However, in the 1988 Little Lon excavations, artefacts were organised and recorded with context as the most important identifier, and the context was used as part of the original ID number in a format such as 01/02/-/-/03. In this example, 01/02 is the trench and unit/context number, and 03 represents the ID number of the artefact. In this system, the ID numbers can be used in the same catalogue up to three times, as special find, inventory or accession numbers. This causes issues where the format of the original ID number is recorded incorrectly when transferred to new systems, or in some cases is misplaced.

As previously reported by Hayes (2011a: 19), the Little Lon recording system seems to have created an issue where artefacts have been put on display.

In some cases, Little Lon objects on display have not yet been assigned new accession numbers, or have been separated from their tags whilst on display. Some artefacts on display which have been excavated from different contexts have been placed together in one record as a group of similar items and are unable to be separated due to the limited nature of the original records. In the movement of these artefacts to the one record, some original contextual information has been lost.

Records can also loose contextual information where the system of part records has been employed. The part record system is usually employed in the museum setting for storage or display of part of an object or set of objects. Part records in the Little Lon collection have sometimes been recorded due to the splitting of records by MV staff. These records generally occur where some fragments from a record are on display, and other fragments have been left in storage. Often part records have been created in EMu but have not been updated to EAMC, and part records have regularly been made for objects that would have been given a new record if recorded by Commonwealth Block project staff, for example one ceramic fragment being removed from a mixed bulk bag.

Within the MV staff cohort, there is a limited understanding of archaeological practices, as is understandable for those without archaeological training. This leads to a misunderstanding of the importance of certain types of information, including provenance. A document introducing historical archaeology, the collection, archaeological methods, and the relationship between EAMC and EMu was created in 2017, and was provided to relevant staff. These concerns will hopefully be lessened in the future if MV staff are aware of this introductory document.

Data Exchanges and Updates

A major source of challenges between EAMC data and EMu data is the process of merging information from the two databases. The process for carrying out these data merges was coordinated with MV staff. The ability to work directly with MV staff on this task was very rewarding and enabled dialogue between not only the various staff members, but also between the two databases. MV staff were able to discuss with Commonwealth Block project staff which fields of data from EAMC were best suited to fields of data in the EMu system, and were able to have data merges checked by project staff post-merge for errors. This also meant that a process which future merges could follow was set up and put into place, allowing each merge to run more smoothly than the one previous.

A concern of MV staff regarding the use of EAMC was that data in EMu wasn't necessarily the most up to date or, in the case of the location system, 'live'. The use of EAMC is integral to the project, and for a collection which throughout the project received little access on a day-to-day basis from staff outside the project, not having current description and location data was not a major issue. It could be considered a downside if the collection was accessed more often, but this is not the case. It is however an inconvenience to project staff when locating artefacts which have been moved and not updated. This concern is ongoing and will continue if one database is accessed and updated without the other. This problem may be remedied by using both systems when accessing the collection, though as there are currently no MV staff with knowledge of the EAMC system, and access to EMu by non-MV staff is restricted except with advanced approval, this solution is not currently practical.

Resource Availability

The main resource which is of limited availability, and by which improvement of the collection and the databases is hindered, is the availability of people's time to work on both the EAMC and EMu databases. This is a major factor in the management and communication of the two databases. As the EAMC database was created with grant funding, the deadline of which has now passed, additional work or support of the database is limited to any spare time that previous staff have and are willing to provide. As the 2015–2017 LTU project was not a joint project, MV staff found it hard to find time to work on the data merge into EMu, as project time was not allocated to them for this task specifically.

The merge process takes many hours to complete, as it is not automated and the data needs to be manually transferred and checked. Mapping each EAMC field to the corresponding field in EMu is not automatic, and MV staff need to remove and combine various columns of data in order to make the information compatible with EMu. For example, data from the four Profile fields in EAMC needed to be merged into one field entry in EMu, the formatting of which is done manually. Before the data merge process was understood, errors were sometimes made due to the manual nature of the process. Where errors existed, the process needed to be redone entirely. If these processes were able to be automated, or semi-automated, fewer resources would be spent on the merge, and a smoother and more reliable process could be put in place.

CONCLUSIONS

Overall, the 2015–2017 cataloguing project was successful, with all high significance features with associated artefacts having their records significantly upgraded and enhanced. More than 7,700 records have either been updated with revised and new information, or created. Multiple uploads of data from the Exploring the Archaeology of the Modern City database have been merged with Museums Victoria's KE Electronic Museum collection management system, and the process for this merge to be carried out has been refined. Other small tasks relating to the wider collection have been completed, ensuring that future research and access can be carried out more efficiently.

The work completed ensures that the collection from the Little Lon and other historical archaeology collections held by Museum Victoria are more easily accessible both in the physical and digital sense. With the improvement of detailed information in records, the research potential of the Little Lon collection continues to grow. This work enables the collection to be more thoroughly analysed, and facilitates the possibility of new interpretations and more detailed studies of the people living and working in Little Lon, as well as comparative analysis between this and other collections.

In order to further improve the data, future projects related to the Little Lon collection could investigate the significant features which have no recorded associated objects, register bones recently returned from a research loan, and more comprehensively catalogue other medium-high significance features.

Museums Victoria staff may need to investigate instructing those who access the historical archaeology collection about archaeological recording, and items on display would benefit from an in-depth audit when they are removed from display. A final excavation of the Commonwealth Block was completed in 2017, after which the artefacts may be stored long term with Museums Victoria.

Despite the above mentioned challenges of the relationship between the EAMC and EMu databases, the current system is largely successful. More than 87,000 records from the Little Lon collection are stored in EAMC, and those records have been successfully merged with the EMu collection management system. With the improvement of technologies, there will always be new directions available for database and collection management. For now, improvements to the current communication between the EAMC and EMu databases will enable the collection to be accessed more readily both physically and digitally, the implementation of which will only be beneficial for both users of the data, and for the institution in which the collection is held.

Acknowledgements

This project was funded by Australian Research Council grants to Professor Tim Murray and partners, and funds from the College of Arts, Social Sciences and Commerce at La Trobe University awarded to Professor Tim Murray.

Thanks go to Dr Sarah Hayes, for her review and comments on this paper.

Thanks also go to the following people for their help and support during the various phases of the project:

La Trobe University:
    Professor Tim Murray
    Dr Sarah Hayes
    Dr Penny Crook
    Paul Pepdjonovic
    Lauren Mitchell
Museums Victoria:
    Dr Charlotte Smith
    Trish Stokes
    Nancy Ladas & staff
    Neville Quick & staff
    Lorenzo Iozzi & staff
    Nick Crotty & staff
    Conservation Dept
    Volunteer Program Dept
    IT Dept
Volunteers:
    Lauren Mitchell (2015–2017)
    Grace Stephenson-Gordon (2015–2017)
    Amalia Major (née Carroll) (2015–2016)
    Claire Nimmo (2016)
    Tiffany Liew (2015)
    Yvette Meades (2015)
    Yajing Zhao (2015)

References

Crook, P., L. Ellmoos and T. Murray, 2003. *Assessment of Historical and Archaeological Resources of the Paddy's Market Site, Darling Harbour, Sydney*. Archaeology of the Modern City 1788–1900 Series 1. Sydney: Historic Houses Trust of New South Wales.

Crook, P., L. Ellmoos and T. Murray, 2005. *Keeping Up with the McNamaras: A Historical Archaeolgical Study of the Cumberland and Gloucester Streets Site, The Rocks, Sydney*. Archaeology of the Modern City 1788–1900 Series 8. Sydney: Historic Houses Trust of New South Wales.

Crook, P. and T. Murray, 2006. *Guide to the EAMC Archaeology Database*. Sydney: Historic Houses Trust of New South Wales.

Hayes, S. 2011a. Amalgamation of Archaeological Assemblages: Experiences from the Commonwealth Block Project Melbourne. *Australian Archaeology* 73: 13–24.

Hayes, S. 2011b. A Historical Archaeology of the Commonwealth Block 1850–1950: Artefact Processing Project Report. Melbourne: La Trobe University and Museums Victoria.

Mayne, A. and T. Murray, 2001. The Archaeology of Urban Landscapes: Explorations in

Slumland. In Mayne, A. and T. Murray (eds.) *The Archaeology of Urban Landscapes: Explorations in Slumland*, pp.1–7. Cambridge: Cambridge University Press.

Murray, T. 2006. Integrating Archaeology and History at the Commonwealth Block: Little Lon and Casselden Place. *International Journal of Historical Archaeology* 10(4): 395–413.

Murray, T. and P. Crook, 2005. Exploring the Archaeology of the Modern City: Issues of Scale, Integration and Complexity. *International Journal of Historical Archaeology* 9(2): 89–109.

Smith, C. and S. Hayes, 2010. Managing the Commonwealth Block Archaeological Assemblage: An Australian Case Study. *Collections: A journal for Museums and Archives Professionals* 6(3): 171–187.

Woff, B. 2015. Commonwealth Block Targeted Context Cataloguing Progress Report 2015. Unpublished report to La Trobe University and Museums Victoria.

Woff, B. 2016. Commonwealth Block Targeted Context Cataloguing Progress Report 2016. Unpublished report to La Trobe University and Museums Victoria.

Woff, B. 2017a. Commonwealth Block Targeted Context Cataloguing Progress Report 2017. Unpublished report to La Trobe University and Museums Victoria.

Woff, B. 2017b. Guide to the Historical Archaeology Collection at Museums Victoria. Unpublished report to Museums Victoria.

11
The 2017 Excavations: 271 Spring Street, Melbourne

Geoff Hewitt

This chapter is intended to present a brief, and preliminary, overview of the excavations conducted during mid-2017 by GML Heritage at the site of Industry Superannuation Property Trust (ISPT)'s redevelopment project known as 271 Spring Street. The project impacted upon what may be the final piece in the Casselden Place/Little Lon precinct jigsaw within urban Melbourne, a precinct that has received considerable and well-merited attention by historical archaeologists over a period approaching thirty years.

As a result of the meticulous research work on this present project carried out by historian Barbara Minchinton and archaeologist Sharon Lane, building upon the earlier work of Justin McCarthy (1989: vol. 5), we have a fine-grained understanding of land ownership and occupancy of our subject area through time. Together with the data resulting from their work, our excavation has led to a quite thorough speculation concerning the history of building within the space; 'speculation' because our understanding is yet to be tested with dates estimated from artefact assemblages.

At the time of writing, cataloguing of the very large number of artefacts recovered during the excavation is yet to be completed. Although analysis of those artefacts that have been catalogued is at a rudimentary stage, it has been possible for Chris Williamson to convey useful impressions of their meaning.

The area impacted during the present project is shown in Figure 11.1. As a portion of that part of the Commonwealth Block identified by McCarthy as site C (Murray 2006: 397), it includes portions of the block bounded by Casselden Place on the west and Spring Street on the east, with Little Lonsdale Street to the north. It also includes a portion of the length of a laneway known as Griffin Lane that leads south from Little Lonsdale Street.

Casselden Place and Griffin Lane were part of the subdivision of Crown allotments 7 and 9 of Section 25 of the City of Melbourne, first alienated during 1847. Surveyor and land speculator Henry Boorn Foot[1] subdivided the corner allotment CA9 beginning in 1848, while CA7 was passed through the hands of further speculators[2] before being subdivided during 1850 by the merchant, squatter and entrepreneur Hugh Glass. A plan of the allotments as subdivided

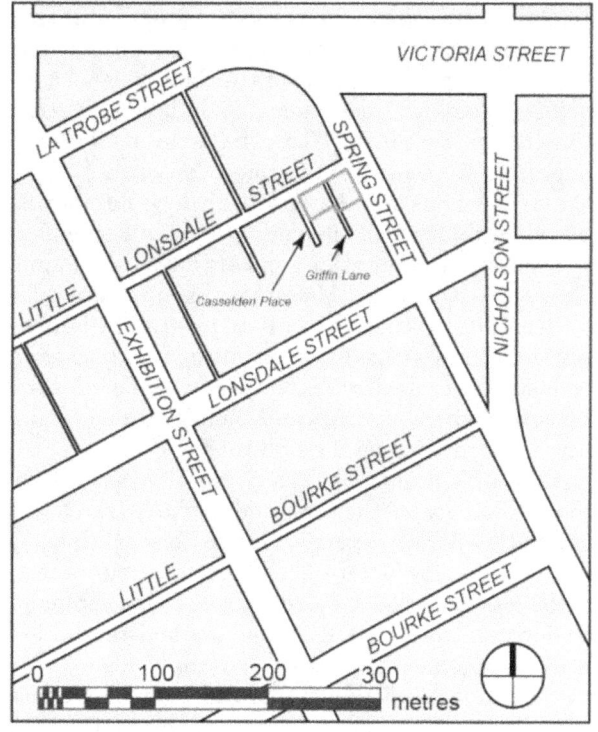

Figure 11.1: Location of the 271 Spring Street site.

---

[1] Henry Boorn Foot(e), surveyor and land speculator earlier in the 1840s, had planned the subdivision of Henry Dendy's eight square mile Special Survey at Brighton. Caught by the financial crash, both Dendy and Foot became insolvent and Foot survived through poorly paid employment as clerk in the office of the Chief Protector of Aborigines, George Augustus Robinson until he resigned in February 1847 (Bate 1983: 33–36, 38–40, 60; Clark 2000: 283; Mouritz 1847: 31).

[2] CA7 was purchased by Phillip Oakden Esq of van Diemen's Land, selling it without changes less than two years later to gentleman squatter Charles Ryan, one of the volunteers led by Snodgrass who captured Daniel Jepps' gang of bushrangers in May 1842 (Finn 1888: 354; de Serville 1980: 183). Still in the same form, CA7 was soon afterwards conveyed by Ryan to merchant, squatter and speculator Hugh Glass, who was to become the wealthiest man in Victoria by 1862, only to die in ignominious poverty nine years later (Senyard 1972: 254–255).

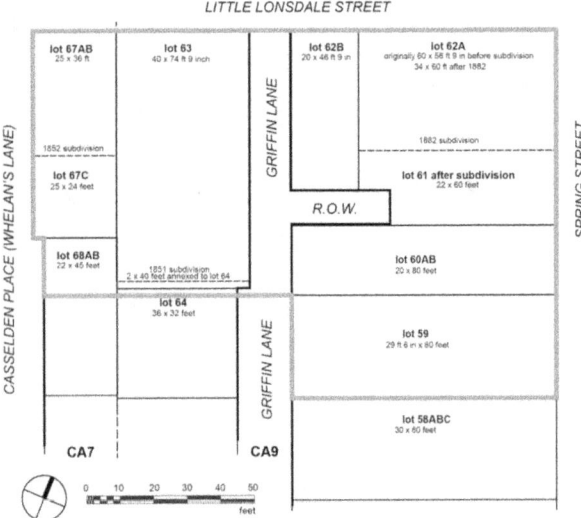

Figure 11.2: Subdivision of CA7 and CA9 of Section 25. The boundary between the Crown allotments is the eastern boundary of lots 67ABC and 68AB. The extent of the 271 Spring Street site is outlined red.

is presented here as Figure 11.2. Original subdivisional boundaries are shown as continuous lines and subsequent subdivision is shown pecked. For continuity with prior investigations in the Little Lon precinct, the allotments are numbered according to the arbitrary system used previously by McCarthy, which appears to have been based on the historic placement of buildings rather than titles research. With McCarthy's allotment boundaries, there are some departures from the true cadastre and his arbitrary numbering bears no relation to the very few instances where original subdivisional lot numbers have been found. However, to be fair to McCarthy, his numbers refer to 'locations' rather than allotments and his data are organised according to habitations rather than cadastral boundaries. This does result in confusion, however, when buildings and their locations within an allotment change through time.

At commencement of the present investigation, lots 67ABC, lot 63, the north end of lot 68AB and very little of lot 64 were occupied by the former Blakeley saw and cutlery factory. This part of the site was to be excavated for a basement during redevelopment. Following demolition of the factory and removal of a modern concrete slab, this portion was subjected to open area excavation to natural ground as phase one. The second phase of investigation, within the lots to the east of Griffin lane, was by targeted trenches in response to planned impacts by piling, footing beams, service trenches and reductions in ground level. A further complication to the phase 2 work was the retention of the mid-1920s façade of the Elms Family Hotel (formerly the site of the Old Governor Bourke Hotel) on lot 62A, together with a large proportion of the former Anglican Mission building remaining on lot 59 and the west portion of lot 60AB.

HISTORIC PLANS AND PHOTOGRAPHS

Figure 11.3 is a compilation of a detail from Thomas Bibbs' ca. 1856 map of Melbourne as a base plan overlaid with the subdivision. Thomas Bibbs' map was produced for the Board of Commissioners for Improvement of the Sewerage and Drainage of the City of Melbourne established by an 1853 Act of the Legislative Council of the Colony of Victoria. Bibbs' map provides a detailed plan view of the city within its contemporary limits. Not only does the map show buildings present at that time, but by means of colour-coding, indicates the materials of their construction (Hewitt *et al.* 2017). Although the Board established by the 1853 Act did construct the Yan Yean water supply which reached Melbourne in 1857, sewerage and drainage were neglected for the next four decades.

The approximate positions of the eight cesspits that were discovered during our investigation are also shown identified with numbers. Buildings shown cross-hatched are present on Parish Plan M325 dated 1850 (a subdivisional plan of East Melbourne in the put-away series) which happens to show structures present on the opposite sides of surrounding streets, including Spring Street. Figure 11.4 combines the allotment plan with a detail from the 1895 MMBW block plan 1019. In both cases, the site boundary is marked.

When the problems with sanitation caused by the lack of sewerage became truly alarming following boom years of development during the 1880s, the Melbourne and Metropolitan Board of Works (MMBW) conducted detailed surveys of the City of Melbourne as a preliminary to the construction of a sewerage collection, pumping and treatment system.

Useful impressions can also be gained from historical photographs of buildings present on the site during the 19th century. Figure 11.5 is a

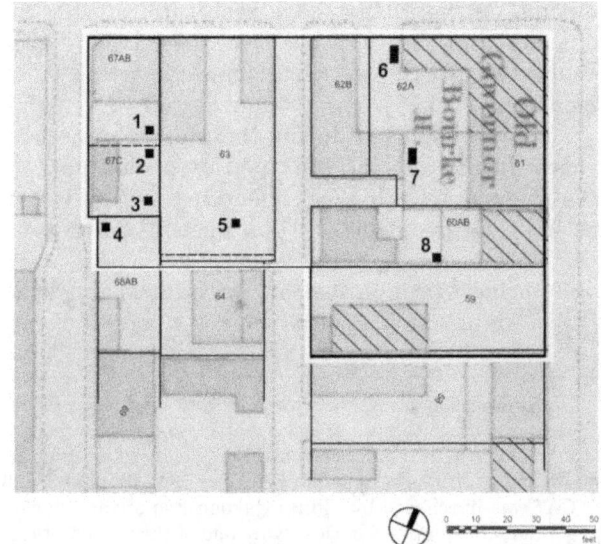

Figure 11.3: Overlay of lot boundaries onto a detail of Thomas Bibbs' ca. 1856 map of Melbourne.

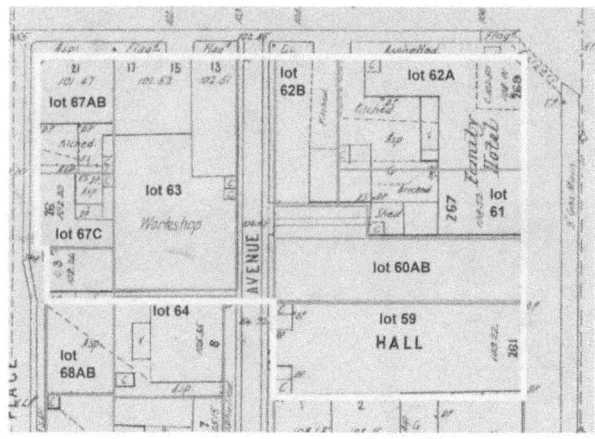

Figure 11.4: Overlay of allotment boundaries onto a detail from the 1895 MMBW block plan 1019.

Figure 11.5: Detail from Charles Nettleton's ca. 1861 photograph of Spring Street from Parliament House, view towards the north-west (Source: SLV H36668/24, LTA642).

detail from a view of Spring Street from Parliament House by Charles Nettleton (ca. 1861), showing the Old Governor Bourke Hotel on the corner of Little Lonsdale Street (lot 62A) with the boarding house adjacent on lot 61 (with lighter-coloured roof), then to the south, the two-storeyed brick house on lot 60 and the front fence of lot 59.

Figure 11.6 is a photograph of Little Lonsdale Street in ca. 1870, looking towards the west. On the left (south) side is the Old Governor Bourke Hotel on the corner, with the earlier kitchen wing adjoining (lot 62A). On the south side of the gate is the hotel stable on lot 62B. Across Griffin Lane is Griffin's hay store with Mrs Griffin's grocery shop adjacent (both on lot 63). Next door is the brick building on lot 67AB (arrowed) on the corner of Casselden Place.

Figure 11.7 is a detail from Paterson Brothers' *Bird's-eye view of Melbourne, taken from the top of Scots' Church spire, Collins Street* (1875). The substantial building in the centre background is a rear view of the Old Governor Bourke Hotel with its kitchen wing with matching gable. The adjacent boarding house follows the architectural style of the hotel. To the right (east) is the brick house on lot 60 and to the south of the hotel and boarding house is the L-shaped plan and iron skillion roof of the stable.

Figure 11.8 is a detail from Charles Nettleton's *'View of Melbourne (south west) from the terrace of the Exhibition Building, Carlton Gardens'* dated 1883. In this image, the licensee of the Old Governor Bourke Hotel on the corner of Little Lonsdale Street is proclaimed as (George) Elms and the adjacent boarding house, then under different

Figure 11.6: View west down Little Lonsdale Street from Spring Street in ca. 1870 (Source: NLA 63909 1870-5).

Figure 11.7: Detail from Paterson Brothers' *'Bird's-eye view of Melbourne, taken from the top of Scots' Church spire, Collins Street'* (1875) (Source: SLV H8014).

Figure 11.8: Detail from Charles Nettleton's 1883 photograph *View of Melbourne (south west) from the terrace of the Exhibition Building, Carlton Gardens* (Source: SLV H845, H4513).

ownership on the newly subdivided lot 61, is painted a different shade. The brick house on lot 60 now has a pedimented neighbour in what had, for a short term commencing in 1877, been William Sweetland Best's 'New Royal Dancing Academy'.[3]

An Overview of the Archaeology of 271 Spring Street

The results of excavation will now be discussed broadly according to phase and lot number.

Phase 1

The open area within the footprint of the former Blakeley saw and cutlery factory was dug in three stages as demolition proceeded within the phase two area towards the east and space allowed a progressive buffer between that activity and the archaeological excavation. The modern concrete slab was initially removed from the west boundary with Casselden Place, revealing substantial remains of architecture and surfaces buried under up to a metre of demolition rubble, fill and recent packing sand. As the excavation moved eastwards up the slope towards Spring Street, the architecture disappeared leaving negative features including robbed-out footing trenches, traces of concrete machinery foundations and pits. The up-slope truncation may be seen in Figure 11.9, a view towards Little Lonsdale Street.

Lot 67ABC

The footings of a building present on both the ca. 1856 Bibbs' map and the 1895 MMBW block plan were revealed at the north end of lot 67AB. In Figure 11.10, the excavated area is bounded on the north and west with the intact brick footings of the

Figure 11.9: A view of the northern part of the phase one area looking towards Little Lonsdale Street. Truncation of the archaeology upslope towards the east is evident (Photo: GML Heritage).

Blakeley factory constructed after 1922 (arrow 1). Construction of those footings had destroyed the north and west walls of the four-roomed structure (148 Little Lonsdale Street until 1892 when the street address became numbers 19 and 21).

The first purchaser of lot 67ABC was George Griffin in May 1850 and Gipps Ward rate valuations indicate that Griffin constructed a two-roomed timber house on his land before the 1851/52 valuation when its occupant was Lawrence Boucher. The rather lightweight single-row fieldstone footings evident for rooms 1 and 2 (arrowed 2 in Figure 11.10) are interpreted as the dado for this timber building which may have been a portable or prefabricated frame structure such as a Manning house or similar (Lewis 1985). This is of interest because the *Building Act* of October 1849 (New South Wales 1849) as a fire prevention strategy did

---

[3] Best, an interesting character, experienced opposition to his application for the necessary operating permits for his dancing saloon, the 'New Royal Dancing Academy'. During July 1877, Councillor Stewart spoke against a motion to grant a permit, pointing out that Best had served two six-month sentences at Sandhurst for harbouring prostitutes. Stewart stated that Best's hall was a nuisance to neighbours and that the Minister for Education too was opposed due to the presence of the Model School across Spring Street (*Argus* 17 July 1877: 6). Best's application to the Council for a permit during March 1877 had been referred to the Health Committee and remained unresolved when Best was summoned to appear in the Police Court charged with operating an unregistered dancing saloon (*Argus* 17 March 1877: 6, 14 April 1877: 6). Best had begun advertising social events at his Spring Street premises earlier in March (*Argus* 19 March 1877: 8). Best, 'a respectable-looking man' had been charged with bigamy at Geelong after his marriage to Ellen Keating in April 1864 (*Argus* 3 May 1864: 4). During 1872, a brawl at Best's saloon in Mitchell Street Sandhurst led to a return bare-knuckle bout in which one of the protagonists died. Best who styled himself 'professor of calisthenics and dancing' was called as a witness by the inquest, where the jury unanimously asserted that Best's establishment was a source of immorality and crime, calling for it to be shut down (*Bendigo Advertiser* 13 March 1872: 2). Best was remanded by the Coroner at Sandhurst on suspicion of arson committed on his own well-insured house during February 1879 but was acquitted (*Argus* 21 March 1879: 6, 11 August 1880: 6). Eighteen eighty seems to have been another tumultuous year for Best who appears to have left both his wife and Spring Street and by then was operating a dancing saloon in Hoddle Street Collingwood where he lived with two young women, sisters by the name of Gaggin (*Argus* 11 August 1880: 6). During February, Best came into the Argus Hotel at 5 a.m. and woke the house by playing the piano. Best was forcibly ejected but then charged the barman with assault. The case was dismissed (*Argus* 27 February 1880: 4). In August, Best was ordered to close his unlicensed saloon in Collingwood which was according to a press report 'well known to police who had often noticed doubtful characters leaving it' (*Mercury and Weekly Courier* 7 August 1880: 2). Less than two weeks later, one Robert Goudie another 'respectable-looking man' was before Mr Justice Barry in the Central Criminal Court charged with malicious wounding of William Sweetland Best by stabbing him in the face. The court was told of Best's 'disgraceful state of immorality' with Goudie's wife and this was compounded by Best's attempt to cast the blame upon the woman. Goudie was found guilty but fined just £2 (*Argus* 18 August 1880: 3; *Age* 18 August 1880: 3).

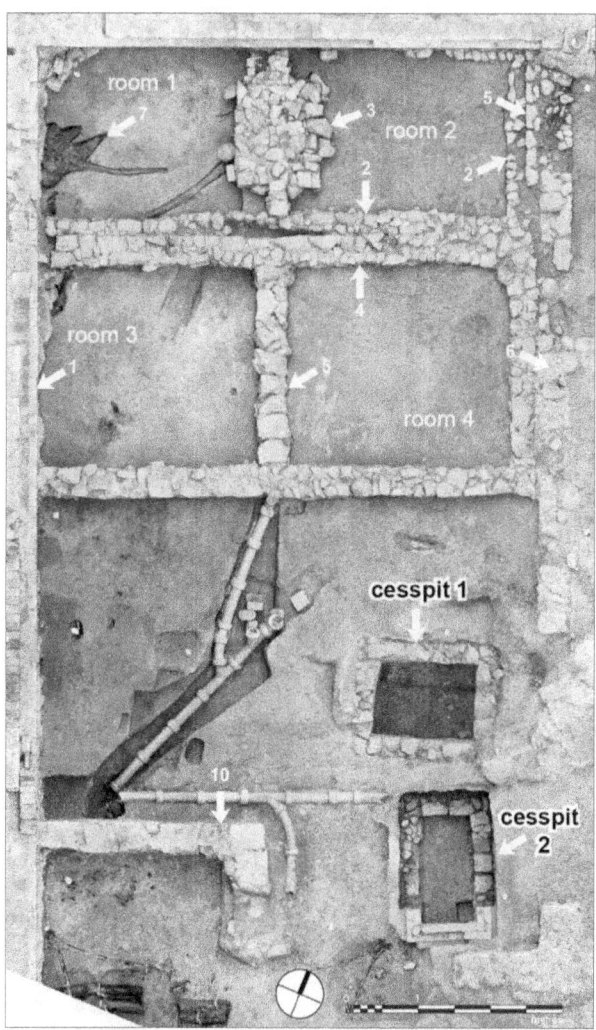

Figure 11.10: Lot 67AB partially excavated (for legend see text). Photogrammetric ortho model by Reeds Consulting, Ref. 23089 version A date 24th May 2017 with added scale and pointers. For explanation of this form of modelling, see for example De Reu et al. (2013).

not permit construction of timber buildings within the limits of the City of Melbourne. This building was constructed over a large tree stump (arrow 7) with minimal attempts at its removal.

In 1851, George Griffin had sold lot 67ABC to Stephen Sherven who subdivided lot 67C and sold it to William Taylor who passed it to William Strahan, a builder, in 1853. Strahan had indirectly become the owner of lot 67AB in 1852 and henceforth, lots 67ABC came again under single ownerships. Strahan mortgaged the land apparsently to construct the four-roomed building in 1854. This appears to have been accomplished by adding the two southern rooms with substantial split basalt footings (arrow 4). Bibbs' colour code suggests that the building was masonry in ca. 1856. The historical images (Figures 11.6 and 11.13), later rate valuations and the evidence from demolition, all confirm that the structure above the footings at least for rooms one and two, was brick. The rear two rooms may have been stone which would account for the description of the building as brick and stone subsequent to the 1856 rate valuations. Further, MCC Notice number 444 dated 6th of March 1854 is an application to construct a 'stone skillion' (McCarthy 1989: vol. 5: 353). As the earlier stone dado for the timber cottage was insufficient to support brickwork, an additional alignment of stone was first placed alongside the dado. This is evident in the surviving east wall (arrow 5).

The adjacent stone footing (arrowed 6 in Figure 11.10) is from a building on lot 63. In addition to the interface between these footings marking the boundary between lots 67 ABC and lot 63, it also marks the boundary between CA 7 and CA9 of Section 25.

A total of 7,925 artefacts were recovered from artefact-rich silty units present in all four rooms of the building on lot 67AB. The lowest of these units rested on the natural clay and are interpreted as earthen floors over which less compact and sometimes stony filling layers have been placed. It appears that timber floors were subsequently installed at least in rooms 2 and 4, apparently over a levelling fill.

Rate valuation data indicates that the four-roomed building was subdivided into two two-roomed tenements before 1863 and the stone party wall footing dividing rooms 3 and 4 (arrow 5 in Figure 11.10) was constructed over earlier deposits at that time. At the time of writing, we are not entirely certain of this, but it appears that the dividing wall and back-to-back hearths between rooms 1 and 2 (arrow 3) may have also been constructed at the same time. McCarthy notes an entry in the MCC Registry of Intention to Build as Notice number 553 dated 21 December 1861, an application 'to make an alteration to a stone cottage' at 148 Little Lonsdale Street East (1989: vol. 5: 353).

In the sub-floor deposits, children's toys are present in large quantities as are children's tablewares of the 'moralising china' genre, suggesting to Chris Williamson (pers. comm.) that money was available to be spent on children. Indeed, the impression from this assemblage is that it reflects a space focused around the activities of women and children. A number of objects associated with lace-making and sewing are present, together with a significant number of buttons and pins which tend to cluster in rooms 2 and 3. According to Williamson, who has considerable experience of artefact deposits within the Little Lon precinct (Williamson 2004, 2006) discretionary spending is also evident in jewellery items, perfume bottles, figurines, pretty china and other decorative items. A range of tea and tablewares, teapots, egg cups and serving dishes are present.

Room 1 had a large proportion of ceramic sherds together with many toys, children's tablewares, jewellery, coins, buttons, ceramic figurines, a metal urethral syringe and a bone and copper alloy pocket knife. Chinese artefacts included a small ivory figure and sherds of several brown-glazed stoneware containers.

Room 2 contained a low proportion of ceramic objects, but a high proportion of organic items, coins, a gaming token, clay smoking pipes, an almost complete gilded copper alloy brooch, a child's ring, 31 buttons, a bone lace-making tool container and a stiletto bodkin, 70 pins, a large metal iron, 12 marbles and part of a child's porcelain tea set.

A high proportion of ceramic objects were found in room 3, along with toys, coins, many clay pipes and fragments, 63 buttons, a crochet hook, three thimbles, two pairs of scissors, and some 75 pins.

Over half of the assemblage from room 4 is glass. Fragments of painted Chinese porcelain and glazed stoneware containers were present, together with clay tobacco pipes, 22 buttons, a bone sewing tool, a sewing needle, and four pins, a piece of jet jewellery, 12 marbles and fragments of approximately six children's plates.

Each room was subdivided into four quadrants for spatial analysis and the artefacts mentioned above are provenanced to many distinct stratigraphic units all well recorded and understood. There appears to be a range of dates, ethnic and occupational associations, together with an interesting variation in the composition of the assemblages between rooms. Further analyses will work towards teasing out the chronology and spatial attributes of these deposits and their possible associations. The artefacts present in apparent earthen floors sealed by later units and structures, including the party wall from ca. 1863, are of particular interest. Tenants of the house at 148 Little Lonsdale Street, prior to subdivision into two tenements, included draper and ex-glover to the Queen, Caleb Williamson (1854–1858?), tailoress Mrs Yates (1862) and dressmaker Mrs Farlow (1863). Although archaeologist Peter Davies has pointed out that the widespread distribution of Chinese material culture found earlier in excavations at Casselden Place indicated their use by people from other backgrounds (Davies 2006), the Chinese artefacts present in lot 67 may reflect the occupancy of Tin Yen followed by Gay Sue who were tenants of number 19 in the early 20th century. However, perhaps the best association with these artefacts is Harry Goong who appears to have been the occupant of number 21 during 1911–1914, just prior to demolition of the building.

A remnant of the northern wall footing of the L-shaped building present on lot 67C on the MMBW block plan is arrowed 1 on Figure 11.11. According to rate valuation data, this building, which was also of brick and evidently set onto a foundation of shaped basalt stones, was constructed during 1877 when lot 67ABC was owned by John Casselden. Very little of this building has survived as the footings had been disturbed and cut through during construction of three brick-lined pits to house and support very

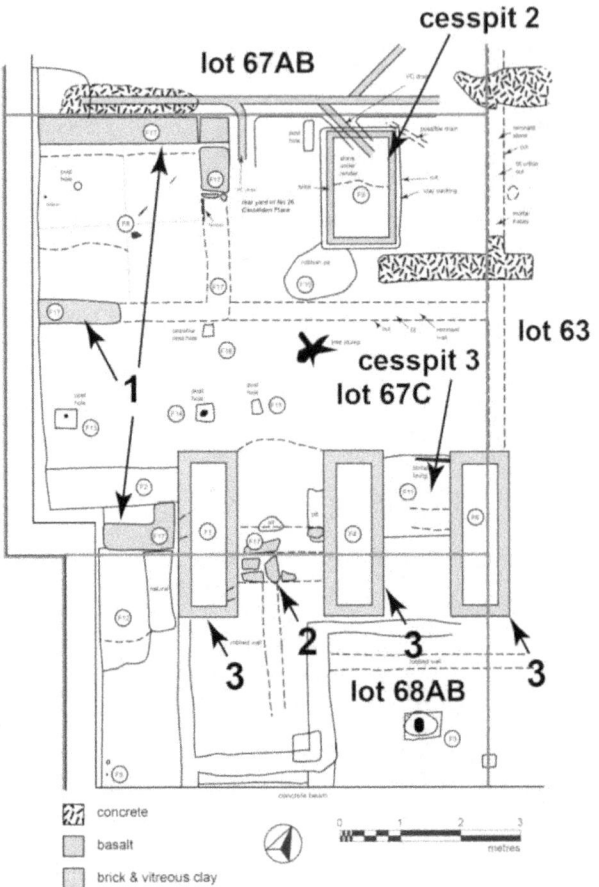

Figure 11.11: Schematic plan of lot 67C and the north end of lot 68AB.

large grinding wheels used to shape, sharpen and polish edge tools in the Blakeley factory (arrowed 3). The 1877 brick building had replaced a two-roomed timber cottage adjacent to Casselden Place shown on Bibbs' map and possibly represented by an alignment of post holes in that location (Figure 11.11). Vagueness in the early rate valuations in Casselden Place, or Whelan's Lane as it was then named, has not permitted the date of construction of the timber building to be definitively determined. However, McCarthy noted a permit application from Stephen Sherven to build a dwelling house in Little Lonsdale Street East dated May 1851 (1989: vol. 5: 53). This application is just prior to transfer of title from Griffin to Sherven, who sold lot 67C to William Taylor in March 1852.

Robbed-out wall trenches evident in Figure 11.11 indicate that the footprint of the later building is in accordance with the 1895 MMBW plan. Possible subfloor deposits with uneven spatial distribution were found within the north-western room, together with evidence of disturbance probably during construction and occupation of the Blakeley factory. There was no evidence of sub-floor deposits in the southern wing of the building.

The 1877 building was constructed over the back-filled timber lined cesspit 3 (Figure 11.11). The timber lining consisted of thin planks of varying width placed edge to edge against a cut into natural clay and secured at the base by timbers wedged into place around the edges. The excavator recorded a packing of clay behind the timber lining but compaction as a result of puddling was not noted. The securing timbers were recycled fence posts cut to fit the dimensions of the pit. They had originally been cut from saplings partly in the round with bark intact and morticed to accommodate rails. Perhaps these timbers represent post and rail fencing of ground used as an animal enclosure or for food production prior to subdivision. This cesspit had been subsequently cut by the easternmost of the three Blakeley-era grinding wheel pits, truncating the upper parts of the timber lining.

Cesspit 3 contained a rich assemblage of early ceramics within a total count of 1,627 artefacts. Chris Williamson's general impression from this assemblage is one of affluence and aspiration to gentility expressed in matching sets of expensive ceramics and tableware having specific functions (Karskens 2001: 71). Examples include a shell-edged covered vegetable dish and a possible creamware asparagus serving dish, a cream-glazed leaf-shaped supper plate and a matching set of bone china plates, serving platters, cups and saucers decorated with overglaze gilding and enamelling. In her analysis of the Viewbank assemblage, Sarah Hayes (2007: 100) concluded that the presence of matching sets of tableware not only indicated that the upper-middle class Martin family had made their purchases in centralised arcades, department stores and by mail, but also that their financial resources allowed large quantities to be purchased at the one time.

Two almost complete clay smoking pipes by Murray of Glasgow (1830–1861) and a complete glass salad oil/vinegar bottle with February 1855 registration diamond are present. Preliminary assessment indicates deposition perhaps before the early 1860s and a strong association with the timber cottage on lot 67C, occupied during 1861 by Thladen O'Don. It is, of course, possible that cesspit 3 serviced both of the cottages on 67ABC and may have been built at the same time as Griffin's first house. One significant find at the bottom of cesspit 3, was a pocket watch possibly of 18th-century date (to be confirmed when cleaned and conserved). The watch was in three pieces, the face, the hemispherical glass and the ornate works, but missing its case. One might speculate that this was disposal of the evidence following theft.

Two further cesspits were present on lot 67ABC. Cesspit 1 on Figure 11.3 (see Figure 11.10) was constructed within lot 67AB while cesspit 2 was constructed partly across the lot boundary between 67AB and 67C. The location of cesspit 2 suggests a build date at a time when the allotments were under a single ownership, in this case probably after 1854 when Strahan had built the brick house at Little Lonsdale Street. Both of these cesspits had been built in the same manner, with partially shaped stone linings placed directly onto natural clay apparently using excavated earth as mortar. As with the timber-lined cesspit 3, cesspit 1 – and cesspit 2 as originally constructed – was intended to allow fluids from the pits to percolate through the lining and dissipate into the subsoil.

The enormous population growth due to gold-rush immigration made this disposal strategy problematic which resulted in the issue during 1861 of a circular produced by the Central Board of Health setting out new design requirements for cesspits. The circular (VPRS 3181 PO364) specified construction methods aimed at eliminating seepage either by lining the pit with brick with a waterproof puddled clay layer behind, or the cheaper option of sinking a timber cask into a pit with a layer of puddled clay outside the staves. The *Public Health Amendment Act* of 1867 gave power to the Board to prosecute occupiers for failure to remedy or close down defective cesspits once these had been identified by Council Inspectors (Hayes and Minchinton 2016: 14).

A cesspit closure notice served upon John Casselden according to Health Committee report 98 dated 17 April 1871 p. 4 (VPRS 3103 PO Unit 14) applies to a cesspit within lot 67ABC. This notice requires the cesspit to be cleaned out and back-filled within seven days and hence gives a useful likely deposition date for artefacts assumed to have been discarded into the pit prior to backfilling (Hayes and Minchinton 2017: 20). As we have seen, there were three cesspits within lot 67ABC so the as-yet unresolved challenge is to determine to which of these the closure notice referred.

The 2,869 artefacts recovered from cesspit 1 have been washed and catalogued by Chris Williamson and her team, also sent for conservation where required. Although analysis is yet to be completed, it is possible to characterise the assemblage as consisting of 25.5% ceramic, 33.5% glass, 7% metal and 32.5% organic objects by count. The earthenwares included expensive matching ceramic tea wares and tablewares as well as figurines. The tea wares included at least four cups and six saucers with the distinctive transfer underglaze (TUG) decoration 'Scrapbook'. Fragments of teawares with this decoration were also found within artefact-bearing floor deposits in all rooms of the house on lot 67AB in contexts apparently earlier than the ca. 1863 party wall subdividing the house into two tenements. Hence it is possible that cesspit 1 went out of use voluntarily at a much earlier date than the Health Committee's 1871 notice to John Casselden. This possibility will be tested with manufacturing date data when artefact analysis is completed.

A high proportion of the assemblage recovered from this cesspit was organic of which 31% was animal bone. The proportion of vegetable material was 28.3% and this included apricot, plum, peach/

nectarine and cherry pips, brazil nuts, hazel nuts and walnuts, melon seeds, grape seeds and coconut shell. Oyster shell represented 13.85% of the organic finds. Egg shells were also present. Juvenile sheep, pig and cow bone indicates a preparedness to spend money on better classes of meat and altogether the food remains suggest a varied diet. Strangely, an intact gilded copper alloy candlestick was present in the cesspit deposit.

Stratigraphy within cesspit 1 indicated that following a rudimentary cleanout of cess, and one or possibly two episodes of dumping, the pit was backfilled with clean clay. Backfilling seems to have been done in two stages, with a lens of nightsoil between. A strong odour of hydrocarbons present in the lower levels of this pit probably reflects subsequent industrial activities on the site.

Apparently in response to the new design requirements of 1861, cesspit 2 had been extensively reconfigured. The stone lining had been demolished down to the lowest course and flat basalt slabs had been placed onto the natural clay base of the pit. A new brick lining had then been constructed within the pit onto a levelled surface leaving a surrounding gap that was subsequently filled with puddled clay. The stone base and the internal walls of the brick lining were then rendered with a cement wash.

According to Chris Williamson (pers. comm.) a total of 176 artefacts were recovered from cesspit 2, with 57.4% being glass, 19.3% ceramic and 18.8% bone by count. Analysis of the assemblage from cesspit 2 is incomplete but the impression derived by Chris Williamson is that the date of deposition is later than the assemblages in cesspits 1 and 3. Current thinking is that cesspit 2 was the one subject to the closure order. At the time of the order, Mrs Hayes was the tenant of 150 Little Lonsdale Street, J. Dunn occupied number 148 and M. O'Regan rented the timber cottage on 67C. It would appear that all shared the one cesspit and possibly the opportunity to add to the rubbish deposit prior to backfilling.

A shallow sub-circular pit was present adjacent to the south-west corner of cesspit 2. This pit contained a dark organic unit with artefacts similar to a cesspit deposit and the contents have been interpreted as evidence of material being removed from cesspit 2, possibly prior to its reconstruction.

Although much disturbed by more recent services, multiple remnant bricked, cobbled and asphalted surfaces were found within the rear yard of number 21 Little Lonsdale Street. Also present was a brick drain in a similar location to a kitchen drain shown on the MMBW plan. Chinese artefacts, including fragments of a large brown-glazed globular jar, a celadon bowl and painted stoneware vessel were recovered from the drain and an adjacent pit. To the south of the area shown in Figure 11.12, the vitreous clay drain system visible in Figure 11.10 connected to a deep abandoned sewer in Casselden Place.

Figure 11.12: Part of the rear yard of 21 Little Lonsdale Street looking north (Photo: GML Heritage).

It is clear from the foregoing that lot 67ABC has yielded a complex archaeology of great interest. Barabara Minchinton (2017) has argued for a cautionary approach regarding linkages between archaeological deposits and households. Nevertheless, we remain cautiously optimistic that data derived from analyses of artefact assemblages applied within the hermeneutic process between historical and archaeological data that Minchinton advises, may permit the establishment of links at a level beyond that of neighbourhood with at least an approach to temporal clarity.

Lot 68AB

The only evidence of a building on lot 68AB is the fragment of basalt footing in place between two of the grinding wheel pits and this is arrowed 2 on Figure 11.11. An earlier feature interpreted as a backfilled cesspit was present in the extreme north-west corner of lot 68AB, cut by the footings of the Blakeley factory. This pit, cesspit 4 on Figure 11.3, appears to have been originally stone-lined and was particularly deep with the bottom at 1.8m below the remnant Blakeley factory footings. Evidently associated with the timber cottage shown on Bibbs' map, the cesspit had been emptied and backfilled prior to construction of the building shown on the 1895 MMBW plan which appears to have the street address of number 3 Casselden Place on the MMBW plan.

The pit was heavily waterlogged and had been severely disturbed during construction of the factory which had needed timber shuttering to locally support the concrete strip sub-footing. Seemingly early artefacts including ceramics, bottle glass and clay smoking pipes were recovered from the lowest level. Continued excavation became an

OHS issue and this pit was quickly backfilled after photographic recording.

Lot 68AB was sold by Hugh Glass to William Mather in February 1850. William Mather is listed in Mouritz (1847: 110) as a carpenter in Bourke Lane. Mather sold to Alexander Morison during August 1856. As interesting as the possibility might have been, Alexander Morison is probably not the person of that name who succeeded William Waterfield as minister of the Congregational Church on the corner of Russell and Collins Street from 1843 to 1864 (see Jenkin 2003). Morison is listed in the 1861 rate valuation as occupier of a brick two-roomed house with an attic. Bibbs' map indicates that this building was at the southern end of the lot and out of the present study area although cesspit 4 is clearly associated with it. Less clear is the sequence of building on lot 68AB during Morison's ownership. The rate valuation for 1862 lists Morison as occupier but there is no description of the house. However, that same year, Morison has tenant John Macreash in an apparently adjoining brick two-roomed house. In 1866, a four-roomed brick house appears to be the only structure on lot 68AB. Thus it is possible that Morison constructed the four-roomed house later known as number 3 (or 23) Casselden Place in ca. 1862 after cesspit 4 had been closed. The Mahlstedt plan dated 1910–1915 reproduced in the 1987 DAS draft conservation plan reveals that the house at the north end of lot 68 was two-storeyed (Figure 11.15), which accords with the building indicated in that position on a detail from De Gruchy and Leigh's 1866 *Isometrical plan of Melbourne and suburbs* (Figure 11.13).

It was this house rented by Kodabux Rohinibaux – described in the historical documents as a 'Hindoo' – that was raided at midnight in 1896 when 16 immigrants from the Subcontinent were found to be inhabiting his upper two rooms (McCarthy 1989: vol. 1: 94).

Lot 63

Historical Background

By 1856, George Griffin had constructed the two masonry buildings shown on Bibbs' map within lot 63, but only one of these buildings was present during the 1849/50 rate valuations. George Griffin and his wife operated a produce store and grocery on lot 63 until 1871 when William John Kerr became mortgagee in possession. Kerr operated the store until 1877, but had sold the freehold to Richard Scoles during 1875. Scoles rented the premises to blacksmiths from 1877 to 1879 when the property was sold by his trustees to James Porta. Porta continued to rent to blacksmith Charles Dowell until 1884 when Porta and Sons were in possession and had constructed the brick and iron workshop evident on the 1895 MMBW detail block plan 1019 (Figure 11.4). Porta's business was the manufacture of bellows but with the opportunistic sideline of patent exterminators during the rabbit plagues of the late 19th century.

Following a fire during October 1919 that destroyed their factory (*Argus* 22 October 1919: 15), Porta interests purchased lot 67ABC indirectly from John Casselden's executors. In 1922, the Porta family, who had also purchased lot 68AB during September 1896, sold their Little Lonsdale Street holdings to W.H. Blakeley and Company Pty. Ltd. who built the saw and cutlery factory demolished during the present redevelopment.

Excavation of Lot 63

Truncation of the Blakeley factory site within lot 63 meant that apart from the bluestone rubble footing of the boundary wall adjacent to lot 67ABC, only negative features remained. These included brick-lined cesspit 5 (Figure 11.14), which had been dug into natural clay and the lining of hand-made bricks with clear hack-marks had been laid directly against the cut with no puddled clay backing. Relatively few artefacts were present and butchered bone

Figure 11.13: Detail from De Gruchy and Leigh's 1866 *Isometrical plan of Melbourne and suburbs*. Alexander Morison's house on lot 68 is arrowed (Source: SLV H26109).

Figure 11.14: Brick-lined cesspit 5 on lot 63 (Photo: GML Heritage).

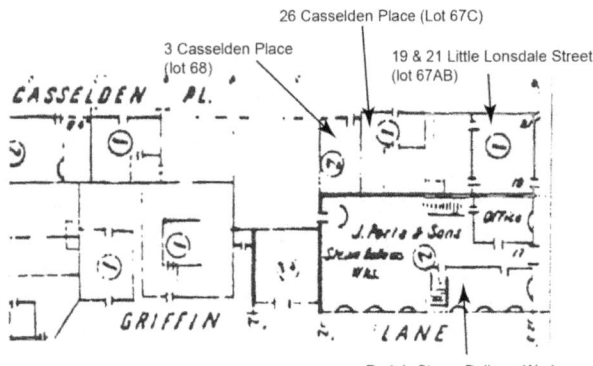

Figure 11.15: Detail from Mahlstedt Plan section 2 sheet 8A 1910–1915 showing internal details of Porta's bellows factory (location of original is unknown, reproduced in DAS draft conservation plan 1987 as Figure 35).

was predominant. Closure of this cesspit almost certainly pre-dates purchase of lot 63 by the Porta family but may have occurred towards the end of the Griffin family ownership and the beginning of ownership and occupancy by William Kerr. Artefact dating will hopefully lend some precision to this understanding.

In addition to an array of concrete column bases formerly supporting the roof of the Blakeley factory, 20th-century concrete machinery foundations were present. Earlier industrial remains included a machinery foundation of basalt blocks at the south end and a pit containing an agglomeration of rusted iron and corroded copper alloy residues, perhaps filings and swarf. The northern end of lot 63 was dominated by the remains of a pit resulting from removal of a very large tree stump.

Figure 11.15 shows the internal arrangements within Porta's bellows factory which the Mahlstedt plan indicates had consisted of two floors. Also of interest is that the small masonry building at the north end of lot 68 is also two-storeyed. The Mahlstedt plans informed fire insurance underwriters of the materials and form of construction of buildings and hence the level of risk. A series of editions was produced from 1888 to 1970 and these were updated (by scissors and paste becoming undated palimpsests between editions) to reflect changes in the built environment. Collections of Mahlstedt plans are held by State Library Victoria, Melbourne University Archives, the Public Records Office Victoria and National Library but unfortunately none of these collections appear to include the relevant section 2 sheet 8A 1910 plan as reproduced in the DAS draft conservation plan 1987.

In the Mahlstedt plan (Figure 11.15), the buildings on lot 67ABC are as shown on the 1895 MMBW plan.

Other than the well-preserved Blakeley grinding wheel pits, insufficient evidence remained from past industrial activities to shed much light on questions of industrial organisation within either the Porta bellows factory or the later saw and cutlery manufacturing establishment. Nevertheless, we were able to quickly recognise the meaning of the wheel pits and from them, the orientation of the photographer in a surviving internal image of the Blakeley factory (SLV H2011 16/10). This orientation gave us confidence regarding some of the massive concrete machinery foundations encountered in lot 63, apparently associated with what appears to be a press in the background of the photograph.

Questions concerning transfer of organisational ideas from traditional Sheffield cutlery industry practice (see Symonds 2002) were perhaps better answered from images than from archaeological evidence, in particular, the photograph of top-hatted William Blakeley seated centrally among his staff and operatives in SLV image H2011 16.5. This group photograph dated ca. 1904–1905 at Blakeley's former factory at 115 Lonsdale Street shows what appears to be a clearly hierarchical arrangement of employer and employees, rather than a collaboration of independent operators.

Phase 2

The locations of the excavation trenches within phase two are shown in Figure 11.16.

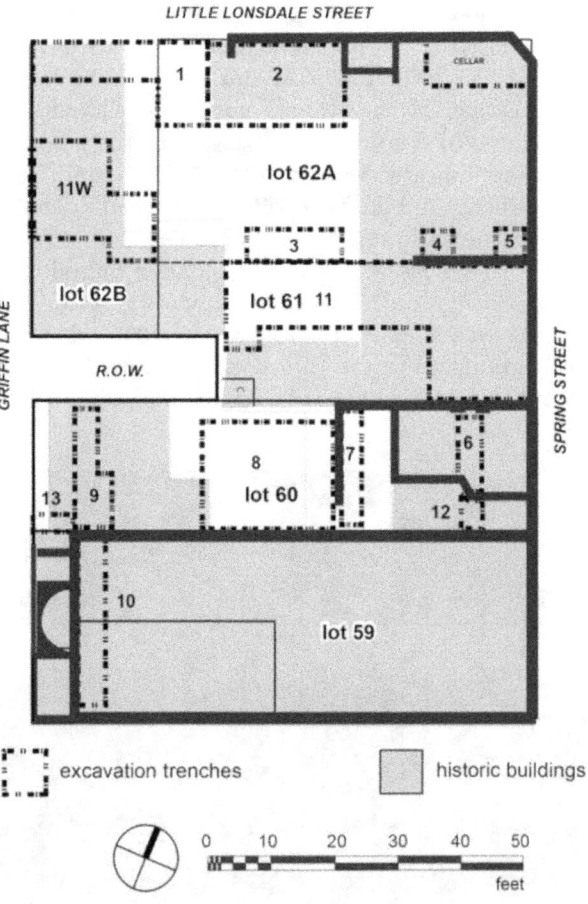

Figure 11.16: The positions of the phase two trenches are shown, together with the outlines of remaining buildings, the historic buildings and lot boundaries.

Lot 62A

Historical Background

Lot 62A was sold by Henry B. Foot to John Brophy in December 1848. John Brophy was a clerk in the Herald Office, Collins Lane, according to Mouritz (1847: 65). Gipps Ward rate valuations for 1849/50 show that Brophy was owner-occupier of an unfinished four-roomed house but before 1850, according to plan M325, there is a substantial building on the corner corresponding to the core part of the Old Governor Bourke Hotel situated on this lot. Indeed, the rate valuation for 1851/52 describes the building then present as having a bar, 12 rooms, detached kitchen plus three rooms and a stable. By ca. 1856, Bibbs' map shows the boarding house also present, adjacent on what was much later to be subdivided as lot 61. The MCC register of intention to build (Notice 291 of 12 March 1855) indicates the date of construction of the boarding house which was described as a 'dwelling house-brick building' (McCarthy 1989: vol. 5: 332).

Brophy's property was held in trust for his wife Eliza following his death in 1862 and remained so until her mortgagee sold the hotel to George Elms in 1879. However, Eliza (who married George Keane Johnston in 1865) retained the adjacent boarding house on lot 61 newly subdivided from Brophy's original purchase. Although the boarding house had been built by Brophy to architecturally harmonise with the hotel, it appears to have been run as a separate business entity in the hands of a procession of tenants. In 1886, George Elms changed the name of the hotel to 'Elms Family'. Elms descendants rebuilt the hotel during 1924–1925 and the only architectural remnants of the older building are some footings of the exterior walls and the original cellar in the north-east corner.

Excavation of Lot 62A

Trenches 2, 4 and 5 plus some 50% of the cellar and the eastern end of trench 1 were excavated within the footprint of the Old Governor Bourke Hotel. The remainder of trench 1 was excavated adjacent to the west end of the Little Lonsdale Street wing of the building and trench 3 was dug in the rear yard. Trenches 1 and 2 partially exposed the footings of the Little Lonsdale Street wing of the Old Governor Bourke Hotel. Most likely, this wing is the first building constructed on lot 62A by John Brophy during 1849–1850. The structure, visible in Figures 11.6 and 11.7, appears to have consisted of two ground-floor rooms divided by a back-to-back hearth with stub walls either side. The description 'four-roomed' possibly refers to two attic rooms having been present under the timber shingle roof evident in Figure 11.6. The plain render apparently over structural brick (showing evidence of rising damp in 1870) differs from the scribed 'ashlar' treatment

Figure 11.17: View of trench 2 looking towards Little Lonsdale Street, within the standing walls of the Elms Hotel (Photo: GML Heritage).

of the stucco on the hotel building and there is no decorative quoining as was present on the hotel.

Before alterations to this wing of the building required the original chimney and hearth to be demolished, a rough brick footing on the east side of the hearth appears to have supported a hearth stone (Figure 11.17) which indicates that the building had a suspended timber floor at that time. Figure 11.18 shows a later wall and hearth constructed from rectangular basalt blocks laid over a silt sub-floor surface. A remnant brick wall and footing of the Elms Hotel is evident to the left of the excavator in Figure 11.18 and to the left of the Elms wall, the west end wall of the original wing is emerging. Although disturbed by drains and other services, this end wall is visible at the top of Figure 11.19.

According to the 1895 MMBW plan, there was a privy within the narrow space between the new and old walls of the Old Governor Bourke, handy to the barrel cesspits adjacent to the older wall. Demolition of the original chimney may reflect the need for an enlarged working space within what is expected to

Figure 11.18: Subsequent view of trench 2 looking towards Little Lonsdale Street, clearly showing the later wall of rectangular basalt blocks (Photo: GML Heritage).

Figure 11.19: View towards the east of trench 1 showing the disturbed western wall of the Little Lonsdale Street wing and the double cask cesspit 6 (Photo: GML Heritage).

have been the kitchen wing of the Old Governor Bourke. The description of the kitchen as 'detached' in the 1851/52 rate valuation perhaps merely refers to an absence of direct access to it from within the main building.

The barrel cesspits adjacent to the Old Governor Bourke Hotel were placed within a mass of puddled clay in accordance with the instructions given in the 1861 Central Board of Health circular. This construction probably dates to soon after the circular. The barrels were placed within a pre-existing rectangular cut evidently an earlier unlined cesspit.

The Health Committee Reports concerning orders for closure of cesspits includes a demand for Mrs Johnston to close a cesspit at the Old Governor Bourke Hotel within seven days from 25 July 1870. It is true that Mrs Johnston was the owner of both the hotel and boarding house, the latter having its own separate cesspit (see Figure 11.22). The common ownership, together with architectural continuity of the buildings, may have confused the inspector. Hayes and Minchinton (2016: 16) point out that *prior* to 1870 most notices targeted hotels rather than private dwellings, so we remain uncertain whether the hotel cesspit (6) or the boarding house cesspit (7) was the subject of the closure order.

As we have artefact assemblages from both cesspits, comparative dating may provide a mofre definitive identification. Although artefact catalogues from the boarding house and hotel cesspits are as yet incomplete, it is possible to state that bottles and bottle glass dominated the hotel assemblage, together with barware and cheap ceramics. Despite the barrel cesspit closest to Little Lonsdale having had much of the contents removed in the past as a consequence of being cut through by sewerage lines, a very large quantity of material was recovered. We are hopeful that this assemblage might address research questions concerning the role of the hotel in local social networks and the possible influence of outsiders upon those networks.

Trench 3 to the north of the footing of a brick party wall between the Elms Hotel and the former garage on lot 61 contained nothing more consequential than an abandoned vitreous clay drain. Trench 4 was placed in a location heavily disturbed by construction of the party wall and, beneath a layer of demolition rubble, revealed a unit of dark silt over natural clay. Trench 5 uncovered a remnant of basalt footing of the Old Governor Bourke Hotel under the brickwork of the Elms Hotel façade. *In situ* hand-made brickwork was present in trench 5, in a remnant of the party wall between the original hotel and boarding house.

A handful of artefacts were recovered from the northern half of the cellar of the Old Governor Bourke Hotel following removal of part of a recent concrete slab floor. The original footings and walls of the cellar had remained *in situ* during reconstruction of the building in the mid-1920s. Traces of lightweight timber bearers placed diagonally over natural clay and rock suggested a crude suspended timber floor. The cellar was drained of water and spillage by running it into a timber-lined sump excavated into the local rock, from which it was removed by means of a stave-built bucket that had been abandoned in place.

Lot 61

A graded entrance lobby is to be located in lot 61 adjacent to Spring Street, so the full width of the lot was to be investigated. This became our trench 11. Excavation uncovered remnant footings of the boarding house including a passage wall and a transverse wall between ground floor rooms, where two courses of hand-made brick survived *in situ*. The passage wall continued west to meet the back wall of the boarding house beyond which was an asphalt surface and a down pipe (Figure 11.20). Removal of the asphalt revealed intact brick paving. This surface was followed westward for the planned

Figure 11.20: The Spring Street end of trench 11 on lot 61, showing the *in situ* brickwork of the dividing wall between rooms (west of a scatter of bluestone rubble) and the passage wall joining to the rear wall of the boarding house and an asphalt surface (Photo: GML Heritage).

Figure 11.21: Excavation in progress revealed the clay capping within stone-lined cesspit 7 associated with the boarding house on lot 61. Note past slumping of the brick paving at left (Photo: GML Heritage).

distance of trench 11, which continued as a narrow slit in the alignment of a proposed service trench. A narrow band of stone pitching was found to be present immediately to the rear of the back wall of the boarding house, but the pitching had been cut by a vitreous clay stormwater drain. Removal of the brick paving and a deposit of yellow clay packing beneath it, revealed a dark silt yard surface layer. Where the trench terminated, a line of basalt stones was found running north–south. Initially we thought that we had found the eastern footing of that part of the stables that remained on lot 61 after demolition of the main bulk of that building. Trench 11 was extended to investigate this possibility. Extension of the trench exposed a more recent brick wall footing resting on a concrete strip, apparently subdividing the Spring Street and Little Lonsdale Street portions of the former motor garage. The found wall intersected the 1920s party wall between the Elms Hotel and the former garage on the north boundary of trench 11. Rather than stable footings, we found that the brick wall had been constructed over a stone-lined cesspit backfilled with yellow clay (Figure 11.21).

Trench 11 was extended a small distance to the south with the aim of exposing the full extent of the cesspit in that direction. Following removal of the

Figure 11.22: Stone-lined cesspit 7 associated with the boarding house on lot 61 (Photo: GML Heritage).

clay capping and backfill, the waterlogged slurry towards the base was mechanically excavated and sieved. Only that portion of the deposit that could be accessed by the backhoe was removed (Figure 11.22). Further excavation was not possible and the remainder of the deposit will be built-over during the present redevelopment. The recovered assemblage had not yet been catalogued at the time of writing, but should provide a most interesting comparison to the domestic and hotel assemblages.

Lot 62B

Lot 62B was occupied from before ca. 1856 by the coursed rubble bluestone stables of the Old Governor Bourke Hotel, an L-shaped building in plan which extended eastwards onto lot 61 reflecting John Brophy's ownership from 1848 of lots 62A, 62B and 61. The Little Lonsdale Street end wall of the stables is visible in Figure 11.6 and the north-south extent may be seen in Figure 11.7. The skillion roof of the stable is also evident in Figure 11.13. Lot 62B was sold by Brophy's executors to Walter Henry Lewis early in 1884. According to rate valuations, the stables had been removed from lot 62B before 1883, except for the remnant on lot 61 evident on the MMBW plan. The latter plan shows a shed in the south-east corner of lot 62B connected to Little Lonsdale Street by a pitched carriageway, but the remainder of the lot is open space. From 1887 to at least 1900, the Porta family used lot 62B as a store yard. During the period 1910 to 1915, this yard was occupied by Louey Weh Hey. By 1929, Elms descendants had purchased, cleared and redeveloped lots 61 and 62B. At that time, Mabel Robertson is listed in the rate valuations as the owner, and Robertson Buckley as the occupier, of a brick garage at 267 Spring Street with 20-foot frontage to Little Lonsdale Street. This building was demolished in the present redevelopment.

There seems to be some confusion regarding the dates of demolition and construction for the rebuilt Elms Hotel and the motor garage on lots 61 and 62B. The DAS draft conservation plan (1987: 66) has argued that construction of the Elms Family Hotel took place in 1907 and that the Spring Street portion of the motor garage was built ca. 1910. This proposition is impossible, since recent demolition has revealed a scar on the north wall of the Mission corresponding to the outline of the south gable of the boarding house on lot 61. This shows that the boarding house was still standing in 1913. Further, our excavation trench 5 revealed a stub of the original party wall between the Old Governor Bourke Hotel and Brophy's boarding house to the *north* of the new party wall between the rebuilt Elms Hotel and the motor garage. Hence the newer hotel and motor garage were built *after* demolition of the boarding house post-1918, the year that Mrs Kate Dunn is listed in the rate valuation records as being the tenant. The DAS conservation plan mentions an MCC building application for a new garage and factory on this site in 1921 (number 3653 £2,800) and this probably included both the Spring Street (lot 61) and Little Lonsdale Street (lot 62B) wings.

Trench 11W was excavated over the inside corner of the L-shaped stable building. A substantial portion of the trench towards Little Lonsdale Street was found to have been backfilled with crushed rock probably after removal of an underground tank. A short length of basalt footing running west from the inside corner of the stable was located, together with an internal post hole, but nothing else of significant interest was uncovered.

Lot 60AB

Historical Background

The Bibbs' map shows two buildings present on lot 60AB, a masonry building with frontage to Spring Street and a timber structure facing towards Griffin Lane. The masonry building, 161 Spring Street, which was present in 1850, is generally described as a brick house of five – but after 1855 six – rooms (Notice number 143 dated 3 February 1855, McCarthy 1989: vol. 5: 328) and it appears to have been rented for its entire existence except when owner James York occupied the house for a short period from 1863. Earlier tenants included Mrs Lucas during 1861 and a resident at that time was John House. During 1861, Thomas Haycock was before the Magistrate's Court charged with stealing a watch from John House at 161 Spring Street. During the recriminations that followed, Haycock accused House of being a brothel keeper (*The Age* 26 March 1861: 7). The final occupants of the house with frontage to Spring Street were the Allessio family from 1883. Joseph Allessio, secretary of the Melbourne Imperial Football Club (*The Sportsman* 4 April 1883: 4), was there until his death in 1886 and his widow continued in occupation until 1890.

The building is visible in Figure 11.5, adjacent to the boarding house wing of the Old Governor Bourke Hotel and next to William Mather's lot 59 which only shows a front fence. The rear view in Figure 11.7 shows a rear skillion-roofed extension and two chimneys. One is at the peak of the south gable and the other at the junction of the skillion roof to the main building.

The timber structure at the rear of lot 60AB, with frontage to Griffin Lane was described as being of wood and brick during 1862 and brick the following year. From 1869 it is variously described as brick having two – but sometimes four – rooms. In 1879, the last year it was let, it had deteriorated to a 'shanty'. In 1881, the rear building disappeared from the rate books. McCarthy's data (1989: vol. 5: 331) notes that this building was brick-nogged (i.e. a form of half-timbering with non-load-bearing brick infill) and plastered externally, hence the successive rate assessors' apparent confusion concerning construction material.

By 1891, the main brick building was unoccupied and lot 60AB was described in the rate valuations as a vacant allotment in 1892. It is shown as such in the 1895 MMBW plan. In the meantime, financier Mark Moss had bought lot 60AB from the York family during March 1884 and was responsible for demolition during the depths of the economic depression. Michael Cannon (1966: 8) describes Mark Moss as 'an eccentric Jewish money lender'. Moss founded the Equitable Loan and Investment Society and at the height of the boom, began building a 14-bedroom mansion named 'Norwood' on The Esplanade at Brighton. Completed in 1891, the mansion was designed by architect Philip Treeby in a strange eclectic style that combined heavy-handed Romanesque with Queen Anne and Arts and Crafts. Within three years, Moss became insolvent.

Successive owners of the vacant lot 60AB were Henry Penketh Fergie, The Bank of Victoria (twice) and Mrs Jane Bowen, before transfer to the Church of England Trusts Corporation for the Diocese of Melbourne during 1911. Presumably referring to lot 60AB, historian Lynne Strahan has stated that 'land in Spring Street adjoining (the) Mission House' was gifted to the Church (Strahan 1988: 50). The north wing of the Anglican Mission House was constructed on lot 60AB during 1913.

Excavations on Lot 60AB

Lot 60AB was investigated with six trenches. Trenches 6 and 12 were dug within the standing north wing of the Mission House, in the public reception room and the passage way leading towards the dining room, kitchen and stairs. Trench 7 was also dug within the standing building in the lobby to the dining room. Trench 8 was dug west of the standing building where the north wing had been removed. This trench targeted the rear yards of both buildings on the lot. Trench 9 investigated the western margin of what had been the basement of the Mission House and trench 13 looked at a small space adjacent to the west end of the Mission hall, west of trench 9.

It was hoped that trenches 6, 7 and 12 might produce sub-floor deposits relating to occupation of the site by the Anglican Mission operated by the religious Sisters of the Community of the Holy Name. Analysis of the sparse artefact assemblage excavated from those trenches may reveal data, but it is to be regretted that the outlook is not overly promising despite very careful digging.

Trenches 6 and 12, did produce evidence of the brick house that stood on 161 Spring Street. This was in the form of basalt rubble footings of an internal (passage) wall in trench 6 and the fireplace that was present at the south gable in trench 12 (Figure 11.23).

Figure 11.23: Part of the hearth and footing at the south wall of the pre-1850 brick house at 161 Spring Street revealed in trench 12 (Photo: GML Heritage).

An asphalt yard surface was exposed in trench 7 under demolition rubble and levelling fills. Further fills below the asphalt were cut by a drain feature containing grey silt with oyster shells, pebbles and crushed brick, bordered by artefact-rich contexts containing charcoal and fragmentary brick. A brick spoon drain was present in the south east corner of trench 7 and this feature continued into trench 8. Four post holes were present below the artefact-rich units.

Figure 11.24: Fragment of the stone-lining of the southern wall of a cesspit in the rear yards of lot 60 adjacent to the boundary with lot 59. The stone footings of Best's dance hall are visible on the right (Photo: GML Heritage).

Trench 9 was excavated within an area that had been extensively disturbed by demolition of the Mission House basement and by earlier services. However, a fragment of a field-stone footing was found adjacent to the boundary with lot 59. This footing was interpreted as being associated with the brick-nogged timber-framed building facing to Griffin lane, but no further data were recovered.

Trench 13 was placed in a location that had been entirely disturbed by earlier services and construction of a retaining wall adjacent to Griffin Lane.

Trench 8 was dug in two parts. The main area was to the north of the passage wall in the area of the demolished dining room. A smaller area was located within the former passage and the two areas were separated by the stub of the passage wall.

In the larger area, under a unit of sandy demolition rubble containing stone chips and fragmentary hand-made and dry-pressed brick, several units described as levelling fills were found. The continuation of a brick spoon drain revealed in trench 7 was found in trench 8, within a cobbled surface and partially covered by a surface of crushed brick, probably a path. This deposit overlayed an intact brick pathway which rested on a dark grey artefact-rich silty yard surface cut by drain trenches and a lead water pipe that had itself been cut during construction of the Mission House.

Excavation within the narrow space between the footings of the passageway wall and the north wall of Best's dance hall on lot 59 revealed the fragment of *in situ* stonework shown in Figure 11.24. A further *in situ* remnant became evident when the passageway footing was subsequently removed by mechanical excavator. These features have been interpreted as the south and east wall respectively of a stone-lined cesspit within the rear yards of the houses on lot 60AB, sited close to the boundary with lot 59. The cesspit, which is marked 8 on Figure 11.3, was most probably closed and backfilled well before construction of the dance hall on lot 59 in 1877.

The pit was comprehensively destroyed ca. 1913 when the Mission House was constructed. Excavators observed that the concrete strip sub-footing of the passageway wall was oddly shaped in this location, as if the concrete had been poured into a footing trench that had intersected a rectangular pit. Concerns about possible undermining of the Mission Hall footings precluded further investigation of this pit and its remains will be built-over in the present project.

Lot 59

Historical Background

A masonry building located towards Griffin Lane is present on lot 59 in Thomas Bibbs' map and appears to have been there before 1850. According to rate valuations, it was initially described as having three rooms and a kitchen and seems to have been occupied by its owner William Mather in 1853. Mather sold the allotment to Isaac Hart in 1857 and it was tenanted by Charles Webb who appears to have operated a bottle-washing yard there before Samuel Walters used the allotment as a wood yard from 1868 to 1870. Following a procession of tenants, the land was transferred in 1877 to William Sweetland Best who constructed a brick hall with the intention of operating a dancing saloon. According to Ryan and Edmonds (1979: 72) Best's application No. 6834 for a permit to build a 'room' was dated July 1876 and Rawlins and Sayers were the builders. In Figure 11.8, Best's dance hall is marked by the triangular pediment at the Spring Street boundary.

The Premier Permanent Building Land and Investment Company[4] foreclosed on Best's mortgage in mid-1880 and sold lot 59 to publican Charles Wright who then leased the dance hall to William Sharp and Sophie Eliza Best. We might assume that Sophie Eliza Best is William Sweetland Best's estranged wife continuing to operate the dancing saloon in partnership with William Sharp. The establishment continued to annoy seekers after moral purity: 'Citizen' wrote to the editor of *The Argus* in October 1881 about an incident outside 'a dancing saloon in Spring Street', calling for police attention and remarking that 'I never met a more complete or insulting member of the larrikin class than the man who claimed to be the manager of the establishment' (*The Argus* 12 October 1881: 11). Their tenancy lasted until 1887. In March that year, renting from Wright, Monsieur Victor[5] became the proprietor of 'Victor's Athletic Hall' where prize fights and wrestling matches together with unstated 'feats of strength and agility' were advertised (*The Sportsman* 8 March 1887: 5). The following March, Victor was in partnership with one Peter Newton but by June 1888, boxing matches were being advertised in 'Boland's (late Victor's) Athletic Hall' (*The Sportsman* 20th June 1888: 7). By mid-July that year, the highlight of the evening's competition was an all-in Chinese-style fight between Ah Kit and Goug Wing refereed by Tee Lung (*The Sportsman* 11 July 1888: 7) after which the venue seems to have folded.

John J. Saqui became Wright's tenant in 1889 and the building is described as a factory in the 1892 valuation records (a cigar factory according to DAS 1987: 136, thus adding one more vice to the building's ripeness for redemption). The hall may have been unoccupied for the years 1893 and 1894, in the depths of the depression. The following year, Wright's tenant was the Church of England Mission, funded apparently through the personal generosity of a member of the committee. This arrangement appears to have continued until Wright's death in 1904. The title was transferred to the Church of England Trusts Corporation for the Diocese of Melbourne during that year. Parts of Best's former dancing saloon, the Anglican Mission Hall, still exist, incorporated into the fabric of the new Mission House during 1913. Ryan and Edmonds (1979: 28) asserted that the original 'secret-nailed' dance floor still existed in the Mission Hall during 1979 and it may well have been still partially present until 2017.

During construction of the Mission House during 1913, the fabric of Best's dance hall was demolished down to the level of the coursed basalt rubble of the footings, much of which were retained and reused, possibly along with the floor. During the present redevelopment, the complete southern wing of the former Mission House was retained. However, the existing timber floor within the Mission Hall covering most of lot 59 was removed for upgrading and a sheet of demolition rubble was found to be present beneath it.

Installation of sub-floor heating ducts in the past had resulted in the presence of trenches approximately 1 metre wide along the north and south walls with additional returns against both ends of the eastern (Spring Street) end wall. Demolition contractors had also made unplanned excavations and bulk movements in several places. These impacts had not penetrated below the rubble layers but may have impacted potential sub-floor deposits.

Excavations within Lot 59

Trench 10, placed at the western end of the former hall, was excavated across its width. Two longitudinal coursed basalt rubble footings, apparently built during Best's original construction

---

[4] The Premier Permanent Building Association was the brainchild of the land booming Congregationalist and Rechabite James Mirams MP, who paid two pence in the pound on his million pound deficiency when bankrupted by the crash of 1890. Mirams was found guilty on a charge of permitting a false balance sheet for the Premier Permanent to be issued and was gaoled for 12 months (Cannon 1966: 71–75).

[5] According to *The Sportsman* (7 May 1884: 1) Monsieur Victor, who was born in Paris in 1847, had trained as a wrestler, but was also a boxer and swordsman. Victor fought for France and was wounded in the Franco-Prussian War. He arrived in the Colony during 1883 and toured the colonies competing professionally before opening Victor's Athletic Hall in Best's former premises during 1887. It is sometimes difficult to know how seriously to consider statements in *Melbourne Punch*, but the issue of Thursday 29 March 1888 (page 16) suggests that Monsieur Victor may have become distracted by the public practice of mesmerism. He disappears from the press after July 1888.

Monsieur Victor (Source: *The Sportsman* Wednesday 7 May 1884: 1)

phase, supported the timber floor and subdivided the underfloor space into three lengthwise bays. Where investigated, the footings of Best's dance hall were found to rest on a yellow clay and mudstone fill which in turn rested on what the excavator described as a lens of demolition debris approximately 175mm thick. This lens in turn rested above a silty natural horizon some 900mm below the top of the footings in that location. Following construction of the footings, a very substantial amount of clay and rubble fill had been placed within them at the downslope west end of the building, apparently to level the sub-floor. Diagnostic artefacts entrained within this fill were retained but these may have no association with activities on lot 59. Apart perhaps from the demolition layer above the natural silt, no trace was found of William Mather's early building on this lot although much of trench 10 was within its footprint. Unfortunately it appears that no significant artefact deposits that might relate to any of the dance hall, athletic hall, cigar factory or Mission Hall occupancies were found.

The Research Questions

Using *Victoria's Framework of Historical Themes*, the outcome of a research project by the Heritage Council of Victoria (www.heritagecouncil.vic.gov.au/research-projects/framework-of-historical-themes/) the research design for the 271 Spring Street excavation posed a range of research questions detailed in Section 6 of GML Heritage (2015). This discussion is intended to briefly examine the present status of the research questions in this early stage of the post-excavation process.

The archaeological record of the 271 Spring Street site, through the 40,000 or so artefacts recovered, does indeed offer the opportunity to explore the possibilities of ethnic diversity and cultural attachment, particularly within contexts that probably relate to the very late 19th- and early 20th-century. We certainly have strong evidence of social interaction within families together with evidence suggesting that occupants gave expression to the notion of childhood, which interestingly appears to be manifest from the earliest stages in the site chronology.

Sub-floor deposits within the duplex house and shop on the corner of Casselden Place and Little Lon even at a high level of rounding up seem to show distinct spatial heterogeneity. Given 60-odd years of occupation by a procession of tenants with highly diversified occupations, this is somewhat surprising and appears to run counter to Murray and Mayne's observation concerning patterns of homogeneity in material culture despite very different forms of occupancy (Murray and Mayne 2001: 102–103). Of course, different scales of analysis may well show distinctly different patterns. There appear to be differences between individual domestic cesspit deposits in terms perhaps of household economic status and habits of consumption. Not unexpectedly, there appear to be qualitative differences between the cesspit deposits of pub, boarding house and the tenanted dwelling houses. On the face of it, the artefact assemblage from 271 Spring Street does seem to offer the opportunity to investigate these questions of patterning and also the possibility of useful comparison to assemblages previously excavated from the Commonwealth Block. There seems no doubt, however, that the former residents of Little Lon who lived within the site known now as 271 Spring Street were also avid consumers and enjoyed access to a wide variety of goods (Murray and Mayne 2001: 102; Davies 2006: 354).

Although we found archaeological evidence of past industrial activity, only very small quantities of artefacts related to this phase of occupation were found and we have gained little in our understanding of industrial organisation or work relationships from this investigation. Unfortunately, it appears that most of the archaeological evidence of the Portas' Steam Bellows Works was lost when lot 63 was truncated by levelling during the Blakeley build.

The phase 2 period 1837–1848 discussed by Tim Murray (2006: 399) does seem to be represented at 271 Spring Street in the form of recycled elements from a primitive post and rail fence reused in the lining of an early cesspit, together with the stumps of substantial trees that probably existed well before the advent of Europeans to the Port Phillip District. Traces appear to be evident also of the earliest part of phase 3, when small timber cottages are being constructed on greenfield sites. These early buildings, of which some were permitted to exist well into the later 19th-century, raise an interesting question concerning approaches to the building code. Schedule E of the *Building Act* of October 1849 required the walls of all buildings within the city limits to be constructed of brick or stone laid in mortar or cement. The limits of the town and the compass of the act were defined by its date. In other words, those parts of the city surveyed and sold before 1849 were subject to the code. In accordance with the act, no timber buildings should have been present in the Little Lon precinct. When the population expansion resulting from gold rush immigration caused acute accommodation shortage, tension certainly arose between executive government and the City Council over application of the building code and largely unsuccessful attempts were made to circumvent it (Hewitt et al. 2017). But these timber buildings pre-date the gold rush and raise questions about the will of the MCC at the time to enforce the code in these newer parts of the city, given that it had the power to extend the city limits if there was any doubt about the then current force of the act.

One striking disappointment from this excavation seems to be the *prima facie* dearth of evidence of the activities that took place within Best's dance hall and the Anglican Mission House. The areas we sampled were relatively small and demolition activities had caused disturbance to the sub-floors. Nevertheless, there was little there. The continued presence of the carefully constructed dance floor in the hall may have prevented the accumulation of lost items in that place and perhaps a similar explanation accounts for the impoverished assemblage in the mission House sub-floor.

Perhaps the most interesting aspect of our site was the strong historical presence of women. Of course we are familiar with Chris McConville's data that shows Casselden Place lined on both sides with brothels, as noted by the police during 1883 and 1884 (McConville 1985: 77). A cottage-scale industry, perhaps encouraged by landlords such as John Casselden, happy enough to accept the proceeds from regular tenants prepared to pay a little more than the usual. Minchinton (2017: 67–68) notes that brothels were conducted in two-room cottages within the Little Lon precinct. Each of the small houses may have been occupied by three or four prostitutes, but very few of their names turn up in the rate books. Although Minchinton has found direct evidence that women used businesses such as grocery stores and draperies as fronts for brothels, there is evidence of much diversity. Affordable rentals, it appears, also attracted industrious women to tenancies at 148 and 150 Little Lonsdale Street, sewing or laundering clothes, making lace, raising children, having tea, making ends meet. John Brophy's widow and George Elms' daughters owned the corner pub, on occasion holding the license. Catherine Gearan ran the adjacent boarding house for years. The pious middle-class sisters of the Mission, rescued the fallen without great success, but educated the racial mix of local children and fed the hungry during the worst of the 1890s depression (Strahan 1988: 31–32, 40–42, 50). All were independent women. Some perhaps fiercely independent, others such as Ada Stack were independently fierce. It would be perhaps an unlikely coincidence that there were two women named Ada Stack in Little Lonsdale Street East but one of them was certainly the tenant of the two-roomed house on the corner of Casselden Place in 1907. An Ada Stack, living in Casselden Place, was charged during March 1903 with the unlawful wounding of her then partner Frederick Payne while in a jealous rage. Payne was stabbed repeatedly in the face and arms with a pair of scissors, losing an eye. Perhaps the same Ada Stack was divorced by her husband in 1908. Some years after her marriage in 1884, Ada began to drink heavily, left him and would not be reconciled (*The Age* 7 March 1903: 12; *The Argus* 12 November 1908: 10).

Historian Alan Mayne focused attention upon the construction of slum stereotypes that demonised the inhabitants of certain precincts of modern cities, distorting, marginalising and obscuring their lives. Universalising 'slum' mythologies were created to serve and reinforce bourgeois social distinctions and to bolster the efforts of social reformers seeking to impose their own systems of belief and behaviour upon their perceived moral inferiors (Mayne 1993; Mayne and Murray 2001: 1).

The significant past presence of independent women revealed at the 271 Spring Street site has prompted further thought concerning gendered processes of 'slum' imagination. It is certain that the interaction and dialogue between poor working class women and their philanthropic middle-class counterparts, as discussed by Ellen Ross (2001), was being conducted in our part of the Little Lon precinct. Sisters of the Community of the Holy Name were active in their attempts to rescue women from prostitution, gather up abandoned children, provide support to the desperate and proselytise their religious faith. Penny Russell has pointed out that, as dictated by their 'genteel performance', only those upper class women consumed with evangelical fervour were prepared to risk contamination 'by other subordinated and sexualised femininities, particularly those associated with working class women and prostitutes' (Russell 1994: 167). So it seems likely that other than the dedicated missioners, the majority of Melbourne's genteel ladies carefully avoided the threat to their status posed by direct association with the non-respectable other. Nevertheless, they were encouraged to exercise philanthropy through donations to the Mission Council by popular press accounts that juxtaposed lurid accounts of 'slumland' with praise for efforts of the Mission Sisters (Strahan 1988: 28–29).

This 'slum' mythology that titillated and alarmed middle-class audiences was drawn from a place where a crowded working-class population inhabited cramped insanitary houses lining narrow streets and lanes, cheek-by-jowl with industries and vice. Racist responses to an increasingly active Chinese population in the Little Lon precinct, together with a concentration of immigrants from the Middle East and Subcontinent, no doubt played a role in its creation. I now suggest that sexism, as a response to the threat to male hegemony posed through the presence of a significant proportion of independent women in this location, may have played a further part. Doubtless, the fears and insecurities of genteel wives, whose role of exercising moral superiority included policing the ill-defined boundaries of gentility (Russell 1994: 199–200), also contributed.

Acknowledgements

Sincere thanks are due to Jarvis Mellor of RCP Pty Ltd and Jason Lourenz of ISPT, also Ben Bugeja, Max Slater and Mark Hughes of Probuild. Caitlin D'Gluyas, GML's site manager, was indispensable.

Richard Mackay, Janine Major, Madeline Shanahan and Abi Cryerhall also of GML, deserve many thanks for input and support. The excavation team led by Cathy Tucker and Sharon Lane was second to none; the strength including Gareth Holes, Haley Banks, Krista Whitewood, Nadia Bajzelj, Paul Freestone, Shane Willis, Jo Wilson (who made most of the photographs), Jen Porter, Luke Wallis, Kerry Platt, Lauren Keating and Anita Barker. Particular acknowledgement is due to Jeremy Smith and his team at Heritage Victoria and to Chris Williamson for management of the artefact assemblage. Barbara Minchinton's and Sharon Lane's historical research was invaluable and I am grateful to Sarah Hayes, Tim Murray and Caitlin D'Gluyas for their useful comments and suggestions on a draft of this chapter.

Geoff Hewitt
(Excavation Director)

References

Bendigo Advertiser, Wednesday 13 March 1872

Melbourne Punch, Thursday 29 March 1888

The Age, Tuesday 26 March 1861

The Age, Wednesday 18 August 1880

The Age, Saturday 7 March 1903

The Argus, Monday 19 March 1877

The Argus, Tuesday 27 March 1877

The Argus, Saturday 14 April 1877

The Argus, Tuesday 17 July 1877

The Argus, Friday 21 March 1879

The Argus, Friday 27 February 1880

The Argus, Wednesday 11 August 1880

The Argus, Wednesday 18 August 1880

The Argus, Wednesday 12 October 1881

The Argus, Thursday 12 November 1908

The Argus, Wednesday 22 October 1919

The Mercury and Weekly Courier, 7 August 1880

The Sportsman, Wednesday 4 April 1883

The Sportsman, Wednesday 7 May 1884

The Sportsman, Tuesday 8 March 1887

The Sportsman, Wednesday 20 June 1888

The Sportsman, Wednesday 11 July 1888

Bate, W. 1983. *A History of Brighton*, 2nd edition. Carlton: Melbourne University Press.

Cannon, M. 1966. *The Land Boomers*. Carlton: Melbourne University Press.

Clark, I.D. 2000. *The Journals of George Augustus Robinson, Chief Protector, Port Phillip Aboriginal Protectorate*, Volume 5: 25th October 1845–9 June 1849. Clarendon: Heritage Matters.

Department of Administrative Services Construction Group, 1987. Interim Conservation Plan, Commonwealth Block, Melbourne, Vic, Site B and C. HV report 0188.

Davidson, G., D. Dunstan and C. McConville (eds.), 1985. *The Outcasts of Melbourne*. Sydney: Allen and Unwin.

Davies, P. 2006. Mapping Commodities at Casselden Place, Melbourne. International *Journal of Historical Archaeology* 10(4): 343–355.

De Gruchy and Leigh, 1866. Isometrical Plan of Melbourne and Suburbs, Coloured Lithographic Map. State Library of Victoria, accession number H26109, LB821.02 EH 1866 DE GRUCHY.

De Reu, J., G. Piets, G. Verhoeven, P. De Smeldt, M. Bats, B. Cherretté, W. De Maeyer, J. Deconynck, D. Herremans, P. Laloo, M. Van Meirvenne and W. De Clercq, 2013. Towards a Three-Dimensional Cost-Effective Registration of the Archaeological Heritage. *Journal of Archaeological Science* 40: 1108–1121.

De Serville, P. 1980. Port Phillip Gentlemen. Carlton: Melbourne University Press.

Finn, E. 'Garryowen', 1888. *The Chronicles of Early Melbourne 1835–1852 Historical, Anecdotal and Personal. Melbourne: Ferguson and Mitchell*. Facsimile edition, no date, Heritage Publications, Melbourne.

GML Heritage, 2015. 271 Spring Street Melbourne Archaeological Assessment and Research Design. Unpublished report prepared for RCP October 2015.

Hayes, S. 2007. Consumer Practice at Viewbank Homestead. *Australasian Historical Archaeology* 25: 87–103.

Hayes, S. and B. Minchinton, 2016. Cesspit Formation Processes and Waste Management History in Melbourne: Evidence from Little Lon. *Australian Archaeology* 82(1): 12–24.

Hewitt, G., N. Paynter, M. Goulding, S. Lane, J. Turnbull and B. Woff, 2017. Salvage Archaeology in Melbourne's CBD: An Opportunity for Reflections upon Documentary Sources and the Role of Prefabricated Buildings in Construction of the 'Instant City' of Gold-Rush-Era Melbourne. *International Journal of Historical Archaeology* https://doi.org/10.1007/s10761-017-0413-6.

Jenkin, C. E. J. 2003. *Alexander Morison: Independent*. Henley Beach: Seaview Press.

Karskens, G. 2001. Small Things, Big Pictures: New Perspectives from the Archaeology of Sydney's Rocks Neighbourhood. In Mayne, A. and T. Murray (eds.) *The Archaeology of Urban Landscapes – Explorations in Slumland*, pp. 69–85, Cambridge: Cambridge University Press.

Lewis, M. 1985. The Diagnosis of Prefabricated Buildings. *Australian Historical Archaeology* 3: 55–69.

McCarthy, J. 1989. Archaeological Investigation of the Commonwealth Offices and and Telecom Corporate Building Sites, the Commonwealth Block, Melbourne, Victoria, vols 1–5. Unpublished report to the department of Administrative Services and Telecom Australia.

McConville, C. 1985. From 'Criminal Class' to 'Underworld'. In Davidson, G., D. Dunstan and C. McConville (eds.) *The Outcasts of Melbourne*, pp. 69–90, Sydney: Allen and Unwin.

Mayne, A. 1993. *The Imagined Slum, Newspaper Representation in Three Cities, 1870–1914.* Leicester: Leicester University Press.

Mayne A. and T. Murray, 2001. The Archaeology of Urban Landscapes: Explorations in Slumland. In Mayne, A. and T. Murray (eds.) *The Archaeology of Urban Landscapes: Explorations in Slumland*, pp. 1–7, Cambridge: Cambridge University Press.

Minchinton, B. 2017. 'Prostitutes' and 'Lodgers' in Little Lon: Constructing a List of Occupiers in Nineteenth-Century Melbourne. *Australasian Historical Archaeology* 35: 64–70.

Mouritz, J. J. 1847 (1979). *The Port Phillip Almanac and Directory, for 1847. Melbourne: 'Herald' Office.* Facsimile edition, Library of Australian History, North Sydney.

Murray, T. 2006. Integrating Archaeology and History at the Commonwealth Block: Little Lon and Casselden Place. *International Journal of Historical Archaeology* 10(4): 395–413.

Murray, T. and A. Mayne, 2001. Imaginary Landscapes: Reading Melbourne's Little Lon. In Mayne, A. and T. Murray (eds.) *The Archaeology of Urban Landscapes: Explorations in Slumland*, pp. 89–105, Cambridge: Cambridge University Press.

New South Wales, 1849. 13th Victoria No. XXXIX. An Act for Regulating Buildings and Party Walls and for Preventing Mischiefs by Fire in the City of Melbourne (12 October 1849), known as the *Building Act*.

Ross, E. 2001. Slum Journeys: Ladies and London Poverty 1860–1940. In Mayne, A. and T. Murray (eds.) *The Archaeology of Urban Landscapes: Explorations in Slumland*, pp. 11–21, Cambridge: Cambridge University Press.

Russell, P. 1994. *'A Wish of Distinction' Colonial Gentitlity and Feminity.* Carlton: Melbourne University Press.

Ryan, A. J. and K.C. Edmonds, 1979. Historical and Architectural Development of the Commonwealth Centre Site, Melbourne, Commonwealth Department of Housing and Construction, Victoria-Tasmania Region, Melbourne. HV report 0187.

Senyard, J.E. 1972. Glass, Hugh (1817–1871). In Nairn, B., G. Serle and R. Ward (eds.) *Australian Dictionary of Biography* vol. 4: 1851–1890 D–J. Carlton: Melbourne University Press.

Strahan, L. 1988. Out of the Silence. *A Study of a Religious Community of Women: The Community of the Holy Name.* Melbourne: Oxford University Press.

Symonds, J. (ed.), 2002. T*he Historical Archaeology of the Sheffield Cutlery and Tableware Industry 1750–1900.* Sheffield, UK: ARCUS Studies in Historical Archaeology.

Trethowan, B. 2015. Draft Heritage Impact Statement. 271 Spring Street Melbourne. Unpublished report, Trethowan Heritage, Richmond.

Williamson, C. 2004. 'Domestic Ceramic and Glass Artefacts', Casseleden Place Archaeological Excavations: Research Archive Report vol. 3i – Draft Artefact Reports, prepared for ISPT and Heritage Victoria, Godden mackay Logan, Austral Archaeology and La Trobe University, Melbourne.

Williamson, C. 2006. Dating the Domestic Ceramics and Pipe Smoking Related Artefacts from Casselden Place, Melbourne, Australia. *International Journal of Historical Archaeology* 10(4): 329–341.

12
Little Lon and the Archaeology of the Modern World

Tim Murray

At its core this book (and the related publications that have appeared in national and international journals) is a testament to over 30 years of excavation and analysis on one Melbourne city block. Each of the chapters either outlines specific passages of work or discusses the implications of that work for heritage archaeology, museum repositories, and creators and managers of databases, as well as for the evolution of urban archaeology in Australia. While urban archaeology in Australia (or elsewhere for that matter) did not come of age as a result of all of this work on the Commonwealth Block, it is nonetheless true that our work has played an important part in its development over the period (see for example Bairstow 1990; Birmingham 1988, 1990; Green and Leech 2006; Kelly 1979).

Throughout this volume the authors have strived to give a sense of the many forces behind the changes in approach and purpose be they the much-cited researches at Five Points in New York City, or in San Francisco, the highly influential work by Godden Mackay Logan and Grace Karskens at The Rocks in Sydney, or our own work at the Commonwealth Block beginning with McCarthy's excavations and finishing most recently with a closing exercise in heritage archaeology led by Geoff Hewitt. I have tried to provide a sense of my own theoretical and methodological journey in urban archaeology that now stresses the supreme importance of comparison, and the properly constructed databases that would support it (Murray 2013).

The analysis of assemblages derived from the earlier research at Little Lon (see e.g. Murray and Mayne 2001, 2003; Williamson 1998) and the more recent work on the Cumberland and Gloucester Street sites (Crook et al. 2005; Gooden Mackay 1999), Riccardi's comparison of Buenos Aires and Melbourne (Riccardi 2015), has allowed us to establish whether there were similar patterns of residence, occupancy, ethnicity and community life in three different cities on the edge of the modern world. However, in doing this we have come to understand the complex and ambiguous nature of urban archaeological deposits from the mid-to-late 19th century, and more fully appreciated that the act of comparison between sites, cities, and continents is neither straightforward nor innocent. Although we have not felt it possible at this point to draw definitive conclusions about 'life at the social and geographical margins' we have greatly expanded our understanding of the historical archaeology of specific sites within those cities and contributed to the construction of new stories about people and places (Mayne et al. 2000; McConville 2000; Murray 2006, 2006; Murray and Crook 2005, in press). At a more general level we have also clearly identified some of the major questions that will continue to drive our research in Australia and elsewhere, and further characterise comparisons between contemporaneous sites in Australia, England and the Americas. Here are just a few of many examples.

First, the broad question of *how to understand domestic assemblages*. This implies a great many subsidiary questions such as: What are the vectors of assemblage formation in 19th-century cities? How did people acquire goods, what did they cost, what was the nature of consumer demand, was social emulation a dominant force in the creation of demand? Is there such a thing as typical poor, working class, middle class, or artisan domestic assemblages?

Second the broad question of *what roles cities have played in the movement of goods from centre to periphery and vice versa*, and then in the distribution of those goods to other population centres. In this reading centre and periphery exists at regional, national and global scales. The operation of Sydney, Melbourne (or indeed London) in terms of their hinterlands is one matter, but the interaction of cities within countries and between cities on a global scale is really only now coming on the agenda of urban historical archaeology in Australia.

Third, the broad question of *what roles cities have played in the movements of people*, either from the metropolitan to the periphery or from the countryside into cites. This last question has itself become a spur to new lines of research into the consequences of immigration both in Australia and in source countries such as England and Ireland. This is not just about exploring conventional issues of how colonies become nations and English people (for example) becoming Australians, but also a consideration of the consequences of immigration for sundered families and sundered communities, via an investigation of memory through written and oral documentary sources and, of course, material culture on both ends of the immigration process. It also directly connects to the complex processes whereby existing cultural and/or ethnic identities can be transformed by the experience of demographic change within settler societies (see e.g. Beaudry and Parno 2013; Brighton 2009; Dawdy 2000; Parker and Rodseth 2005; Voss 2008).

To develop the kinds of methodologies necessary to exploit this broader comparative agenda, we must remain sensible to the complexity of the landscape we are trying to interpret. The integration of history and archaeology occurs at many levels, and in some cases, rigorous analytical comparison is best teamed with individual stories – speculative though they may be – to more fully explore the archaeology of the modern city. Conversely, analyses of historical data (such as the mean value of building stock in a given area) and individual artefacts (such as the appearance of 'high quality' wares), may be a more appropriate level at which to integrate archaeologically derived information – be it at the household, site or other scale. We must employ all the armoury of archaeological enquiry – both deductive and inductive reasoning, attention to the detail of *both* documentary and archaeological datasets, and a commitment to their effective integration – to make a significant contribution to the histories of modern cities.

The business of practising archaeology provides an excellent introduction to frustration, paradox and irony. Historical archaeology has more than its far share of all three, and its worth reflecting that the garbage we paw through was created by societies that were grappling with the concepts of the past and the present in their own ways, and consciously working through what are now considered to be quite modish issues of otherness and self.

I have written before of the English essayists of the late 19th century, and their strongly held views of the reality of history, change, and decay. In closing I want to quote Andrew Lang from a great essay 'A Reverie at Christie's' written in 1892, in order to characterise a viewpoint about the possibility of interpreting 19th-century archaeology which I hope we can get past when we seek to comprehend the archaeology of the modern city. Lang saw closure and distance in the archaeology of his time:

> Here are pieces made by dead artists, whose very art ... is dead too, and can never be revived ... Here are ... Aztec relics which almost make one shudder; they are so marked with the hideous mark of a fiendish people ... We can make none of [those beautiful things]; we have not the ideas, the cultivation, the skill nor the time to bestow. We can make telephones ... we can litter continents with jam pots and sardine tins, but we cannot create the beautiful, we cannot make the splendid and gracious. We can only collect all the spoils of all the past, and store it is glass cases, and be learned, or sentimental, over the lot of dead ages and the rubbish heaps of fallen empires. (1892: 478)

There is absolutely no need for us to limit ourselves in this way. If there is one lesson to learn from the archaeology of the Commonwealth Block is that the historical archaeology of such places, though difficult and at times frustrating, has many new things to teach us about living in cities – either then or now.

REFERENCES

Bairstow, D. 1990. Urban Archaeology: American Theory, Australian Practice. *Australian Archaeology* 33: 52–58.

Beaudry, M. and T. Parno (eds.), 2013. *Archaeologies of Mobility and Movement*. New York: Springer.

Birmingham, J. 1988. The Refuse of Empire: International Perspectives on Urban Colonial Rubbish. In Birmingham, J. et al. (eds.) *Archaeology and Colonisation: Australia in the World Context*, pp. 149–171, Sydney: Australian Society for Historical Archaeology Incorporated.

Birmingham, J. 1990. A Decade of Digging: Deconstructing Urban Archaeology. *Australian Historical Archaeology* 8: 13–22.

Brighton, S. 2009. *Historical Archaeology of the Irish Diaspora: A Transnational Approach*. Knoxville: University of Tennessee Press.

Crook, P., L. Ellmoos and T. Murray, 2005. *Keeping up with the McNamaras: A Historical Archaeological Study of the Cumberland and Gloucester Streets Site, The Rocks, Sydney*. Sydney: Historic Houses Trust of NSW.

Dawdy, S. (ed.), 2000. Creolization. *Historical Archaeology* 34(3): 1–133.

Godden Mackay Heritage Consultants, 1999. *The Cumberland/Gloucester Streets Site, The Rocks: Archaeological Investigation Report*, Volumes 1, 3–5, prepared for the Sydney Cove Authority. Sydney: Godden Mackay Logan Pty Ltd.

Green, A. and R. Leech (eds.), 2006. *Cities in the World, 1500–2000: Papers Given at the Conference for Post-Medieval Archaeology, April 2002*. Leeds: Maney Publishing.

Kelly, M. 1979. Roads to Yesterday. In Stanbury, P. (ed.) *10,000 Years of Sydney Life: A Guide to Archaeological Discovery*, pp. 2–9, Sydney: Macleay Museum.

Lang, A. 1892 A Reverie at Christie's. *Longman's 20* (Sep. 1892): 473–479.

McConville, C. 2000. Big Notes from a Little Street: Re/newing Social History in Melbourne? *Australian Historical Studies* 32: 325–327.

Mayne, A., T. Murray and S. Lawrence, 2000. Historic Sites: Melbourne's Little Lon. *Australian Historical Studies* 31(114): 131–151.

Murray, T. 2005, Images of Little Lon: Making History, Changing Perceptions. In Murray, T. (ed.) *Object Lessons: Archaeology and Heritage in Australia*, pp. 167–185, Melbourne: Australian Scholarly Press.

Murray, T. 2006. Integrating Archaeology and History at the Commonwealth Block: Little Lon and Casselden Place. *International Journal of Historical Archaeology* 10(4): 395–413.

Murray, T. 2013. Expanding Horizons in the Archaeology of the Modern City: A Tale in Six Projects. *Journal of Urban History*, first published on March 6, 2013 as doi:10.1177/0096144213479308.

Murray, T. and P. Crook, 2005. Exploring the Archaeology of the Modern City: Issues of Scale, Integration and Complexity. *International Journal of Historical Archaeology* 9(2): 89–109.

Murray, T. and P. Crook, *in press. The Archaeology of the Modern City in 19th Century Australia: In Search of the McNamaras.* New York: Springer.

Parker, B. and L. Rodseth (eds.), 2005. *Untaming the Frontier in Anthropology, Archaeology and History.* Tucson: University of Arizona Press.

Riccardi, P. 2015. A Tale of Two Cities: Nineteenth Century Consumer Behaviour in Melbourne and Buenos Aires. Unpublished PhD dissertation, La Trobe University.

Voss, B. 2015. What's New? Rethinking Ethnogenesis in the Archaeology of Colonialism. *American Antiquity* 80(4): 655–670.

Williamson, C. 1998. Slums and Sluts: Lonsdale Street Project Report. Unpublished report for La Trobe University, Melbourne.

Plates

Chapter 2

Plate 2.1: The Casselden Place site interpretation scheme, installed 2004 (Photos: Renee Gardiner).

Chapter 6

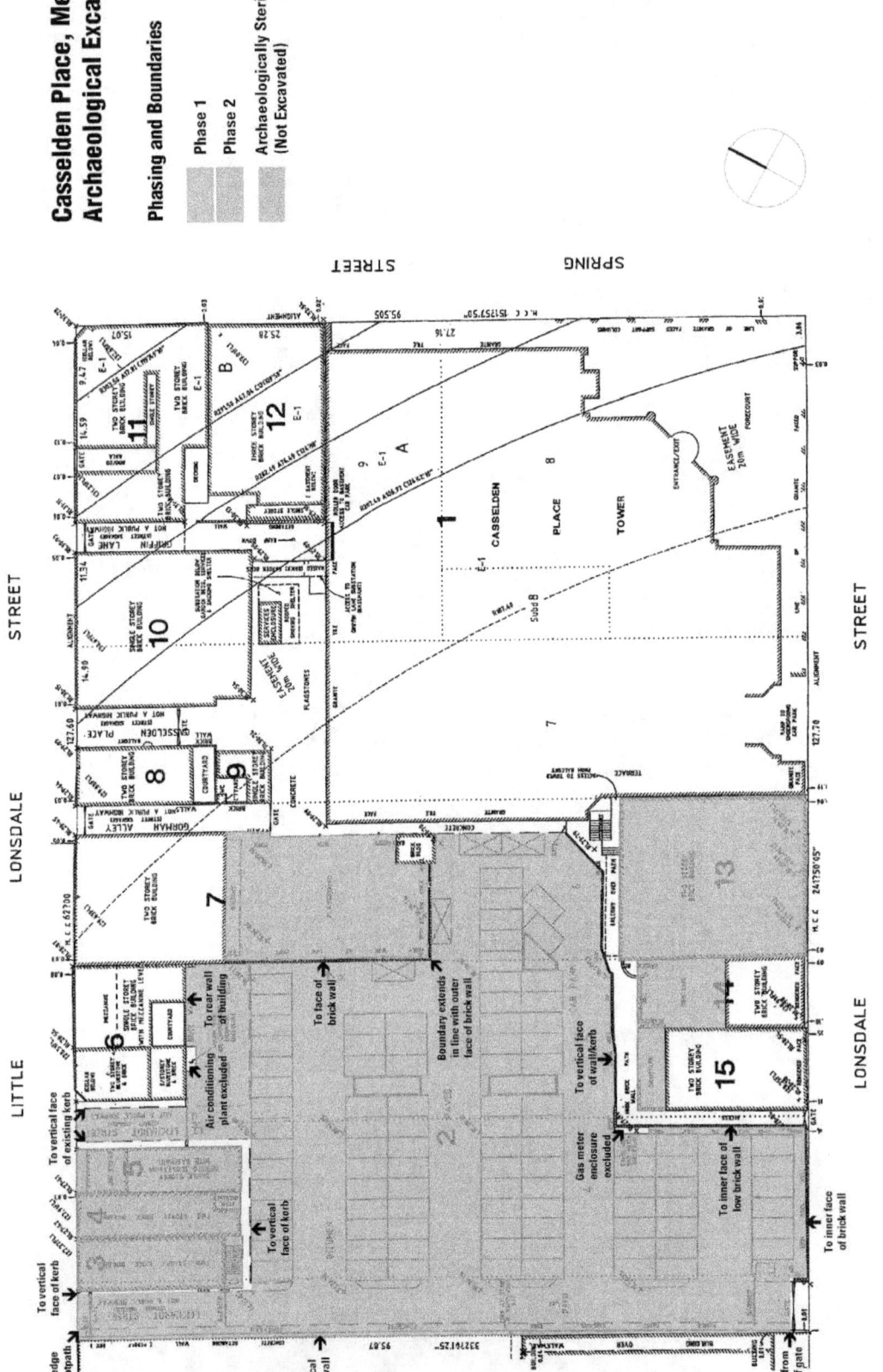

Plate 6.1: The Casselden Place Site, 50 Lonsdale Street, Melbourne (Reproduced from Mackay *et al.* 2006).

Plates

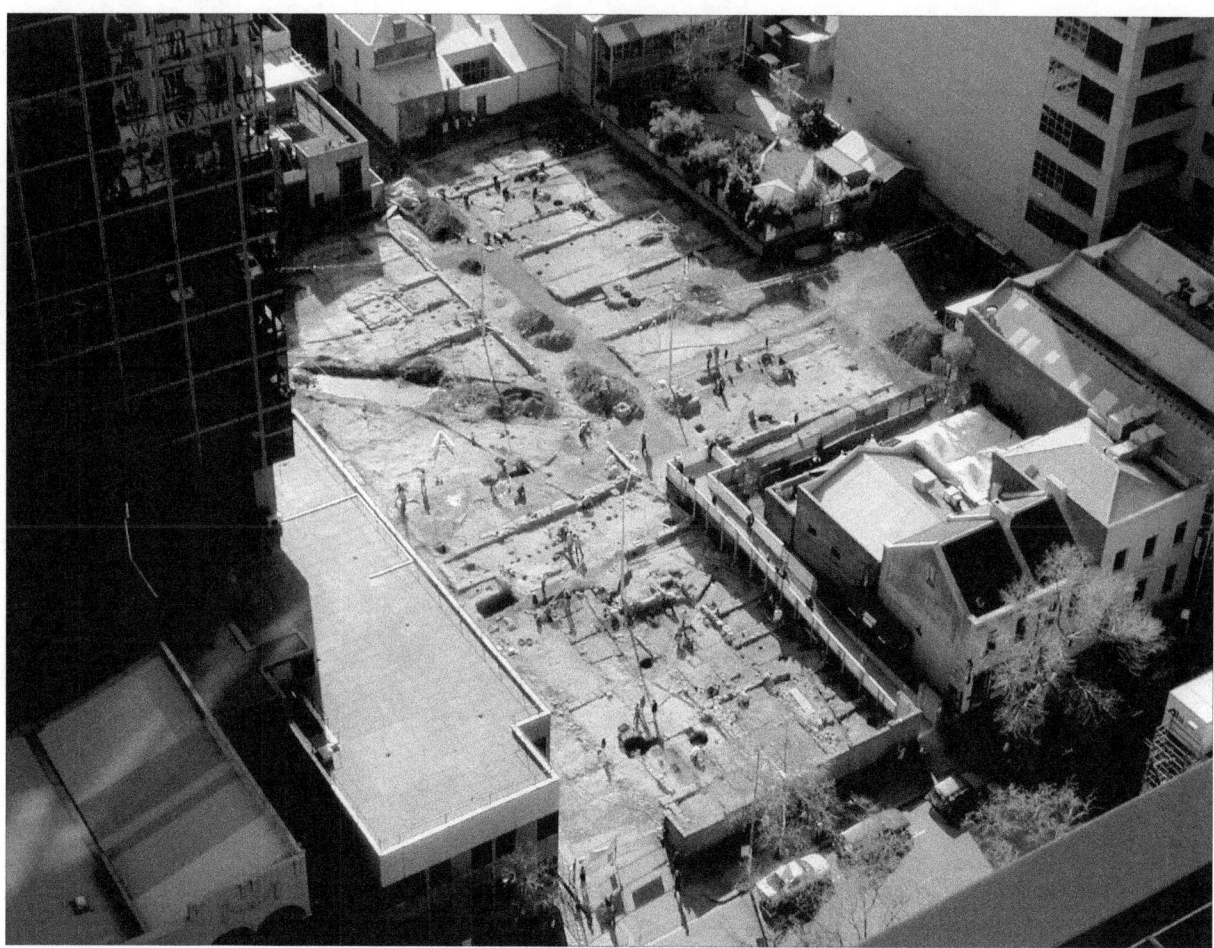

Plate 6.2: Casselden Place Site, aerial perspective, looking northeast from Lonsdale Street during Phase 1, 2002 (Photo: Tony Jenner for Godden Mackay Logan, Austral Archaeology and La Trobe University).

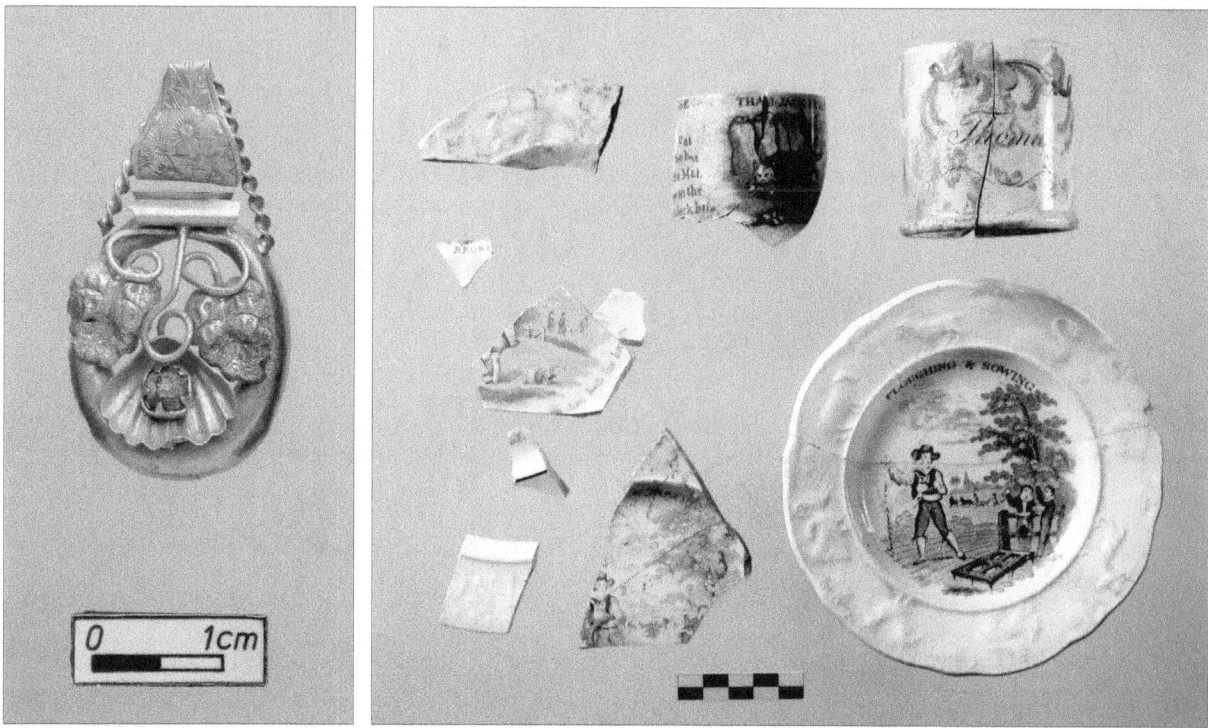

Plate 6.3: Artefacts such as this gold pendant and 19th-century 'moralising china' provide alternative perspectives about the socio-ecomonic status and morals of the 'Little Lon' community (Photos: Ming Wei, La Trobe University).

145

The Commonwealth Block, Melbourne

Chapter 8

Plate 8.1: Stories from a City: Little Lon, Australia Gallery, Melbourne Museum, 2000–2007 (Source: Museum Victoria).

Plate 8.2: Artefacts displayed in cabinets outside Little Lon's recreated cottages, The Melbourne Story, Melbourne Museum, 2007 (Source: Benjamin Healley, Museum Victoria).

Index

Aboriginal Affairs Victoria 61
Aboriginal and Torres Strait Islander Protection Act 1984 8
Aboriginal archaeology 89
Aboriginal Australians 8, 55, 60, 61, 76
Adelaide University 19
Ah Kit 134
alcohol 34, 51, 105–106
Allen, Jim 22
Allessio, Joseph 132
Amiet, Louis 36
Andrew Long and Associates (heritage consultants) 53, 79
animal bones 36, 39–40, 60, 90, 125–126
Annear, Robyn 25, 31
anthropology 56, 75
Archaeological and Aboriginal Relics Preservation Act 1972 7–8, 88
archaeological archives 92–93
archaeological recording systems 26, 60, 62
Archaeology Advisory Committee (Vic) 13, 14
archival research 22, 31, 47, 57, 62, 79–80, 82
artefact cataloguing 12, 14, 27, 33, 60–61, 88–91, 95, 101, 113–117
artefact conservation 14, 15, 90, 94
artefact retention policies 95
asbestos 9
assemblage analysis 43–46, 90
Auckland Hotel 71
Austral Archaeology 27, 33, 35, 55, 66
Australian Defence Industries assemblage 89
Australian Heritage Commission 8, 10
Australian Heritage Commission Act 1975 8
Australian Historical Archaeology Database (AHAD) 94
Australian Museum 93
Australian Research Council 1, 70, 88, 113
Australian Survey Office 26

Bannear, David 13, 20, 24, 31
Barker, James 78
Barnett, F. Oswald 77
Baum, Caroline. *See* Brussels, Madame
Beaudry, Mary 44
Best, Sophie Eliza 134
Best, William Sweetland 134
Birmingham, Judy 19
Black Eagle Hotel 36–37, 53, 74, 90–91, 93
Blakeley saw factory 122, 124, 126, 127–128
Blamey, Sir Thomas Albert 78
bluestone 31, 38, 46
boarding houses 36, 39, 129, 130
Bond, Mrs 105

Bond, William 105
Boucher, Lawrence 122
Bowen, Jane 132
Bracchi, Carlo 87
Brandt, William 39
British Hotel 71
Brophy, John 129, 131
brothels 3, 36–37, 56, 66, 72–79, 99, 105–106, 109, 136. *See also* sex workers
Brussels, Madame 39, 72, 73, 75, 78, 79
Buchan, Rosemary 7, 17, 19, 22
Buckley, Kristal 19, 22
Buckley, Robertson 131
building codes 135
Burra Charter 8

Cannon, Michael 132
Carlton United Brewery 89, 91
Casey, Mary 2
Casselden, John 46, 47, 124, 125, 136
Casselden Place, Melbourne
    excavation and analysis 45–51, 53–68, 82, 100
    heritage management 14–16
    occupancy patterns 47, 71–75, 100, 104
ceramics 34, 36, 39, 64, 104, 107, 123–124, 125, 126
cesspits
    and occupancy patterns 103–109
    closure dates 99–100, 125, 128
    excavation and analysis 31–35, 56, 59–60, 124–127, 130–133
Cheok Hong Cheong 72
children's toys 38, 64, 104, 107, 123–124
Chinese residents 7, 36, 37, 38–39, 71–75, 78–79, 103, 124, 136
church buildings 73, 74, 77, 132, 134
clay pipes 34, 36, 102, 104, 124, 125
Cleary, Timothy 103
Cohen, Janet 25
Cohen Place, Melbourne 54
coins 36, 62, 123
collections management 92–95
colonisation 8, 61
Commonwealth Centre, Melbourne 3, 9–10, 32
Commonwealth Department of Administrative Services 10, 19, 21
Commonwealth Department of Housing and Construction 22
Commonwealth government
    funding 10
    legislation 8
    ownership of sites 8–9, 11, 19

147

community engagement 14–15, 65–66, 76, 87
comparative archaeology 1, 81, 82, 139–140
compulsory acquisition 3, 11, 77
computer technology 22, 26, 40, 93
consultant archaeologists 10, 12, 19, 55
Cornwell family 107–108
corporate sponsors 27
cottages 31, 33, 46–47, 79
Coultas, Diana 25, 31
Council for British Archaeology 94
Coutts, Peter 8, 22
crime 55–56, 99, 103, 122
Crook, Penny 49, 81
Cumberland Gloucester Street, Sydney 1
Cumberland Place, Melbourne 3
Cunningham, Anne 87

dance halls 133–134
databases 1, 2–3, 81–82, 88–90, 93–95, 101, 113–117
Davies, Peter 124
Davison, Graeme 22
de Beaumont, Diana 105–106
Dennis, C.J. 3, 77
developers 1–2, 3, 11, 13, 70
diet 31, 39–40, 63–64, 125–126
digital repositories 94–95
domestic consumption habits 81, 88, 99–108
Donati, Laura 57
du Cros, Hilary 24
Dunn, J. 126
Dunn, Kate 131
Dunstan, David 22

EAMC database 113–117
economic depression, 1890s 62, 73, 74, 81, 109, 132, 134, 136
economic depression, 1930s 62, 72
Ellson, David 25, 31
Elms, Emma 73
Elms Family Hotel 73, 129, 131
Elms, George 73, 121, 129
ethnography 56, 61, 75–76
excavation methods 69–71, 80, 81–82, 119
   at 271 Spring Street 122–138
Exhibition Street, Melbourne 3, 27

factories 28, 32, 71–75, 78–79, 81
Farlow, Mrs 124
faunal material. *See* animal bones
Fergie, Henry Penketh 132
Film Victoria 26
First Government House, Sydney 2
First World War 3, 62, 72, 77
Foley Square, New York 77
Foo, Henry B. 129
Foot, Henry Boorn 119
Footscray, Melbourne 12
Fowell, Derek 10, 22

funding 1, 10–11, 22, 27, 70

Gay Sue 124
Gearan, Catherine 136
Glass, Hugh 119, 126
glassware 34, 35, 39, 106, 126
Godden Mackay Logan 27, 33, 66, 81
gold mining sites 13
gold rushes 76, 103, 108, 109, 125, 135
Goong, Harry 124
Gorman Alley 72, 75
Gott, Beth 31
Goug Wing 134
Governor Bourke Hotel 71
Griffin family 121, 122
Griffin, George 127
Griffin Lane 73
Grinblat, Samuel 71

Harris, Edward 26
Harris Matrix System 26, 62
Hart, Isaac 134
Haycock, Thomas 132
Hayes, Marie 87
Hayes, Mrs 126
Hayes, Sarah 2, 125
Heritage Act 1995 (Vic) 13, 16, 19, 89–90, 92
heritage archaeology
   and developers 1–2, 8, 11, 69, 95
   and governments 7–8, 13
Heritage Council of Victoria 135
heritage management 12–13, 65, 70
Heritage Victoria 13, 14, 39, 55, 60, 64, 90, 94, 101
Hey, Louey Weh 131
historical archaeology 22, 43, 48, 75, 80, 81
   increasing interest in 12, 39
   in universities 8, 12
Historic Buildings Act 1981 (Vic) 13
Historic Buildings Council 13
Historic Houses Trust of New South Wales 43
Historic Shipwrecks Act 1981 13
Hope Inquiry into the National Estate 8
hotels 71–73
House, John 132
house numbering 32
Howes, George 103

immigrant communities 3, 78–79, 103, 109, 136
Indian residents 47, 78, 103, 127, 136
industrial heritage 13
Industry Superannuation Property Trust 14, 66, 119–137
International Council on Monuments and Sites (ICOMOS) 8, 19
Irish residents 47, 81, 87
Italian residents 75, 78, 81, 87
itinerant residents 82

Jameson, George 106
Jenner, Tony 25, 33
jewellery 64, 123–124
Johnston, George Keane 129
Judd, Honora 100, 108

Karskens, Grace 44, 81, 107
Kennan, Jim 8
Kennett, Jeff 13
Kennon, William 74
Kerr, William John 127
Knox, David 25

lace-making tools 123–124
Lands Department 31
land titles records 28, 31, 34, 80, 100
Lane, Sharon 119
Lang, Andrew 140
La Trobe University 1, 8, 25, 27, 33, 35, 66, 88, 90, 93, 94
Lebanese residents 74, 78, 136
Leckey, John 78
legislation 7–8, 12–13, 16, 19, 40, 92
Leichardt Street, Melbourne 28, 35, 54, 57
Life at Little Lon (film) 26–27, 40
Little Lonsdale Street, Melbourne
  changes in community over time 99–103
  in popular culture 3
  lessons for future digs 14
  reputation as a 'slum' 3, 44, 47, 55–57, 64, 66, 76–77, 81, 99, 103, 108–109, 136
Lonsdale Street, Melbourne 3, 35, 37, 55
Lucas, Mrs 132
Lugton, Alexander 72, 74, 78

Mackay, Richard 15
MacLellan, Robert 13
Macreash, John 127
Mahlstedt plans 128
Maloney, John 87
Malouf, Joseph 74
mandatory reporting of sites 13
mapping 13
maritime archaeology 13
Martin family 125
Martin, Sara 57
Mather, William 126, 132, 134, 135
May, Andy 23
Mayne, Alan 43, 44, 45, 49, 55, 57, 64, 71, 103, 136
McCarthy, Justin 12, 15, 43, 45, 47, 53, 78, 80, 106, 119
McConville, Chris 22, 136
McIlwaine family 75, 79
McIntyre, Mike 13, 22
McKillop, Sister Mary 77
McLelland family 38
media reporting 7, 14, 26
Melbourne
  public interest in 8, 12, 87
  sesquicentenary (1985) 8

Melbourne City Council 31
Melbourne City Mission 77
Melbourne Museum 71, 87. *See also* Museums Victoria
Metropolitan Board of Works 31
Miller, Patrick 27
Minchinton, Barbara 119, 126, 136
Minerals Council of Australia 13
Mission House 132–134
Mission to the Streets and Lanes 77, 87
Moline, Dick 25
Moloney family 46–47, 104, 107
Monks, Anne 100
Morison, Alexander 126
Moss, Mark 132
Mrozowski, Stephen 44
multimedia technologies 2
Murray, Tim 15, 22, 44, 45, 49, 55, 64, 71, 95
museum curation 88–97, 115
Museums Victoria 1, 12, 15, 34, 39, 87–97, 101, 113, 117

natural soil 60
Nelsen, Ivar 7, 8, 19, 22
Nettleton, Charles 121
Newtown, Peter 134
Neylan, Margaret 47

Oddfellows Hotel 29, 35, 36, 39, 53, 72, 75, 78–79, 90–91, 93
O'Don, Thladen 125
office blocks 9, 77
Old Governor Bourke Hotel 73, 121, 129–131
Old Melbourne Cemetery 12
open access 1
opium dens 3
oral history 22
O'Regan, M. 126
overcrowding 47

packing 12
Parliamentary Standing Committee on Public Works 11
Payne, Frederick 136
Pearson, Michael 10
photographic records 12
Piggott, Rosslynd 16
Planning and Environment Act 1987 (Vic) 13
police 78
policy development 12–13
pollen samples 59
Porta, James 127
Porta, Joseph 72–73, 78
Port Arthur, Tasmania 22, 26
prefabricated housing 122
public interest 8, 11, 12, 14, 65–66, 76
publicity 10, 14, 26, 65–66

Queen Street, Melbourne 2, 54, 89
Queen Victoria Market (Melbourne) 12

Ranson, Don 31
rate books 28, 31, 32, 57, 62, 99–100, 103, 132
Rawson, Robyn 25
Relics Act. See Archaeological and Aboriginal Relics Preservation Act 1972
rental market 47, 105
rental records 100–102, 109–110
research design 56–57, 69–71, 75–76, 80, 102–103
Rhodes, David 24
risk assessment 93
RMIT 25
Robertson, Mabel 131
Rocks, The (Sydney) 1–2, 44, 55, 76, 77, 81, 100
Rohinibaux, Kodabux 127
Ross, Ellen 136
Royal Exhibition Building, Melbourne 89
rubbish pits 28, 32–33, 35, 60
Russell, Penny 136

Saltwater Crossing site (Melbourne) 12
Salvation Army 77
sanitation 35, 47, 81, 99, 125, 130. *See also* cesspits
Saqui, John J. 134
schools 73, 77
Schuyler, Robert L. 22
Scoles, Richard 127
Second World War 8
sesquicentenary of Victorian colony 8
sex workers 100, 103, 104–109, 136. *See also* brothels
Sharp, William 134
Sherven, Stephen 123, 124
Sister Esther 87
Sisters of the Community of the Holy Name 73, 77, 132, 136
site phasing 61
slums 3, 44, 48, 55, 76–77, 99, 136
sly grog shops 3
Smith, Jeremy 14
social history 8, 87
social mobility 107–108
South Australia Heritage Branch 20
South Australia Museum 19
Southbank (Melbourne) 12
Spring Street, Melbourne 3, 27, 119–137
Spring Street Mission 73
Stack, Ada 136
St Joseph's elementary school 77
storage of artefacts 12, 15, 24
Strahan, Lynne 132
Strahan, William 123, 125
stratigraphy 28, 56, 79, 80, 81, 126
Stuart, Iain 7, 22
St Vincent de Paul Home 77
Summerton, Michele 16
Sydney 1–2, 77, 81, 90, 113
tableware 123, 125
Taylor, William 123, 124

Tee Lung 134
Telecom 9, 10, 21, 25, 28, 77
textiles 36, 60
Thomas, Jane 15
Thorp, Wendy 44
timber cottages 28, 33, 46, 75, 79, 122, 124, 135
Tin Yen 124
Townrow, Karen 13
Tucker, Peter 103

University of Melbourne 8, 25, 93
University of Sydney 19
urban archaeology 1–2, 12, 43, 44, 48–49, 55, 66, 71, 81, 82–83, 139
urban poor 8, 36, 44, 47, 51, 64, 76, 81, 136

Vandersluiys, Rebecca 25
Vanished Communities project 2
Varley, Henry 78
Victoria Archaeological Survey 7, 9–11, 13, 22, 39
Victorian Heritage Council 13
Victorian Housing Commission 77
Victorian Ministry of Planning and Environment 7
Victor, Monsieur 134
Vines, Gary 13
volunteers 10, 14, 21, 24–26, 28, 33, 39, 66, 90

Walters, Samuel 134
Warrington, George 75
Waterfield, William 126
Webb, Charles 134
West Oakland, California 77
Whelan's Lane, Melbourne 46, 124. *See also* Casselden Place, Melbourne
Whitlam, Gough 8
Williams, George 106
Williams, Mary 105–107
Williamson, Caleb 124
Williamson, Christine 43, 51, 119, 123, 125, 126
Wills, Henry Charles 72
World War I. *See* First World War
World War II. *See* Second World War
Wright, Charles 134

Yates, Mrs 124
York, James 132

Zygmuntowicz, Kasia 51

www.ingramcontent.com/pod-product-compliance
Lightning Source LLC
Chambersburg PA
CBHW080856230426
43662CB00013B/2119